Cigar Taste Terminology

- Mouth Taste: What we perceive or taste in the mouth—there are only five tastes: Sweet, Sour, Salty, Bitter and Savory (or Umami)
- Palate: Word commonly used to describe the mouth-nasal cavity we use to smell and taste
- Olfactory Bulb: Nerve structure in the nasal cavity that is responsible for sensing odorants and then sending a coded sensory message to the brain so it can process and identify the stimulation based on previously familiar references
- Odorant: Invisible airborne molecules that can be considered pleasant or unpleasant, also referred to as aromas or odors
- Aroma: Pleasing odorants experienced through an ortho or retro hale
- Ortho hale: What we smell by inhaling through our nose
- Retro hale: What we smell by exhaling through our nose what we have inhaled through our mouth
- Taste association or reference: Mouth Taste + Smell (both ortho and retro) = Flavor
- Flavor and Taste: Words commonly used interchangeably to denote the overall stimulation
- Threshold: Minimum number of airborne aroma/odor molecules necessary to detect an aroma/odorant, typically, 1 part per billion

Must Learn Spanish Words

Agua—Water	Disfruta—Enjoy	Muy fuerte—Very strong	Un tabaco—A cigar
Cenicero—Ashtray	Fuego—Fire	Ron—Rum	Vitola—cigar ring gauge
Cerveza—Beer	Fuerte—Strong	Tripa—Filler leaves	Wiki—Whiskey

Tobacco Belt Map™

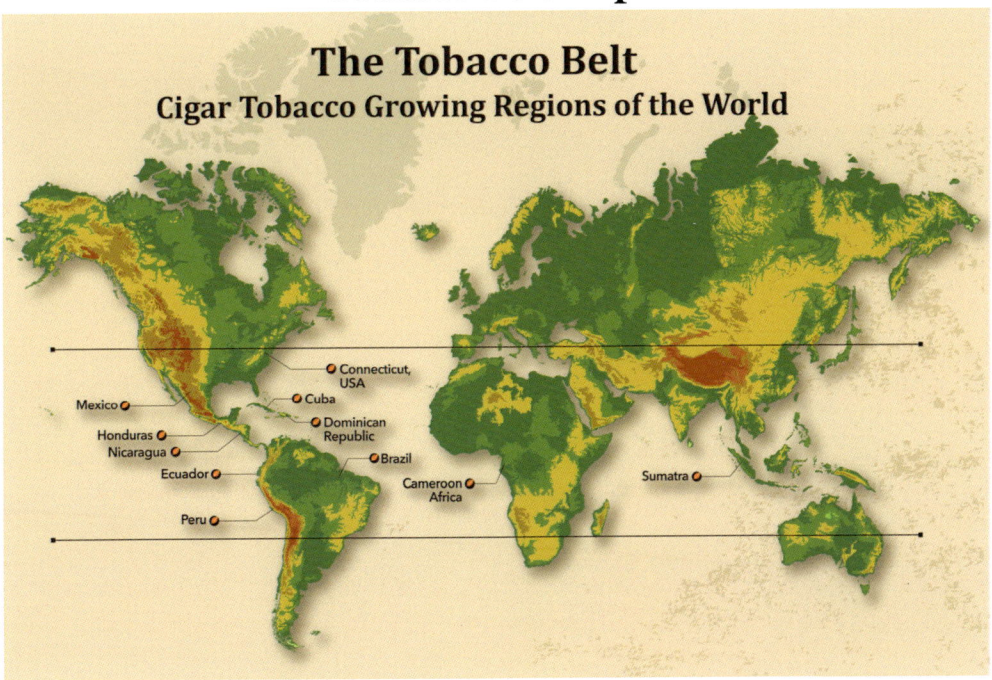

DEMYSTIFYING the ART of TASTE

Written by **Nick Cutro**

Foreword by Manolo Quesada

Cigar Bliss – Demystifying the Art of Taste
Copyright © 2020 Nick Cutro

All rights reserved. No part of this book may be reproduced or transmitted in any form or by any means without written permission from the author or publisher. This book and its contents are to be used for informational purposes only. No income claims are to be construed or inferred and results are neither promised nor guaranteed. By purchasing this book, the reader agrees to hold the author and publisher harmless of any cause or action resulting from any application or implementation of the content of this book by the reader.

FIRST EDITION
Published in 2020

www.ProPalate.net

ISBN: 978-1-7361967-0-0

Category: Cigar Tasting, Cigar Connoisseur, Tobacco, Education, Manual

Library of Congress Cataloging-in-Publication Data

Written by: Nick Cutro | Email: info@ProPalate.com

Facebook: https://www.facebook.com/propalatesystem/

Instagram: https://www.instagram.com/propalatesystem/

Edited by: Denise McCabe | www.McCabeEditing.com

Photo Credits: Mike Coppin

Cover Designed & Formatted by: Eli Blyden Sr. | www.EliTheBookGuy.com

Published & Printed in the United States of America

Disclaimer

This book is not intended as a substitute for the medical advice of physicians. The reader should regularly consult a physician in matters relating to his/her health and particularly with respect to any symptoms that may require diagnosis or medical attention.

Although the author and publisher have made every effort to ensure that the information in this book was correct at press time, the author and publisher do not assume and hereby disclaim any liability to any party for any loss, damage, or disruption caused by errors or omissions, whether such errors or omissions result from negligence, accident, or any other cause.

Some names and identifying details have been changed to protect the privacy of individuals.

The author and publisher are providing this book and its contents on an 'as is' basis and make no representations or warranties of any kind with respect to the book and its contents. The author and publisher disclaim all such representations and warranties, including, for example, warranties of merchantability and medical or legal advice for a particular purpose. In addition, the author and publisher do not represent or warrant that the information accessible is fully accurate, complete or current.

The statements made about products and services have not been evaluated by the U.S. government. Please consult with your own legal and accounting professional regarding the suggestions and recommendations made in this book.

Except as specifically stated in this book, neither the author or publisher, nor authors, contributors or other representatives will be liable for damages arising out of or in connection with the use of this book. This is a comprehensive limitation of liability that applies to all damages of any kind, including (without limitation) compensatory, direct, indirect or consequential damages; loss of data, income or profit; loss of or damage to property and claims of third parties.

You understand that this book is not intended as a substitute for consultation with a licensed legal or accounting professional. Before you begin any change in your lifestyle in any way, you will consult a licensed professional to ensure you are doing what is best for your situation.

This book provides content related to emotional intelligence topics. As such, use of this book implies your acceptance of this disclaimer.

Table of Contents

Cigar Taste Terminology i
   Must Learn Spanish Words i
   Tobacco Belt Map™ i

Disclaimer vii

Foreword xiii

Introduction 1

Excerpt from an Interview with J O C H Y   B L A N C O 5

CHAPTER 1

Why All the Confusion? 7
   The Death Spiral of Whole Foods 7
   Additives, Irradiation, and Taste Preferences 9
   Manufacturing Food 10
   A Junk Food Plague 11
   Old World Cigar Era 13
   Cigar Gene Pool Expansion 16
   A Modern Cigar Boom 16
   A List of Innovators 17
   Seemingly Endless Choices 18
   Avoiding Deception 20

Excerpt from an Interview with J H O N Y S   D I A Z 21

CHAPTER 2

The Basics of Sensory Perception and the Science Behind Taste 23
   Our Five Sensory Tools 23
   Sight (Visual) 24
   Sound (Auditory) 25
   Touch (Tactile) 25
   Taste (Gastronomic) 26
   Smell (Olfactory) 27
   The Anatomy of Smell 28
   Getting the Terminology Right 29
   Humans' Versus Other Species' Ability to Smell 30
   Threshold 30
   Nasal Cycling: How It Affects Your Sense of Smell 30
   Five Smell Disorders 31
   The Causes of Smell Disorders 32
   DNA: How It Affects the Way We Taste 32

Excerpt from an Interview with M A N O L O   Q U E S A D A 37

Excerpt from an Interview with J O S E L I T O   D O M I N G U E Z 39

Excerpt from an Interview with J O H N   O L I V A , J r 41

Your Palate and Beyond......42
Palate Development Exercises......45

Excerpt from an Interview with K L A A S   K E L N E R......48

CHAPTER 3

Tools of the Trade......51
  Books, Magazines, Websites, Podcasts, and Blogs......52
  From the Color Wheel to the Flavor Wheel......53
  Taste Models and Training......56
  Aroma Kits......57
  A New, Effective Approach to Training......58

Excerpt from an Interview with L i t t o   G o m e z......59
  Essential Cigar Language: Subjective versus Objective Descriptions......62
  Tools to Keep Your Palate Razor Sharp......64
  The Smoking Environment and Why It Matters......69
  Palate Developing Exercises......72
  Recommended Cigar Books for Your Library......75

Excerpt from an Interview with J h o n y s   D i a z......76

CHAPTER 4

The Psychology Behind the Art, Part 1......77
  Taste References and Associations......78
  Taste Associations: References Required......78
  A Surprising Lesson Learned During a Training Session......81
  Neuro-Linguistic Programming (NLP)......82
  Calibration......83
  Most Common Taste Associations and Their Unique Characteristics......85
  Defining the Cigar Connoisseur......89
  Understanding Your Primary Frame of Reference......90
  How Our Brains Influence Our Taste Perception......91
  An Exercise for Stubborn Associations......93
  Taste Triggers......94
  Adaptation......96
  Smoker's Nausea......97
  Nicotine: What You Should Know......98
  Secondhand Cigar Smoke: What You Should Know......101
  Virgin Palate......101
  Palate Cleanse and Your Body's pH Level......102
  A Cigar Taste Dilemma......103
  Barrel Aging Tobacco: How It Influences a Cigar......104
  The Life Cycle of an Oak Barrel......107
  What Affects Cigar Costs......111
  Thinking in Thirds......115
  Palate Development Exercises......116

    Excerpt from an Interview with Eric Newman 119
    Excerpt from an Interview with Manolo Quesada 120

CHAPTER 5

The Psychology Behind the Art, Part 2 121
    Ortho Hale and Retro Hale 122
    Taking Control of Your Palate 124
    Taste Associations 127
    Next Steps in Calibrating Your Palate 129

Excerpt from an Interview with Joselito Dominguez 131
    Cigar Ritual: Getting in the Zone 132
    The Importance of Exercise 133
    Mucus-inducing Foods 133
    Mucus-inducing Environments 135
    Medicines and Their Effect on Taste 136
    Common Sense about Scents 138
    Alcohol and Cigars 139
    Pairing Your Cigar with a Beverage: Two Distinct Approaches 140
    Life: Complicated—Retro Hale: Not 143
    Types of Blind Tasting 144
    Budgeting 147
    Tasting and the Environment 147
    Eliminating Bias 148
    The ProTip™ 151
    Terroir 153

Excerpt from an Interview with John Oliva, Jr. 157
Excerpt from an Interview with Fito Maruschke Mendez 159
    Tobacco: Understanding the Raw Material 161
    Cigar Aging 165
    Cigar Ambassador 167

Excerpt from an Interview with Klaas Kelner 171
Excerpt from an Interview with John Oliva, Jr. 172

CHAPTER 6:

The Ultimate Experience: CIGAR BLISS 173
    Closing Thoughts 176
    My Story: Why I Wrote This Book 177

Understanding Humidity & How it Effects Your Cigars 186
    Relative Humidity Chart 186
    Two Ways to Describe a Cigar 186

Foreword

In July of 2019 at the IPCPR show is Las Vegas Nick Cutro approached our booth. I have known Nick for over twenty years and his visits always meant an interesting conversation that centered around new ideas with projects that he was working on.

I told Nick we would have to meet after show hours for we had customers visiting the booth and I knew I needed time to listen to Nick's ideas. At 5:00 pm, Nick came back to the booth and we had a wonderful conversation about his extraordinary idea to write a book to go along with the ProPalate® training system which he developed for cigar smokers. I congratulated him and told him I was impressed with the courage it takes to tackle the art and science of what we taste in cigars.

In this world where immediacy has become the rule of our activities, Cigars are the perfect answer to our immediacy needs. They require no mixing, no cooking, no freezing, and no boiling or frying or steaming. Cut, light and you're on your way to immediate pleasure and enjoyment.

This being said, there are certain aspects of Cigars that, if understood and mastered, will allow the smoker to truly enjoy the experience of smoking a Cigar even more. The Cigar delivers smoke into your mouth and it is here where a basic knowledge of your palate can enhance your enjoyment.

Cigar Bliss is a comprehensive guide to understanding all the elements that come together making Cigar smoking a truly wonderful experience in both pleasure and enjoyment. Having this book handy will help you better understand the basics of how we taste and the many dimensions of your unique palate.

I have been smoking Cigars for 60 years and, after participating in Mr. Cutro's knowledge and exercises, I can truly say I have greatly enhanced my Cigar smoking universe and have become much more aware of what happens in my palate when I smoke all the Cigars that I smoke.

Manolo Quesada

Introduction

Cigars are a perfect balance between art and science. Consider that for a moment. While the currently available information regarding methods to develop your cigar palate involve plenty of artistic flair and intuition, scientific awareness has often been overlooked, if not ignored. This book corrects that imbalance, explaining and identifying the science behind the art.

In most people's minds, science feels like a mystery wrapped in an enigma. Until I did research for the book you are holding, I felt the same way, believing that science is tedious activity conducted in secret laboratories, with experiments funded by big government and huge pharma: in other words, a little "out there" and not to be trusted.

But that's nonsense. Science can be extraordinary and enlightening—and even entertaining. The best definition was offered to me by a retired NASA rocket scientist while we relaxed in a—you guessed it—cigar lounge. Yes, rocket scientists do exist. They walk on two legs like we do, but they lean forward more than the average person, due to the extra weight of their oversized brains. I met Max when he was working in a cigar shop after his primary career had ended. We went to dinner and frequented cigar lounges together. His scientific discourse went something like this:

> *Sonny (that's what he called me), the best way to understand science is to identify what it's not. It's not about fancy testing equipment, white lab coats and safety goggles. It's obviously not about sounding pretentious, using big words most people would have trouble pronouncing and a zero chance of spelling.*
>
> *Science is about making discoveries: new ways of looking at things, not an end in and of itself. You could look at it as a process to help us better understand the world around us and help us speculate or forecast how things will act in the near or distant future.*
>
> *The scientific process is two-fold. First, the scientist makes observations and keeps detailed records of those findings while looking at patterns that he can replicate. When he identifies a pattern, he forms a hypothesis to explain that occurrence. Second, he, oftentimes with the assistance of his colleagues, designs and performs tests that are aimed at disproving the hypotheses. If they are unable to disprove it, then the hypothesis is considered to be true. That is science.*

Simple, yet profound.

I would venture to say that most of you practice a little science in some form or other every day without even realizing it. To illustrate this theory, in a real-world cigar situation, let's assume that you notice a repeating pattern. Every time you light up one of your favorite cigars in the bitter cold, the wrapper cracks and unravels. During summer months, when you step outside into ultra-steam-bath-like weather (because your significant other doesn't allow you to smoke in the house), the wrapper still unravels.

Instead of hypothesizing that cigar wrappers will never remain intact, you persist until you discover that your cigars just don't fancy extremely low temperatures or extremely high humidity. So the only recourse, apparently, is to either trade in your significant other for a more open-minded one and smoke in the house or find a cigar lounge close to your work or home (the latter is probably much less expensive).

Science can be quite basic, as in the anecdote above, or it can be as complex as determining the probability that your firstborn child will inherent your spouse's dominant taste gene and your recessive taste gene, which would produce a child with a 75% chance of being a dominant taster and a 25% chance of being a recessive taster. The point is that most of us conduct scientific experiments from time to time without even realizing it: Science is a never ending quest for knowledge, and no matter how much we know about the world around us—including the world inside a hand-crafted cigar or inside a tobacco plant seed the size of a grain of salt—the amount we don't know will always be greater than what we do know.

But we need art just as much as science. In this book, we will discuss how art and science merge to create the fabulous experience we refer to as taste, aroma, and flavor. Once you understand the biology behind our perceptions, you free yourself from the shackles of mystery. You will no longer blindly follow someone else's opinion or advice. Only by understanding the underlying principles involved in first selecting the right cigar, gently roasting the foot of the cigar, then tasting its rich, silky, seductive, and oftentimes intoxicating aromas can you start to form your own opinions that are grounded in your knowledge, life experiences, and present state of mind.

I invite you to read this book with a skeptic's mindset. Galileo didn't blindly accept what the "experts" of the day declared, nor did he conclude that the Earth revolves around the Sun before he could prove his hypotheses. He challenged conventional wisdom and developed a new hypothesis to describe the universe around him, and only then did he ask people to believe his seemingly outlandish claim. No pun intended.

History recounts that Galileo died under house arrest after being tried by the Inquisition for his trouble, paying a huge price for redefining the center of the solar system and therefore the center of the very universe. Let's hope that doesn't happen to us cigar aficionados, since we might be embarking on an even *bigger* issue: How does one identify a cigar's taste notes and make taste associations without suffering from palate fatigue, confusion, and frustration?

This book is not an end in itself, nor the final word on any topic. You will find observations that I have made, researched, and tested over and over again, covering a span of 25 years in my quest to better understand two of our most elusive senses: taste and smell. To help you gain an appreciation for the interplay of art and science while reading, I invite you to do the following:

- Taste every food and drink at least once.
- Smoke every style cigar at least two or three times.
- Challenge everything you believe and hear.
- Live, laugh, love, and relax more.
- And remember: It's only a cigar.

Galileo Resting from His Labors

Excerpt from an Interview with
JOCHY BLANCO

TABACALERA LA PALMA, TAMBORIL, DOMINICAN REPUBLIC, FEBRUARY 2020

Nick: Earlier we were discussing how you nurture the tobacco plants. Would you share with our readers what we discussed regarding how you raise a tobacco plant from a tiny seed the size of a grain of salt into a large, lush plant in 90 to 120 days—one that's going to produce aroma and taste characteristics that is going to excite cigar smokers?

Jochy: The tobacco plant is a child; we have to take extra good care of it when it is small. We must give it the right amount of nutrients that it needs, not making a mistake of giving it too much or too little; if we do, it will change the flavor of the tobacco. Also, at a certain time during the growing stage, we need to stress the plants a little by holding back irrigation—this will cause them to take on their own unique flavors and characteristics: it's incredible how smart the plants are, and nature in general.

Nick: So creating a little bit of stress at the right moment and in the right amount causes the tobacco plant to take on different characteristics or stronger characteristics? So timing is critical.

Jochy: Yes, and we have stressed the plants a couple of times during the growing season. Not in the early growing stage, not in the late. It has to be somewhere in the middle.

Nick: So you guys are like scientists out in the tobacco fields. The only difference is you're not wearing a white lab coat—you're wearing a guayabera.

Jochy: [Laughter] Well I guess you can put it that way.

Nick: I know this is going to be a hard question to answer, but I am going to ask it anyway. Of all the cigars you've blended in your career, which one stands out as exceptional in terms of aroma, taste, and flavor characteristics and how are you able to achieve it?

Jochy: It's hard to pick only one cigar. To create a really good blend with lots of taste and flavor, you must start by using the best tobacco seeds, and there aren't that many seed varieties to choose from. It's like wine grapes used to make excellent wine: There are probably seven or eight main varieties. In tobacco, it's the same, just a handful. We use about four or five seed varieties to create really good tobacco plants.

For me, the most important thing is to create blends using combinations of same seed grown in different regions. Why? Because sometimes we grow the same seeds in La Canela and Acao, work with them in the same way, giving them the same treatment in terms of irrigation and fertilization. And, surprisingly, the taste of the tobaccos from the same seed grown in different areas is different. Sometimes the tobaccos from one area have more strength or they are sweeter. We mix and play with those tobaccos to find the best combinations.

Chapter 1

Why All the Confusion?

The closer you get to nature, the closer you get to the truth.
—Albert Einstein

Our journey to developing a more sophisticated palate will not be easy: Several forces are against us. We will demystify each, one by one.

In the Introduction we briefly discussed science and art—now we add *history* to the equation: A (Art) + S (Science) + H (History) = T (Truth). In order to fully understand why we sense certain flavors and not others, we need to study America's history; oddly enough it will shed some light on this dilemma. Let's take a hard look at facts and figures and clear up the confusion. You might want to light up.

The Death Spiral of Whole Foods

The 20th century ushered in the death of whole foods—no, not the Whole Food chain often called "Whole Paycheck"—but intact food from nature with a single ingredient: beef, fish, nuts, whole wheat, brown rice, cabbage, beans, figs, eggs. As the old saying goes, "There's nothing like the real thing." After World War II, the US population expanded by leaps and bounds, in what is commonly referred to as the Baby Boom. I like to refer to it as the Wonder Bread Era because this product sums up the movement so well. Take a wholesome grain that has sustained humans for millennia and remove the bran (the outer fiber-rich layer) and the wheat germ (the inner layer rich in nutrients) and what is left is the endosperm, the starchy part of the grain that white flour is made from.

> ### SLIM PICKINGS
> The world today relies on just 150 food plants. Of these, only 20 produce 90% of our food. Only 9 are widely used and associated with 75% of the human diet. Fifty percent of our diets include rice, corn, and wheat. This is slim pickings considering that there are over 32,000 edible plants and grains.

This byproduct of the whole grain is very light brown, so it is chemically bleached, making it snow white. But the processing doesn't end there. To make the flour silky smooth to the touch, improve dough's elasticity, and produce a higher rise when baked, potassium bromate is added as an oxidizing agent. What is left is a product that is almost pure starch.

After all the inherent nutrients are removed from the whole grain, they are replaced with synthetic vitamins, resulting in *enriched* flour (I confess that, when I started reading food labels years ago, I naively thought that enriched flour was better than whole grain flour because it was, well, *enriched*). The wheat byproduct is then formed into a loaf, and baked until it rises into a fluffy white, almost weightless loaf. The iconic version of this loaf was, and is, Wonder Bread, marketed during the 1950s as a product that "builds strong bodies 12 ways."

In order to keep up with the population explosion and consumer demand, companies made large capital investments in food laboratories to create and produce synthetic substances, commonly referred to as "imitation." Unless the label on a product reads, "Contains only 100% certified organic ingredients," it contains one or more of the 85,000 FDA-approved synthetic substances, including artificial flavors, dyes, fragrances, and preservatives.

What motivates this synthetic insanity? The bottom line is money—it's all about the money, the main advantage of synthetic over organic.

For instance, one of the most widely used flavor additives in the world is imitation vanilla. The average retail price of natural vanilla is $18.75 per ounce versus imitation vanilla, at $0.12 per ounce. The vanilla plant is very fussy. It originated in Mexico, only allowing a single bee—the Melipona Beecheii, commonly referred to as the "mountain bee"—to pollinate its precious flower bud. Attempts to grow vanilla in Spain were met with no success. Importing mountain bees for pollination did not work as they didn't take kindly to being removed from their homeland and would not pollinate the vanilla flower. To this day, every vanilla flower is pollinated by human hands, one flower at a time. To make matters even more challenging, the vanilla plant blooms only once a year, for 12-14 hours. Can you image the daunting task of the vanilla orchard farmers having to hand pollinate the entire orchard during such a small window of time? I think it is fair to say that the vanilla flower bloom epitomizes the saying, "Timing is everything."

NOTHING LIKE THE REAL THING

Real vanilla has 250 flavor compounds versus imitation vanilla, which has a grand total of one: "vanillin." Imitation vanilla is made from wood-tar creosote, wood pulp, or petro chemicals. Less than 1% of the world's real vanilla extract comes from actual vanilla orchids.

Vanilla beans are ready to harvest 9 months after blooms are pollinated, after which the curing process begins with drying the beans in the sun. Immediately following the curing process is the sweating stage where the beans are wrapped in cloth and stored in a wood crate for one year before they are ready for the final drying process. In this stage, they are preserved: usually air-dried, partially in sun and partially in shade, preventing them from drying too quickly, which affects quality.

To ensure that the beans dry out evenly, they are often massaged by hand. To reach their peak quality, they are wrapped in wax paper and stored in boxes for about a month, then packaged and sent to market for us to savor. Producing a high quality vanilla bean is a very intensive, long process. Now you won't get sticker shock when you see a single, tiny, dried vanilla bean costing $4.00 or more.

Additives, Irradiation, and Taste Preferences

Consider this for a moment: A cigar is made from the highest quality tobacco in the world and goes through several forms of fermentation for six months to several years. Tobacco is a pure, 100% agriculture substance: no additives, no fillers or preservatives, no color dyes, no stabilizers. It is just tobacco, the way nature made it. How could synthetic chemicals mimic tobacco's complex flavor footprint, which consists of hundreds of flavor molecules and compounds?

Baby Boomers and Millennials grew up eating foods flavored with imitation substances such as vanilla, bitter almond, strawberry, grape, orange, etc. Countless foods have been diluted to the point that they taste entirely different from their natural state. Chocolate provides a prime example. In an 8-ounce milk chocolate candy bar, one finds only 10% of the lowest-quality cacao on the market or about one cacao bean. Herein lies the problem for many of us raised since the Wonder Bread Era began: We may have had only rare opportunities to taste whole foods and beverages in their natural state. This might explain why so many of our sensory perceptions have inaccurate references and need to be recalibrated to the original organic substances.

Most herbs, spices, flours, grains, and fruits purchased at grocery stores have been irradiated to extend their shelf life tenfold, eliminating the possibility of little bugs showing up in your outdated rice or flour. I remember as a young boy asking my mom how the little black bugs got in the bag of rice and cream of wheat? Mom would tell me to go ask dad. Dad's answer was that bug eggs are always there, and when they hatch, its nature's way of telling us that the food is too old for us to eat and it is time to give it to the chickens.

If you are not familiar with the food irradiation process, it is simple: Herbs, spices, flour, grains, and fruits are run through a radiation machine on a conveyer belt, essentially killing any and all living organisms and enzymes. One day I brought an apple home that was included in my meal at a restaurant, and it just didn't look right—almost fake. So I decided to put it to the test. I put it in clear sight on the countertop so that when it started rotting, I could catch it early, before it stunk up my kitchen. To my surprise, the apple sat there for four months without showing any signs of rotting. I wouldn't feed it to my hens or put it in the compost or worm bed—this apple was bionic.

Many young and old cigar smokers alike have never tasted certain organic flavors in their natural state. As a result, they have developed false taste associations, which do not offer the wide range of complex flavor compounds that natural organic substances do. I can't image walking into a cigar shop and asking the salesperson if they carry the new premium cigar brand that is handcrafted with synthetic wrapper leaves.

During the 20th century, with the use of newly developed processes and additives, the cost to make food dropped tremendously. Margins sprang sky-high. Once corporate America realized it could make *big* money in food, it dove right in. Today, Fortune 500 food and Ag companies hire the most highly educated, talented, and creative minds straight out of the best universities in the country—not to discover the cure for cancer, diabetes, or obesity, or to minimize our carbon footprint without giving up any of our vices or luxuries, but to create foods that we will like, buy, and continue to buy.

Their mission: to create the tastiest and sometimes borderline addictive products. They do so by (1) using the least expensive ingredients; (2) making the products as visually appealing as possible, including using an array of synthetic chemical dyes; (3) preserving them with one or a combination of thousands of preservative chemicals; and (4) irradiating them to achieve a possible two- plus years of shelf life. We can only imagine what happened to the living organisms that once resided inside that apple.

THE AMERICAN PALATE

Say hello to the American palate. Ever consider why the greatest—in many ways—country in the world has an obesity epidemic, a diabetes crisis, a coronary heart disease pandemic, and a cancer scourge? By now you are probably wondering, *What on Earth does this have to do with cigars?* Hang in there, take a couple puffs, and you will soon find out.

Most of the artificial ingredients, dyes, and preservatives are now considered carcinogenic—that is, poisonous to the human body, with one caveat: in *certain amounts*. I don't know about you, but I'd rather not put anything poisonous in my mouth regardless of the amount. And we consume many of these substances in our food every day.

Manufacturing Food

Getting the FDA to approve toxic additives has proven easy for food manufacturers: A business meeting with FDA buddies may transpire at an exclusive golf resort in the Bahamas or, for high-dollar deals that may require some arm-twisting, in Hawaii. These all-expense-paid outings are disguised as new product development workshops. What overworked, underpaid FDA examiner would say no to a free vacation, spouse included?

Food processing is one of the largest industries in the country and hence one of the most powerful. This industry uses its financial clout to influence politicians as well as the FDA. A 1998 study showed that almost half of the leading officials at the FDA previously worked for the same organizations they were mandated to regulate. Universities have equally powerful ties to the food processing industry. They receive huge grants from food manufacturers, which ensures test outcomes that benefit their donors: the processed food manufacturers.

If the Fortune 500 food companies don't have an in-house food laboratory, they hire one of the major food development companies out there—and there are many. These companies *are* scientific food laboratories. If you had the opportunity to visit one, you'd walk away with your head spinning. You would think they were splitting atoms or mapping the complete human genome. These companies, along with the well-equipped major brands, hire PhDs from various academic disciplines to address all five senses:

- Visual (the way a product looks)
- Auditory (the sound packaging makes when touched)
- Tactile (the way a product feels to the touch and when chewed)
- Gastronomic (the way a product tastes)
- Olfactory (the way a product smells)

The lineup of their team includes (but is not limited to) neuroscientists, neurologists, biomechanical engineers, microbiologists, enologists, plus chemosensory, auditory, and tactile scientists. After a product is made, they need to sell it, so they hire a world-class marketing team comprised of behavioral scientists, physiologists, psychophysics, psychologists, physiologists, and pneumonologists. In this department the visual sensory division will decide which color dyes make food most visually appealing.

Food labs are equipped with taste-profiling departments that may use salaried employees or college students to wear nose clips while tasting different combinations of foods, artificial ingredients, etc. Teams of human tasters approach food in an unusual way: *by design*. They seek to guide consumers to inexpensive products—I mean foods—that will excite our sensory organs. The taster functions as an analytical machine.

We may wonder why the process isn't more fully automated, like bank ATMs or Home Depot and Walmart checkouts. Well, companies do plan to pursue automation, but, so far, the machines are very expensive and still pale in comparison to the gold standard: a person. It is still cheaper to overwork and underpay a human than to buy a gas chromatography machine. Do your fellow man, your kids, and your grandkids a big favor and boycott any and all forms of automation when possible. This movement builds machines to take the place of humans, increasing the corporations' and shareholders' profits at the cost of putting people out of work and creating unnecessary hardship for their families and communities.

A Junk Food Plague

Potato chips, an American invention, paved the way for our contemporary metamorphosis toward craving junk food, comparable in impact to early man's ability to control fire and ferment food. The chip's exact origin remains hazy. The most popular story suggests that it was born in 1853 at Moon Lake Lodge in Saratoga Springs, New York, when a diner found his side dish of scalloped potatoes soggy. The waitress took them back to the kitchen where a tired short order cook at the end of his shift tossed them into a pot of hot oil. The waitress served the dish to the patron, and the rest is history.

Potato chip manufacturers had very little knowledge of biology when they began to flavor their products with spices in the 1950s, so they basically used salt—a lot of it. Gradually, the food industry started to develop its own insights into flavor and appetite. Howard Moskowitz, a graduate of Harvard's Department of Psychology, worked in the psychophysics lab, experimenting with perceptions of sweet and salty solutions. He was hired as a young scientist at the US Army Natick Laboratories in the early 1970s. His assignment was to make the canned food rations that soldiers ate in the field more palatable. The food was so awful that many soldiers were skipping meals, becoming undernourished. Moskowitz added monosodium glutamate, commonly referred to as MSG, to the canned food rations. It was so successful that the food industry giants caught wind and jumped on the bandwagon, adding MSG to their processed foods.

The Japanese were first to identify MSG in miso, a fish-based broth and very healthy soup. But American food scientists found a shortcut at a fraction of the price by rearranging the atoms in corn flour, creating the US version of MSG, which many people are slightly or very allergic to. If you eat food seasoned with MSG as a flavor enhancer, it may taste great going down, but later you may find that you can't seem to quench your thirst and may feel bloated for several hours after the meal. Most fast food and low priced buffet style restaurants use MSG to make their low quality foods taste, at best, good. Next time you are dining at a mid-tier or high-end Asian restaurant, ask the server if they use MSG. If they say yes, tell them you do not want any soup, appetizer, or entrée that is prepared with MSG. Ask which dishes are not prepared with MSG. I simplify the process and tell the server that I am severely allergic to MSG. Rest assured, they won't prepare my dish with it. The last thing they want is a customer rolling on the floor with an adverse reaction to their food.

I still remember the first time I had an Asian meal prepared without MSG. It was the mid-90s, during the cigar boom. An investment group was interested in buying my company, and they offered to fly me to New York to discuss the deal. One night we dined at an upscale Asian restaurant. After we were seated, the waitress came to the table to bring us hot tea. I kept looking around the table for the fried noodles. I was accustomed to filling up on them while waiting for the main dish. To my surprise, but not to my disappointment, fried noodles were not served, nor was vanilla ice cream with a fortune cookie at the end of the meal. In the soup, appetizers, and entrée, I tasted flavors I had never experienced before. And after eating my fair share, I didn't feel bloated like I usually felt after a typical American Asian dining experience.

Fascinating Cigar History

Old World Cigar Era

1492

Christopher Columbus accidently makes two great discoveries: the Americas and tobacco. The Spanish keep their tobacco secret to themselves for the next 250 years.

1731-1750

Spain establishes the Royal Tobacco Manufacturers of Seville to oversee the expanding business in tobacco and cigars. Dutch traders introduce cigars and tobacco to Holland and Russia.

1751

Empress Catherine II has silk bands wrapped around the cigars so her glove won't become stained while she smoked. Little did she know that 100 years later cigar bands would decorate most cigars.

1762-1763

King George III goes to war with Cuba and British-occupied Cuba for only one year, but it was enough time to introduce Europe to the exotic and opulent aroma of tobacco.

1800-1810

France creates a government tobacco monopoly. Cigar-making spreads to Italy and Switzerland. In 1810 the first cigar factory is built in America. The Victorian Era helps cigars find a place in high society.

1823

In 1823, 15,000 cigars are imported into Britain. In 1840, 17 years later, that number would grow by leaps and bounds to 13 million. Cigars become a status symbol for wealth, success, and elegance.

1845-1855

Tobacco becomes Cuba's number one export, replacing coffee. Cuba exports 360 million Havana cigars. US President Franklin Pierce tries to buy Cuba from Spain but is unsuccessful.

1870

The first Cuban counterfeit cigars appear in the marketplace. Havana Cigar Brands Association is formed to protect Cuban brand names and stop counterfeiters.

1880

Leopold de Rothschild instructs the Joya de Monterrey factory in Havana to produce a short cigar, 4.5", with a large ring gauge so he could get into the heart of the cigar quickly—a precursor for the Nub?

1875

Tobacco farmers in the US improve tobacco strains and produce fillers with unique taste characteristics in Florida, Connecticut, Pennsylvania, New York, Ohio, and Wisconsin. Immigrants help the US gain traction in a new cigar industry.

1880

First signs of government harassment: Boston passes a law prohibiting anyone from carrying a lit "see/gar" on public streets. This leads to the birth of the smoking room or smoking parlor.

1885

Vincent Martinez Ybor develops a small subdivision named after him, "Ybor City," later nicknamed "Cigar Capitol of the World." In 1929, production peaked at 500 million hand-rolled "clear Havana" cigars.

1898

America becomes a cigar making and cigar smoking nation. There are over 500 factories of size in West Tampa, Ybor City, and Key West and a whopping 7,000 throughout of the country.

1898

The Spanish-American War leads to the first Cuban embargo, causing wrapper shortages that encourage tobacco farmers to start growing wrapper leaf. The surprising result: U.S. Conn. and Broadleaf.

1898

A good, American-made cigar with Havana leaf costs five cents, while an imported Havana costs ten to fifteen cents. The least expensive cigar, a stogie, costs one penny.

1901

After his coronation, King Edward VII utters four words that will go down in history: "Gentlemen, you may smoke." King Edward becomes the #1-selling cigar in the world in 1940.

1920

US President Woodrow Wilson's VP Thomas Marshall tells the Senate, "What this country needs is a really good 5-cent cigar."

1921

VP Marshall's wish becomes a reality. With 5 cents you could buy a good cigar, a beer, or a quart of milk. A box of good cigars costs $5 to $10.

1921-1930

Cigar sales decline due to less expensive cigarettes. Swisher and Cuesta Rey pioneer all tobacco machine-made cigars. Swisher produces 100 million per year.

1929-1935

During the Great Depression, the cost of a good machine-made cigar is 3 for 5 cents or about one and a half cents each.

New World Cigar Era

1930-1960

This was quite a time for the cigar industry due to World War I and World War II and the Surgeon General's warning regarding smoking cigarettes. A premium cigar costs 10 cents to 65 cents.

1962 Forward

President Kennedy imposes an embargo on all goods imported from Cuba. Twelve hours before the embargo, Pierre Salinger, Kennedy's press secretary, is instructed to purchase 1,000 H. Upmann Petit Coronas cigars.

1962 Forward

Havana tobacco prices soar. The price of a bale goes from $150 to $1,000 each. Unknown to anyone at the time, the Cuban Revolution would do more for the advancement of premium cigars than any prior historical event.

1963

Due to the political turmoil in Cuba, expatriates explore other regions outside of Cuba. Cigar maker Frank Llaneza and tobacco grower Angel Olivas set up operations in Honduras.

Cigar Smoking Renaissance

1972

The Dominican Republic (DR) becomes a cigar industry giant. Cuban expatriates Benji Menendez, Manolo Quesada, and Charlie Toraño find a more stable home to make cigars. By the mid-90s, the DR is the #1 producer of premium cigars in the world.

1989

The world's love affair with Cuban cigars is on the rocks due to issues with quality. Davidoff of Geneva sets fire to 130,000 Cuban-made cigars and moves production to the DR.

1991-1996

The US Embargo in Nicaragua is lifted in 1991, and in 1996, six privately owned factories are opened including: Padron, Plasencia, and Joya de Nicaragua. Nicaragua exports 4 million cigars in 1995.

1992

A magazine called *Cigar Aficionado* debuts in 1992, giving the industry what it needs to break orbit. In 1992 in the US alone, there are 400,000 cigar smokers. By 1995, the number more than doubles, and today there are 5 million premium cigar smokers.

Cigar Industry Revival

1995

Cigar imports to the US soar 66%. Smokers seek richer, spicier, fuller bodied cigars with larger ring gauges. Robusto and Toro are the most popular sizes. Diamond Crown introduces the cigar market to a monster cigar size: a 54rg

1998

The cigar boom ends, leaving a graveyard of new brands behind. A handful of anomalies emerge that will push the cigar making envelope, resulting in some of the most exciting blends ever.

2001

Sales are back to the cigar boom highs, and the old and new icons are creating new blends every year, with tobaccos from around the world that are extraordinary. There is never a better time in cigar history for smokers than now.

2019

Global Exports of Premium Cigars*:

Country	Total	US Only
Nicaragua	196M	169M
Dominican Republic	137M	106M
Honduras	77M	60M
Cuba	90M	N/A

*All figures are estimates.

Cigar Gene Pool Expansion

If necessity is the mother of invention, then we could say that curiosity drives innovation. How did cigar options increase from a handful to hundreds? The cigar gene pool expansion changed the industry forever.

The verdict is still out whether the gene pool or just people from different walks of life converging in one place is the reason for the cigar boom. Allow me to share with you my thoughts regarding the gene pool, and I'll let you decide what to believe.

The gene pool is the sum of a population's genetic material at a given time. Aleksandr Serebrovskii, a Russian geneticist, first introduced this concept in the 1920s as *genofond* or *gene fund*. This concept was exported to the United States by Theodosius Dobzhansky, a Russian linguist, who translated *genofond* into English as *gene pool*. A diverse gene pool offers genetic diversity, which leads to a robust population. Livestock breeders import outside genetic material via a stud from different genetic lines for a more robust herd. In humans, a large gene pool results in a more robust and dynamic population. America is a perfect example, populated by people from Europe, Asia, the Middle East, Africa, and South America, as well as those descended from indigenous Native American tribes.

A Modern Cigar Boom

The cigar boom of the mid-90s attracted many successful, intelligent, and passionate men to the cigar industry. Passion is a common thread that connects most of those in the cigar world, because making cigars is not what someone does to get rich quick. Quite the contrary: Manufacturing cigars is one of the most challenging and difficult businesses to survive in. Mother Nature can bless the tobacco crop with good weather or destroy it with a hurricane in a few hours. Cigar manufactures also have an ever-changing consumer to satisfy. A cigar maker must reinvent himself year after year, staying up to date with market treads, consumer tastes, and now government harassment. Today, the cigar consumer is much more educated than two decades ago, and with a more educated palate comes a demand for more complex and interesting taste profiles. Gone are the days when a cigar smoker buys and smokes the same cigar day after day.

The cigar industry expanded with many new players, most without Cuban lineage, who brought different skillsets, pushing the envelope and challenging conventional practices. They were wise enough to learn from the Cuban masters but broadened the possibilities through experimentation and innovation.

These newcomers had their fingers on the pulse of the marketplace. I am sure many, if not most, of their experimental ideas were failures, but some resulted in blends that offered novel and rich flavor profiles and taste characteristics. Their curiosity and passion to create something new and different expanded the possibilities exponentially.

A List of Innovators

Let's take a look at the most interesting and surprising newcomers who have challenged conventional wisdom and thus changed the landscape of the cigar industry.

The year ranges are plus or minus a year and listed in alphabetical order.

ANOMALIES, 1995–2003	
COMPANY	OWNER
Alex Bradly	Alan Ruben, 1996
Camacho	Julio and Christian Eiroa, 1995
Aganorsa Leaf f/k/a Casa Fernandez	Eduardo Fernandez, 1998
Gurkha Cigars	Kaizad Hansotia (revived 1992)
Drew Estates	Johnathan Drew and Marvin Samel, 1995
La Flor Dominican	Litto Gomez, 1996
My Father Cigar	Pepin Garcia, 2002
Perdomo Cigar	Nick Perdomo, 1992
Rocky Patel	Rocky Patel, 1995
Tatuaje	Pete Johnson, 2003
LATE BLOOMERS, 2003–2013	
Just when everyone thought the market had enough brands, and new ones would go up in smoke, these were launched successfully:	
Aging Room	Rafael Nodal, 2011
AJ Fernandez	Abdel Fernandez, 2009
Curivari Cigars	Andreas Throuvalas, 2012
El Artista Cigars	Ram Rodriguez (revived 2012)
Esteban Carreras Cigars	Craig Cunningham, 2012
EPC	Ernesto Carrillo, 2010
Fratello Cigars	Omar de Frias, 2013
Gran Habano	Guillermo and George Rico, 2003
Kristoff Cigars	Glen Case, 2004
La Palina Cigars	Bill Paley (Revived 2010)
La Zona	Erik Espinosa, 2012
Illusione	Dion Giolito, 2005
Mombacho	Cameron Heaps, Markus Raty, 2006
PDR	Abe Flores, 2008
Recluse	Jose Dominguez, Jr., 2012
RoMa Craft Tobac	Mike Rosales and Skip Martin, 2012
Room 101	Matt Booth, 2009
Venture Cigars	Kretek Group, 2006
Warped Cigars	Kale Gillis, 2009
Willie Herrera (Blender)	Drew Estates Blender, 2011

TWILIGHT NEWCOMERS, 2014–2019

As the ball dropped marking the first day of 2014, anyone in the cigar industry would have bet the farm that the tobacco gods would not give birth to any new stars. Low and behold, rising stars emerged from the abyss.

Caldwell	Robert Caldwell, 2014
Casa Cuevas	Luis Sr. and Luis Jr. Cuevas, 2017
D'Crossier	Santana Diaz, 2015
Dunbarton Tobacco Trust	Steve Saka, 2015
Foundation Cigars	Nick Melillo, 2015
JRE Tobacco	Julio and Justo Eiroa, 2015
Micallef Cigars	Al Micallef, 2017
MBombay Cigars	Mel Shah, 2014
Plascencia Cigars	Plascencia Cigar Family, 2017

*If I missed anyone, you probably forgot to send me a free box of cigars, so my apologies. **Just kidding**.*

Seemingly Endless Choices

> **OPTION MADNESS**
>
> Frito Lay offers over 200 varieties of flavored chips. There are 65 major brands of Tomato Sauce: Prego alone offers 20 varieties.

Ever wonder why today there seems to be an endless number of foods, wine, coffee, and cigar choices? We can thank Moskowitz, mentioned earlier. His most noted accomplishment was the development of the food tasting process called Cluster Tasting, which is why I refer to him as him the Father of Food Options.

In the early 1980s, Campbell Soup, the maker of Prego tomato sauce, hired Moskowitz to help them compete with Ragu, the number one canned tomato sauce maker. The Cluster Tasting method he developed was different from the standard taste-testing system of the day, which consisted in hiring 100 random tasters and asking them to taste and rate tomato sauce from three different recipes: creamy, chunky, and spicy. It would be the equivalent of giving 100 random cigar smokers a light, medium, and full-bodied cigar and asking them which one they liked best. The inherent problem with this type of testing was that the mean, or average, was rarely greater than 55% to 60%. You could flip a coin and have the same odds at a fraction of the cost of the taste test.

In Cluster Tasting, by contrast, 100 tasters were divided into three groups: the tasters who liked creamy, chunky, and spicy sauce. The mean shot up to 70% to 80%. This was a game changer, and the results were extraordinary. Prego quickly surpassed Ragu as the leader in the industry. Maxwell House, the second largest coffee maker, caught wind of Moskowitz's new approach and hired him to do what he did for Prego: make them number one in their industry. Using the same method, he divided 100 coffee tasters into three groups: those who liked light, medium, and dark roast. The results were the same, and within a few years Maxwell House was the number one coffee sold in America. During the following decade, Prego and Maxwell House increased their sales by $800 million.

Moskowitz's cluster tasting method was adopted by the rest of the players in the food industry. Next time you stand in front a variety of purchasing options and can't decide which coffee to buy or which bag of potato chips to break your New Year's resolution with, or which cigar blend or wrapper—whether a small batch, reserve, grand reserve, or vintage—to enjoy, you can thank Moskowitz.

Food companies exploit tricks to nudge consumer buying habits. They design names, colors, and packaging to leap out at the shopper from supermarket shelves, forming wonderful taste images. The most powerful of these tools is *branding*.

An entire set of memories, feelings, and associations coalesce around a name and logo, which the brain accesses with each view. In 2004, scientists at Baylor University in Houston ran experiments to show exactly how brands make such deep impressions, studying reactions to Coke and Pepsi. The two colas have similar chemical compositions, flavors, colors, and consistencies. In a taste test with no labels, volunteers rated both equally delicious. Once the labels appeared, Coke won, hands down. Labeled Coke also beat unlabeled Coke.

Avoiding Deception

As the 21st century arrived, food and beverage manufacturers seemed to reach the limits of their ability to manipulate our senses. Every known technique, device, and trick had been exploited. If you choose to rebel against the tyranny of the food industry while improving your palate, read the ingredients before buying products. Return to natural ingredients and simple, natural flavors. There are many ways to do this, such as the Paleolithic diet commonly referred to as the Paleo diet, based on the idea that our genes and bodies are better suited to eat foods that could have been acquired by hunter-gatherers, or a more modern version of the Paleo diet, the Mediterranean diet, that offers a broader food footprint, such as lean meats, wild-caught fish, aged cheese, eggs, veggies, fruit, and nuts. More regarding your options in Chapter 5.

And vote with your dollars. Every time you buy healthy, unprocessed food, you hit the processed food tyrants where it hurts most: their pockets. CEOs of these companies might wake up when their bonuses, stock options, and pensions are decreased.

Taste preference now sits at the intersection of many sciences. It's driven more by forces outside the kitchen than inside. Chefs, artisans, and cigar blenders do have one thing working for them: the mystery at the heart of taste has never been cracked. Science has still not explained how taste can encompass the whole range of human emotions and experiences, from memories of pleasure and joy to those of disgust and pain.

These chefs, artisans, and cigar blenders continuously recreate themselves using their tools, be they foods, grapes, grains, or tobacco leaves, into something new. With each bite, each sip, each puff, bliss!

Excerpt from an Interview with
JHONYS DIAZ

General Cigar Santiago, Dominican Republic, February 2020

Nick: Do you feel that the ability to detect and identify different taste nuances and make taste associations, such as, *I'm sensing a dried lemon peel, dried fruit, a hint of cedar and chocolate,* could enhance a cigar smokers experience?

Jhony: Yes, very much, of course you know it's not that simple. You have to be an experienced smoker to actually go that far and be able to appreciate those nuances. But having this ability will of course enhance your experience and in the end, you will have a much better picture of the cigar's taste profile.

Nick: Earlier before the interview I was given a tour of the facility and I saw firsthand the long fermentation processes the tobacco leaf goes through. I also noticed that each tobacco bulk or "pilon" had a birth certificate. You guys are like modern day alchemist.

Jhony: Yes, you could say that. But a cook is also a perfect name for what we do. What we have to go through when putting together a blend is a lengthy and cumbersome process. Picking different varieties of tobaccos from different origins, I guess you could refer to it as a cook or even an alchemist. Maybe an alchemist is too much, but I think at least a cook.

Nick: Well, I think you're very humble and I admire you for that. I might add, some of the best meals I have had, have been in simple homes with a cook.

Chapter 2

The Basics of Sensory Perception and the Science Behind Taste

Smell is a potent wizard that transports you across thousands of miles and all the years you have lived.
—Helen Keller

Chapter 1 served up a lot to digest, no pun intended. It angered me to learn that our food industry has no regard for our health and well-being, and it infuriates me to think that they have the FDA and our politicians in their back pockets. Our palates—whether savoring fine cuisine or, in the case of this book, fine cigars—have been severely compromised due to the processed and imitation foods we've been consuming for decades.

We are going to look at the science behind taste to clear up false assumptions and misinformation in order to reset our palates. You might find it helpful to get in the right mindset before delving into the science of taste. We will be challenging conventional wisdom and seeing it in a new light. As we do, keep this in mind: *One of the biggest mistakes most of us make is knowing enough about a subject to think we are right, but not enough to know when we are wrong.*

Beginning in the 1990s, exciting new research into the senses of taste and smell has yielded more knowledge than in all the previous millennia. In this chapter, we'll draw on this research to help us explore how our intricate palates—the olfactory and gastronomic systems, to be more precise—really work.

I will do my best to make the science we encounter easily palatable.

Our Five Sensory Tools

1. Sight (Visual)
2. Sound (Auditory)
3. Touch (Tactile)
4. Taste (Gastronomic)
5. Smell (Olfactory)

We experience the world, as well as premium cigars, through these five senses. Some play a more significant role than others, but all have an effect. Let's take a brief look at each one and then delve into taste and smell. These two play the most significant roles in our smoking ritual and experience. To use more technical jargon, each sensory perception influences a cigar's overall taste impressions and our sensorial experience.

Sight (Visual)

Sight is our most familiar and most developed sense. Of course, we don't smoke with our eyes, but we can appreciate a visually appealing cigar band and wrapper leaf. Many connoisseurs look for a cigar that has a wrapper with a sheen from the still-intact natural oils and a wrapper leaf that is tightly stretched around the cigar bunch (filler leaves). When a true artisan handcrafts a cigar, it will usually have a shiny surface due to the wrapper leaf being tightly stretched over the bunch (the cigar's core of filler leaves).

The smoother the surface, the more light it will reflect. For me, though, this sheen serves as a general guide, but not the gospel. I've enjoyed many great cigars without a sheen and encountered some cigars with one that did not impress me in the least.

Although sight is our most familiar sense, it is also the easiest to fool—evident in optical illusions that we have all experienced—whereas, taste and smell are both very difficult to fool.

Sound (Auditory)

We live in a world of amplified distractions, a punishing drumbeat of constant input, broadcast through our cellphones, tablets, iPad, TV news channels, and radios, and so on. We need to be conscious of how these distractions potentially influence our smoking experience.

Listening to pleasant sounds, for example, will definitely improve your smoking experience. Whether the echoes of nature in a waterfall, ocean waves breaking on the shoreline, or your preferred music, pleasing sounds all work in your favor. On the other hand, if you hope to leave the problems of the world behind and someone has cranked up annoying music, or if you are in an environment with eight TV screens blaring from all directions, your chances of having an enjoyable smoking experience are slim to none—unless someone dipped the head of your cigar in CDB oil when you went to the restroom.

Touch (Tactile)

Like sight and sound, touch also plays a role in a smoking experience. The size of a cigar and how it feels in your hand and mouth can make a big difference. Common cigar sizes range from *Lancero* (or 38 ring gauge) to *Gordo* (or 60 ring gauge) and lengths from 5 inches to 7 inches. If you are not yet a seasoned cigar smoker, you nonetheless will come to know your preferences over time. Some sizes may suit you better on different occasions, so don't get locked into one size: You may discover a welcome surprise if you are willing to explore different cigar sizes from time to time as you develop your palate.

Taste (Gastronomic)

There is the common use of the word taste to refer to everything we experience when we eat or drink, but for our purposes taste, or gustation, refers to what is detected by the taste receptors in the mouth, located on the front, back and both sides of the tongue, along with the all the tissue inside the mouth and throat. These taste receptors react to the flavor molecules from the food or drink we consume and send signals to the brain. The way our brains perceive these stimuli is what we refer to as taste. There are only a handful of different tastes that we detect, which we will examine in detail.

Only in recent years have taste receptors been accurately identified. One of the first breakthroughs in taste research came in 1974 with the realization that the Tongue Map was essentially an unchallenged, decades-old misunderstanding. The map dates back to research published in 1901 by a German scientist, D. P. Hanig, who set out to measure the relative sensitivity of the tongue for the four known basic tastes.

1. Bitter
2. Sour
3. Salty
4. Sweet
5. Savory/Umami

Based on the subjective whims of his volunteers, he concluded that sensitivity to the four tastes varied around the tongue. Then in 1942, Edwin Boring, a noted experimental psychologist and later historian of psychology, took Hanig's raw data and calculated numbers for the levels of sensitivity. These numbers merely denoted relative sensitivities, but they were plotted on a graph in such a way that other scientists assumed that areas of lower sensitivity were areas of no sensitivity. With this, the modern—and misleading—Tongue Map was born.

You might have been introduced to the Tongue Map in grade school. The theory goes something like this: Taste buds for bitter are way in the back of the tongue, the sour taste buds are in front of them to the sides, the salty taste buds are in front of those and also to the sides, and the sweet taste buds are on the tip of the tongue.

You can disprove the map in the comfort of your own kitchen. Place salt on the tip of your tongue, where our sweet taste receptors supposedly reside. You'll taste salt. Carefully place some sugar in the middle of your tongue, close your mouth, wait for it to dissolve, and you'll taste sweet. For reasons unknown, scientists never disputed this inconsistency. The map has frustrated many a grade-schooler, including me, who couldn't get the experiment right in science class. I, along with a few of my brave classmates, failed the lesson for insisting we could taste sugar in the middle, sides, and back of our tongues. Training not to challenge conventional wisdom starts at a young age.

In fact, there's more to taste than sweet, sour, salty, and bitter. Most scientists agree upon a fifth distinct taste called *umami*, also referred to as *savory*. Kikunae Ikeda, a Japanese scientist, identified umami in the early 1900s, but the West ignored his finding for most of the 20th century. Umami is associated with glutamates, which are found in foods containing animal fat and in fruits and vegetables high in omega-3 oil, such as avocados, coconut, and tree nuts, as well as sea vegetables such as kelp.

The latest research suggests that there just might be a sixth: the taste of animal fat. The problem with this theory is that human tasters have difficulty differentiating between the fifth taste (umami or savory) and the sixth (animal fat).

In 1974, Virginia Collings, a faculty scientist at the University of Pittsburgh, reexamined Hanig's work and agreed with his main point: Disparities in sensitivity to the four basic tastes do exist on various parts of the tongue. Collings discovered that all tastes can be detected anywhere taste receptors are found: around the tongue, on the soft palate at back and roof of the mouth, and even on the epiglottis, the flap that blocks food from the windpipe.

The kindest way I can find to describe the Tongue Map is that it is a vast *oversimplification.*

Smell (Olfactory)

Our sense of smell is crucial to the enjoyment of a fine cigar, not to mention to a great glass of wine, whiskey, a snifter of brandy, or a delicious meal. Innumerable pleasures abound. A person with a keen sense of smell delights in the aromas of a fine cigar, a slow-roasting turkey, or a Chateaubriand smothered with caramelized onions and shitake mushrooms.

On a more scientific level, our sense of smell emanates from an internal warning system that dates back to early man, alerting him to the danger of smoke from a fire, spoiled food, or tiger excrement. In a more positive light, he might be alerted by the smell of a herd of grazing game, signifying the possibility of a delicious meal, or the sweet fragrance of apricot or orange blossoms, announcing soon-to-harvest fruit. Smell just might be our most treasured sense. Many cigar smokers I know think so.

Any loss in our sense of smell can have a negative effect on quality of life. It can also be a sign of serious health problems. The good news is that only 2% of North Americans report issues in this area. If you partake in the ritual of enjoying premium cigars, you probably do not fall into that 2%.

Problems with the sense of smell increase as people's health diminishes, not necessarily as people get older. Many studies say that a person's sense of smell diminishes with age, but these are poorly designed studies that test individuals based on age only, instead of basing them on age and health. Remember, *question everything*. Expect to run into junk science, good science, and excellent science.

If you have the opportunity to travel to a cigar event in Nicaragua, Honduras, or the Dominican Republic, you will see many old-timers who are either factory owners, cigar blenders, production managers, or cigar makers. They are living examples who can prove that our palates don't diminish with age.

About a decade ago, I met José Daniel Sanchez, who at that time was 86 years young. He was in charge of quality control, making sure of proper cigar blend and construction. When creating a premium cigar, the placement of the tobacco leaves is critical. If the ligero leaf isn't positioned in the center of the cigar bunch, the cigar will not burn well or taste good.

I asked José, "Do you remember when you started smoking cigars?" His face lit up as he reflected on his early days in Cuba working on a tobacco farm.

"I was fourteen. Since then, I haven't gone a single day without smoking at least one."

I asked him if he could tell what kind of tobaccos were used in a cigar blend just by smoking the cigar. "If I couldn't, I wouldn't be here, walking the factory floor eight hours a day, making sure the cigar makers are making the correct blend and putting the tobacco leaves in the correct position."

I wondered how I could I test his palate without insulting him. In a flash, an idea came to me. "José," I said, "I have what I think is a good cigar that someone gave me, but I don't know what kind of tobacco was used to make it." Someone had indeed given me the cigar, but I had removed the band to test friends' palates as part of my "research."

José asked me if it was okay if he took a puff of my cigar, which isn't commonly done among cigar connoisseurs. He wasn't a connoisseur, though. He was a master. He needed only a couple draws, not a whole cigar.

He grabbed a napkin from his desk and wiped the head of my cigar to absorb the moisture, took a puff, then waited for a moment and took a second puff. As he was gently blowing the smoke from his mouth, he grinned. "The wrapper is probably Corojo; the filler is a mix of Criollo 98 grown in Condega, and Corojo grown in Jalapa."

Incredible! This octogenarian who had been smoking cigars every day for 72 years had a razor-sharp palate. And he was still healthy enough to work full time in subtropical heat.

The Anatomy of Smell

Our ability to smell comes from sensory receptor cells, which are present in very large numbers (millions), clustered within a small area in the back of the nasal cavity, forming the olfactory bulb (see illustration). Each receptor cell extends to the surface of the epithelium and connects with a large number of long, slender extensions called cilia. The cilia are covered with mucus, facilitating the detection of odor molecules by the olfactory receptors. These receptor cells are connected directly to the brain. Each olfactory neuron has one odor receptor. Microscopic molecules released by substances around us—whether it is the aroma of coffee brewing or a neighbor's cigar smoke drifting by—stimulate these receptors. Once the neurons detect the molecules, they send messages to the brain, which filters the input through a library of stored references. Our amazing gray matter identifies the specific odor, and we have a eureka moment: Aha—got it! Cigar connoisseurs, and wine and whiskey snobs refer to these as Taste Associations.

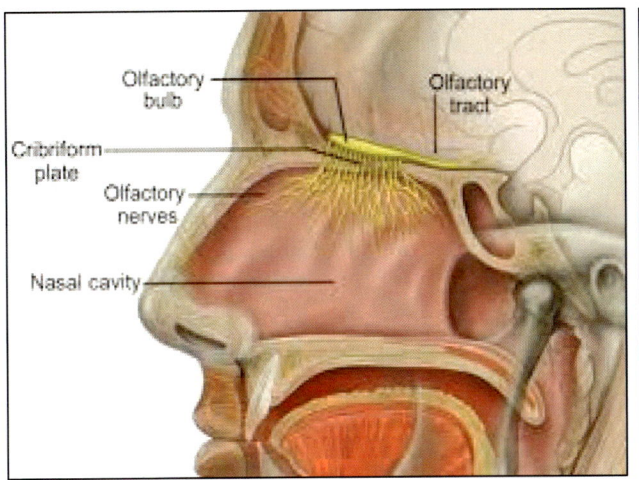
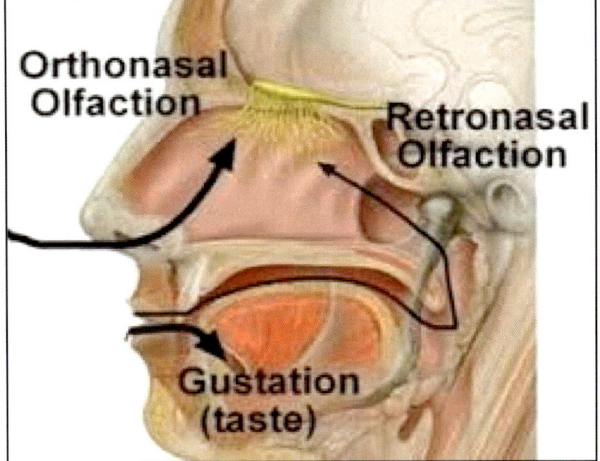

Smells reach the olfactory sensory neurons through two pathways. The first, through the nostrils, is called ortho hale by cigar aficionados (see illustration). The second pathway is through the mouth then up into the nasal cavity, referred to as retro hale. Chewing food releases aromas that access the olfactory sensory neurons through the second pathway. If the pathway is blocked, such as when our nose is stuffed up due to a cold, odors or aromas can't reach the sensory cells. As a result, we lose much of our ability to enjoy the flavor in foods, drinks, or cigars.

In this way, the senses of smell and taste work closely together.

Without the olfactory sensory neurons, familiar flavors such as dark chocolate, caramel, or dried figs would be hard to distinguish, and food in general and cigars in particular would tend to taste bland.

For cigar aficionados, the olfactory bulb plays a critical role in the enjoyment of our smoking experiences. In later chapters, we will learn about ways to improve, protect, and repair your sense of smell.

Getting the Terminology Right

In the context of food, the term *flavor* is used to refer to the perception that results from both mouth taste/gustation and smell/olfaction. To avoid confusion, we will use the term *mouth taste* to refer to the sensation experienced only in the mouth. For the overall sensation experience in the mouth and smell/olfaction, we will use the commonly accepted terms *taste*, *flavor*, and *palate*.

- Mouth Taste/Gastronomy
- Nasal: Aroma/Smell/Olfaction
- Combination of Mouth Taste and Smell = Taste, Flavor, or Palate

Humans' Versus Other Species' Ability to Smell

It is estimated that humans have around 12 million olfactory receptor cells that can distinguish approximately 10,000 odors or aromas. Although it's yet to be proven, this theory is based on the laws of probability using the sheer number of sensory receptors present in the average human's olfactory bulb.

Man's best friend, the beloved dog, can have from 100 to 200 million-plus sensory receptors, depending on the breed, with the bloodhound leading the pack with as many as 300 million.

The grizzly bear is the king of kings in the four-legged animal world. If the winds are blowing in his favor, he can smell a dead animal or beached salmon up to eight miles away. So you hunters out there, "be aware" when a known man-attacking bear is on the loose: I would highly suggest smoking your favorite cigars in the safety of the hunter's camp, not when you are in the wilderness following a hot animal trail. As painful as it might seem, a vicious bear will inflict far more pain than an afternoon without a cigar!

Threshold

Threshold is the number of odor molecules that need to be present in the air we breathe in order to detect an aroma. Depending on the aroma, it may take only one part per billion, in other words, one aroma molecule mixed with one billion parts of air. We could think of this ratio in visual terms: If we put one tablespoon of dye in an Olympic swimming pool, it would represent one part per billion, and the dye would soon go unnoticed to the eye.

Once I understood this fact, I saved myself the unnecessary pain experienced from a forced retro hale, not to mention the possibility of damaging my olfactory bulb. (Retro hale is discussed at length in Chapter 4.)

Nasal Cycling: How It Affects Your Sense of Smell

During the cigar boom of the 1990s, all of my vacations were what many would consider work vacations to one destination: the Dominican Republic. When the cigar boom went plop, I was long overdue for a real vacation that didn't involve work.

When I traveled to Ireland and Scotland to visit whiskey distilleries, I noticed that most distillers, and all the master distillers, would tilt their head from side to side as they nosed a whiskey. When they tilted their head to the right, it lined up the right nostril over the center of the glass and then to the left with the same affect. I asked several distillers why they did this, and the common answer was "Because it works; try it." I tried it and noticed that, depending on the tilt of my head or the nostril over the center of the glass, I would sense different taste notes. I started using this technique when I took a pre-lit smell of the cigar wrapper and experienced the same effect. Years later, I would look for the science behind this phenomenon, which is quite simple.

Have you ever noticed that one nostril seems clear and the other congested or slightly congested even when you don't have a cold? This is caused by our autonomic nervous system—it happens automatically, like the beating of your heart, your digestion, your breathing, and so on. There are two reasons why this happens: (1) to allow your sensory receptors a chance to rest and not dry out from their nonstop job of sensing the air you breathe with the 23,000 breaths you take per day, and (2) some odor/aroma molecules are highly volatile and dissipate very rapidly, while others are very faint and linger, so in the nostril that is uncongested, you will detect the molecules that dissipate rapidly. The nostril that seems congested will detect odors that are faint, because the molecules spend more time in this nasal passageway.

Try recording your times here.

UNCONGESTED NOSTRIL (right or left):		
○ Right	○ Left	Time:
○ Right	○ Left	Time:
○ Right	○ Left	Time:
○ Right	○ Left	Time:

Put your finger on your right nostril and inhale, then on your left nostril and inhale—which nostril was clearer? In 1.5 to 4 hours, the nostril that is a little congested will clear and the nostril that was clear will be congested. Try writing down the time and which nostril is clearer and come back to it in a few hours after you finish reading so you can experience the phenomenon firsthand. Nasal cycling is more pronounced in the late evening just before you go to sleep and while you are sleeping, and also when you first wake up in the morning. The congested nostril is not filled with mucus; the nasal turbinates (which warm inhaled air) in your nasal cavities are swollen, caused by the autonomic nervous system, so no matter how hard you try to clear the congested nostril, it will be to no avail. Usually after a morning shower or your first cup of coffee, the congestion will subside and move to the other nostril.

It is estimated that 80% of the population experiences nasal cycling; those who don't may have a more sensitive or heightened sense of smell for certain aromas and less for others and are prone to experience palate fatigue more quickly.

Five Smell Disorders

- ***Hyposmia*** is a reduced ability to detect odors.
- ***Anosmia*** is the complete inability to detect odors. In rare cases, someone may be born without a sense of smell, a condition called congenital anosmia.
- ***Parosmia*** is a change in the normal perception of odors, such as when the smell of something familiar is distorted, or when something that normally smells pleasant now smells foul. (Ask a pregnant woman!)
- ***Phantosmia*** is the sensation of an odor that isn't there.
- ***Hyperosmia*** is an unusually high sensitivity to odors.

The Causes of Smell Disorders

Smell disorders have many causes, with some more obvious than others. Most afflicted folks have experienced a recent illness or injury. Common causes include the following:

- Poor health
- Obsessive smoking
- Head injury
- Ear infection
- Sinus and other upper respiratory infections
- Exposure to certain chemicals, such as insecticides and solvents
- Numerous medications, including some common antibiotics and antihistamines, allergy medications, etc. (Chapter 5 lists the most common medications.)
- Radiation for treatment of head and neck cancers
- Conditions that affect the nervous system, such as Parkinson's disease or Alzheimer's disease
- Dental problems

DNA: How It Affects the Way We Taste

Having knowledge of three specific genes that determine your mouth taste sensitivity can shed some new light on your cigar, food, and drink preferences. You can begin to understand personal preferences in cigars, wine and spirits, and foods. Thus, better choices become possible the first time, every time. One no longer wastes money on unsuitable indulgences.

Understanding the role DNA plays in how we perceive taste has challenged scientists since it was first identified in the late 1860s by Swiss chemist Friedrich Miescher. It wasn't until the 1930s that two chemists turned a mishap into a groundbreaking discovery.

Arthur L. Fox, a scientist working at Dupont chemical laboratory, was experimenting with formulas for blue dye when he accidentally poured a substance called Phenylthiourea (PTC), sending a puff into the air. His colleague, Carl Noller, a visiting professor from Stanford, was standing nearby and inhaled some of the powder and had a strong reaction. It tasted sharply bitter. Fox also inhaled some of the powder but tasted nothing. Fox put a pinch of PTC on his tongue and assured Noller it was tasteless. Then Noller moistened his index finger, dipped it into the powder, and put it in his mouth and winced.

A spontaneous experiment unfolded as they asked other lab workers to do the same, scientists and technicians acting as their own guinea pigs. Their hypothesis shattered conventional wisdom, paving the way for a new frontier into the world of DNA and how it affects our taste.

For the better part of the last century, scientists believed that people's tastes were essentially the same, and when they differed, it was attributed to a person's temperament or mood. If a child snubbed his nose at broccoli, it was considered a matter of poor discipline, not biology. Then in the 1970s, Linda Bartoshuk, a scientist at Yale, noticed that individuals who could taste PTC were also more sensitive to sour, sweet, and salty tastes. They tended to avoid the powerful kick of wasabi or hot peppers and overly sweet, sour, or salty foods. Bartoshuk started looking into the mouths of her volunteers and found that most of those who tasted bitter in the PTC saliva litmus test had a radically different tongue anatomy from those who did not. The ones who tasted bitter (PTC) typically had more fungiform papillae (taste buds) on their tongues [see Duffy, V. B. and Bartoshuk, L. M. (2000), "Food Acceptance and Genetic Variation in Taste," Journal of the American Dietetic Association, 100, 647-655; and Tepper, B. J., (1998), "6-N-Propylthiouracil: A Genetic Marker for Taste, with Implications for Food Preference and Dietary Habits," American Journal of Human Genetics, 63, 1271-1276].

Taste buds are tiny structures consisting of nub-like papillae found on the surface of the tongue. The average tongue of the group Bartoshuk refers to non-tasters (people who can't detect PTC in a saliva litmus test) contains about 10,000 taste buds, whereas a supertaster's tongue can have as many as 30,000 taste buds. This means that they have more hard-wired connections between the mouth and the brain, causing them to perceive more intense taste sensations and sometimes more flavor information overall than non-tasters. The way supertasters experience flavor differs not so much in the taste of the food but in the intensity felt.

The terms Bartoshuk used to describe the different levels of taste sensitivity worked in the science laboratory, where she needed empirical data, but I feel these terms may cause some confusion when used outside of the laboratory, so I will substitute the following terms:

LABORATORY LANGUAGE	CIGAR SPEAK
Non-Taster	Normal Sensitivity (N)
Taster	Moderate Sensitivity (MS)
Supertaster	Sensitive (S)
Supertaster	Ultra-Sensitive (US)

Cigar smokers are complex creatures, living in their own individual, sensorial world. Each is biased and influenced by their anatomy, genetics, medical history, culture, and life experiences. So remember that your mouth taste sensitivity is just one factor among many that influence your food, drink, and cigar choices.

Once you know your mouth taste sensitivity level, you will be able to make better choices when purchasing cigars and wines and spirits and ordering in a restaurant. Also you will know how to make adjustments, such as toning down a bitter espresso with a little sugar or adding a little lemon and salt to a plate of steamed green leafy veggies to tone down their inherent bitterness.

I am often asked the best level of taste sensitivity to have, and my answer is this: There is no best level. Knowing what your DNA mouth taste sensitivity is, along with knowing how to use the knowledge, is what is important. For instance, if you are an N, then you have a distinct advantage over 75% of other cigar smokers because some bitterness or sourness in the wrapper leaf may excite your palate, whereas it may turn off MS, S, and US individuals, not allowing them to fully enjoy the other flavor notes that a well-made premium cigar has to offer.

If you are a US, your cigars, drink, and food options may be limited or reduced dramatically, especially if you don't know how to smoke a heavy, full bodied, intense cigar or drink a robust, rich cab, or peaty single malt scotch. There are many great cigar blends that may have a very rich, robust wrapper leaf draping exotic filler leaves, but the wrapper leaf may have too much of a bitter, sour, or salty mouth taste for a US smoker, and his palate may rebel, sending a message to the brain that the cigar is too harsh, too sour, or too salty.

Below are some suggestions on how to apply DNA knowledge to cigars, drinks, and foods.

DNA TYPE	OPTIONS TO CONSIDER
Normal Sensitive (N) *Typical cigar preferences: Medium-plus to full bodied with all wrapper types* *Drinks: All, even high-alcohol drinks, served neat or on the rocks* *Foods: The richer and spicier, the better*	*Cigars: The sky is your limit for any well-made cigar. If you are not a connoisseur yet, you may need to learn how to enjoy a light bodied blend.* *Coffees: Black or with sugar or cream* *Wines: Bold, full bodied reds, young or aged in oak with high acidity and strong tannins* *Liquors: Rich bourbons, whiskeys, scotch (neat or on the rocks), ports, and cognacs*
Moderate Sensitive (MS) *Typical cigar preferences: Medium to full bodied with all wrapper types* *Drinks: Almost all, neat or on the rocks* *Foods: Rich and spicy*	*Cigars: The sky is your limit for any well-made cigar. If you are not a connoisseur yet, you may need to learn how to enjoy a light bodied blend.* *Coffees: Black or with sugar or cream* *Wines: Bold, full bodied reds, young or aged in oak with high acidity and strong tannins* *Liquors: Rich bourbons, whiskeys, scotch (neat or on the rocks), ports and cognacs*
Sensitive (S) *Typical cigar preferences: Light to medium-plus with most wrapper types, but U.S. Conn. mouth taste perhaps a little too acidic* *Drinks: Somewhat picky, preferring your alcohol on the rocks or with a splash of water* *Foods: Medium rich and medium spicy*	*Cigars: You are a little picky about what you smoke. You know what you like and stick to your favorites unless you are a connoisseur: Then you venture out from time to time and try new blends.* *Coffees: With just enough cane sugar to balance the inherent bitter and sourness* *Wines: All high-quality wines that are balanced, aged in oak with medium acidity and tannins* *Liquors: Aged bourbons or whiskeys with a splash of water or on the rocks, aged ports, and cognacs*
Ultra-Sensitive (US) *Typical cigar preferences: Light to medium-plus with most wrapper types, but U.S. Conn. mouth taste perhaps a little too acidic* *Drinks: Picky and not eager to try something different* *Foods: Medium to full flavored. Seasoned with a well-balanced blend of herbs and spices, but never too spicy*	*Cigars: You are very picky about your cigars. If a connoisseur, you may not always reach for a full bodied cigar, but when you do, you know how to adjust your smoking technique to bypass the sometimes aggressive mouth taste stimulation and higher nicotine of a full bodied cigar.* *Coffees: With just the right amount of cane sugar to balance the inherent bitter and sourness* *Wines: All high-quality wines that are balanced, aged in oak with medium acidity and tannins* *Liquors: Aged bourbons, whiskeys with a splash of water, aged ports, and cognacs*

Excerpt from an Interview with
MANOLO QUESADA

An Inductee in the Exclusive Cigar Aficionado's Hall of Fame Class of 2012

QUESADA CIGAR FACTORY, LICEY AL MEDIO, DOMINICAN REPUBLIC, NOVEMBER 2019

Nick: I really appreciate you having me here today. You were one of my first inspirations on my journey to demystify the art of taste going back to the mid-90s. I used to read and reread all the articles that you were in, which inspired me to think about cigars and taste differently and develop my palate to identify and appreciate different aroma and taste characteristics.

Manolo: You make me blush, because being inspiration to anyone is certainly an achievement, and one doesn't set out to impress anyone; one does what has to be done when it feels right. But I do have to give you credit because of the courage it takes to enter into the world of taste, not setting boundaries, but suggesting setting certain limits and standards. For instance, hay smells like hay and pepper tastes like pepper and cinnamon is cinnamon—it is not pepper or leather. It takes…a lot of work and a lot of experience and tasting and testing and a lot of courage to enter into the world of taste. It's a world that is very closely guarded by individuals, because it's my taste, not yours. But when you take that whole thing and combinations thereof, which could be many, yes, I value your taste, but are you really in charge of your taste?

Nick: What are your thoughts regarding the use of DNA testing to determine your mouth taste sensitivity to better understand your taste preferences?

Manolo: Definitely a good idea, because it gives you a better feel for what your thresholds may be, and thresholds are very important, because they are dynamic, not static. They move and they change. This may sound strange, but it is important, because those thresholds will be at a certain point in a given moment when you put your cigar in your mouth, and knowing that you are sensitive to one thing or less sensitive to another will give you an approach, an entrance into the experience that's coming at you.

Excerpt from an Interview with
JOSELITO DOMINGUEZ

TABACALERA VICTOR SINCLAIR IN GURABO, DOMINICAN REPUBLIC, NOVEMBER 2019

Nick: You allowed me to test your DNA for mouth taste sensitivity to see if it would shed some light on your understanding about how a person's DNA can affect their taste references. What would you like to share with our readers regarding your test?

Joselito: After I took the test, a light bulb came on. I started understanding all those things that happened to me in the past; for instance, when a cigar smoker felt a cigar was strong that was not strong to me, or that was mild but not mild to me. I now realize it has a lot to do with the sensibility of your DNA. It also shed some light on my and my family's food choices and why one of us always needs to add more salt, while another is complaining the dish is too salty.

Excerpt from an Interview with
JOHN OLIVA, Jr.

Tampa, Florida, September 2020

Nick: What are your thoughts regarding using a DNA test to better understand your palate and help you make better choices when selecting a cigar to smoke?

Johnny: I think this is an excellent approach. I had no idea how much it could influence my taste: I think it's critical from a knowledge standpoint. It makes sense to me now, why there are certain cigars and certain types of tobacco that I just don't enjoy and now I understand why. It's just part of my DNA palate.

Your Palate and Beyond

Mucus is not widely considered a polite conversation topic, but because it plays a significant role in our ability to smell and taste, I feel it is important that we understand its basic function. *Jeffrey Spiegel, an ear, nose, and throat surgeon at Boston University, wants us to know this:*

> *Mucus is essential for the protection of your body. It's a protective barrier and it allows you to breathe comfortably. If you had no mucus, you'd be quite sorry you didn't. You produce 1 to 1.5 quarts of mucus a day—and swallow the vast majority.*

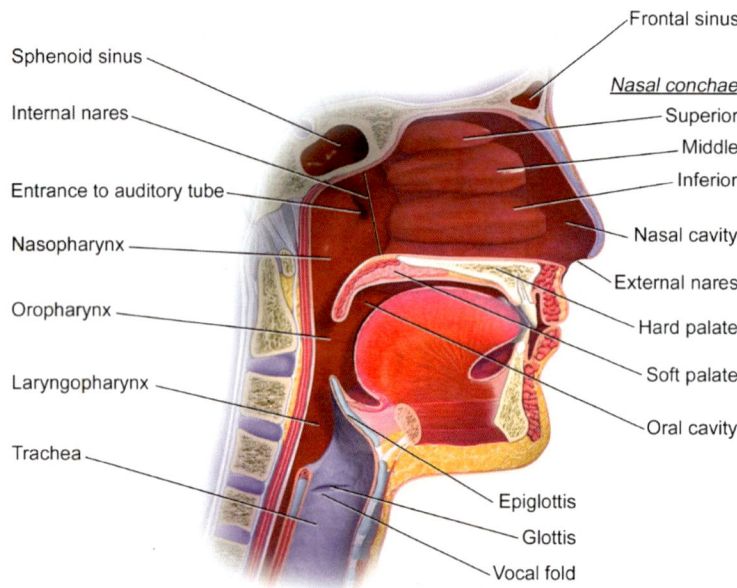

The inside of your nose is filled with structures called *conchae*, or *turbinates*. Their primary function is to warm the inhaled air and humidify it so that the air will enter your lungs without causing discomfort.

According to Dr. Michael Ellis, an ear, nose, and throat specialist at Tulane University,

> *A stuffy nose occurs when the conchae rapidly swell in size in response to cold, dry conditions, so there's more surface area for the air to flow over. Additionally, if you're fighting an infection, the conchae can swell further with blood, in order to bring more white blood cells to the site of the infection.*

This should not be confused with nasal cycling discussed earlier.

Most people think of this congestion as a result of too much mucus, but in reality, it's just swollen conchae. This explains why many people are congested when they wake up in the morning (after breathing cold, dry air all night), especially because central air and heating systems dry out air significantly.

Most ENT doctors agree that the best way to decongest your nose is with steam, because cold, dry air is what most often causes your conchae to swell; the best remedy is hot, moist air. Hot shower and facial steamers are also effective treatments to ease congestion and open up a clogged nose.

Nasal decongestants (such as pseudoephedrine and phenylephrine) can also help de-swell the conchae, but in some cases, there's a downside: They dry out the nasal cavity by reducing the amount of serous fluid. So if you're also experiencing excessively thick, dry mucus, you're better off avoiding decongestants.

The nasal decongestant spray Afrin (which has the active ingredient Oxymetazoline) works really well, and maybe too well, according to Ellis: "I caution my patients from using this product because it's not just habit-forming, it's totally addictive, because the lining of the nose becomes completely dependent on it." If you read the fine print on the Afrin bottles, you will find a warning statement telling you not to use the medicine for more than three days, but few people read the ingredients and warnings. In the case of Afrin, so many people have misused this product that there are Afrin addiction support groups online.

Below are some questions you can ask yourself if you find that you are experiencing an unusual amount of nasal congestion.

First, am I nasal cycling or congested? If you are nasal cycling, one nostril is clear and the other is congested.

Is it allergy season? Fall or spring, falling leaves, high air pollen counts, etc.?

In the summer months, do you sleep with the air conditioner thermostat set below 76°?

In the winter months, do you sleep with the heat set above 72°?

Do you consume too much dairy or mucus-producing foods?

Did you drink too much scotch or other alcohol the night before?

Are you smoking too many cigars a day?

Are you force retro haling too much?

Are you breathing too much secondhand smoke in a cigar lounge with poor ventilation?

Do you have indoor pets that are creating too much hair or fur dander?

Are the carpets in your home or office old and in need of a cleaning or replacement?

The majority of the pleasure we get when smoking a cigar happens in our mouth and nasal cavity or palate, and it happens in fleeting seconds, so keeping your nasal cavity in good shape is critical for a cigar connoisseur. When your nasal cavity is clear and your palate razor sharp, you will pick up taste nuances that come to you like rainbows of flavor. When this happens, take note of what you did that day or the day before, and hopefully you will start to see a pattern that you can repeat over and over again.

Mouth Salinity and Taste

A half an eyedropper of saliva can spell out your entire genetic blueprint and ancestral history.

Saliva transports substances and protects the taste receptors and taste buds and is responsible for your sense of taste. If your food isn't dissolved in saliva, the receptors on your tongue can't detect food, beverage or smoke molecules.

To fully appreciate taste and flavor, your mouth must be in its natural state of salinity. It typically takes from 40 seconds to a minute to obtain this natural state after swallowing a liquid or food or taking a puff from a cigar.

For instance, if you place salt or sugar on a dry tongue, the taste buds will not be able to identify it until saliva dissolves the substance; then the taste sensation takes place. This holds true for drinking and smoking: If you take a sip of your whiskey and immediately puff on your cigar, you will find that you experience little to no cigar taste.

Palate Development Exercises

Exercise 1: Mouth Salinity—How It Affects Taste

What to Do

1. Light one cigar.

2. Have one beverage: a glass of water or a snifter of whiskey.

3. Take a drink of your beverage and immediately after you swallow (within 3 seconds) take a puff on your cigar.

    What did the cigar taste like? _____

    Did you enjoy the taste?
    >there was none/very little/a little/the same/a lot/a lot more

4. Take a drink of your beverage and wait 40-60 seconds after you swallow and then take a puff on your cigar.

    Did the cigar taste different?
    >no/very little/a little/the same/a lot/a lot more

Exercise 2: Calibrating to the Bitter Taste

What to Do

1. Brew 8 to 12 ounces of coffee (no sugar), about 2 coffee cups.

2. Gather cane or white sugar, a measuring teaspoon, and 1 glass of water at room temperature.

3. Pour even amounts of coffee (4 to 6 ounces) in each of the two cups.

4. Add one teaspoon of sugar in one cup and stir (the purpose of the sugar is not to make the coffee taste sweet but to balance the bitterness).

5. Take a small sip or a teaspoon full of black coffee first.

    Did you notice any bitterness or acidity, and if so, how much?
    >Bitterness: no/very little/a little/a lot/a lot more
    >Acidity: no/very little/a little/a lot/a lot more

6. Rinse your mouth with a sip of water.

7. Take a small sip or teaspoon full of coffee with the added sugar.

    Did you notice any bitterness or acidity and, if so, how much?
    >Bitterness: no/very little/a little/a lot/a lot more
    >Acidity: no/very little/a little/a lot/a lot more

8. Repeat the exercise several times.

    Did you notice more coffee flavors in the cup with a little sugar?
    >no/very little/a little/a lot/a lot more

The takeaway: The sugar did not add to the coffee's flavor; it toned down the bitterness and acidity, allowing inherent coffee flavors to come forth. Drinking black coffee, you probably tasted a little to a lot of bitterness and acidity. Drinking coffee with a little added sugar, you probably tasted less acidity and even less or no bitterness but more overall coffee flavor and nuances.

Exercise 3: Understanding Retro Hale

What to Do

1. Have small piece (1/2 to 1 teaspoon) of any food item. If a common cigar taste association item is available, use one of them; for example, dried fruit, licorice, nuts, chocolate, caramel. If not, you can use a candy bar or cracker.

2. Pinch your nostrils shut, then put the piece of food in your mouth and gently chew while breathing through your mouth for about 5 to 10 seconds. During this procedure, ask yourself, *What am I tasting? Sweet, sour, salty, bitter, savory? Chocolate, caramel, licorice, dried fruit, etc.?*

3. Swallow the food, then release your pinched nose. The burst of flavor you experience is caused by a natural retro nasal or retro hale.

4. With your nostrils pinched shut, did you taste anything other than sweet, sour, salty, bitter or savory?
   ❏ Yes ❏ No

5. If you did, you allowed some air to enter through your pinched nose. If so, do the exercise again and this time pinch your nose a little tighter. When your nose is pinched and air can't enter your nasal cavity, it is impossible to taste anything except sweet, salty, sour, bitter, or savory.

   When you released your pinched nose, did you consciously retro hale (push air through your nasal cavity)?
   ❏ Yes ❏ No

Exercise 4: Mouth Taste Versus Retro Nasal While Calibrating to Milk Chocolate and Dark Chocolate

What to Do

1. Have small pieces (½ to 1 teaspoon) of milk chocolate and dark chocolate (preferable 70%).

2. Pinch your nostrils, put a piece of milk chocolate in your mouth, and let it gently dissolve while breathing through your mouth for about 5 to 10 seconds.

   What do you taste?

   sweet/salty/sour/bitter/savory

3. Swallow the chocolate, then release your nostrils. What did you experience? _____

4. Rinse your palate with a little water, or with a cracker and water, and repeat the exercise, this time with the dark chocolate.

   What did you taste? _____

   How was it different?
   less sweet/richer flavor/more chocolaty/more complex/more taste nuances?

Excerpt from an Interview with
KLAAS KELNER

Grand Ambassador, Davidoff of Geneva

USA Corporate Headquarters, Pinellas Park, Florida, USA, December 2019

Nick: Your father is an inductee in the exclusive *Cigar Aficionado's Hall of Fame* Class of 2012, and is one of the most respected tobacco grower, blender, and cigar ambassadors in the industry. What were the most important lessons he taught you about a cigar's taste and aroma?

Klaas: First, I want to say thank you on behalf of my father for saying such nice words. In regard to the question, what did my father teach me about taste and aroma, I would say it's two main things. The first thing is that when you're blending cigars for consumers, for people that are going to enjoy your cigar, you have to make a cigar that is balanced in the palate, meaning that it's not overly bitter, overly sweet, or one-dimensional, but all your palate is being stimulated one way or another, some places more than others, but it's not one-sided: That is what creates complexity.

The other thing that he taught me is consistency, because you can have the best cigar in the world, but if you can't make it over and over again and be able to produce it year after year offering the same palate stimulation you were able to provide the first time, then everything is to no avail. Being able to deliver the same cigar is the most important thing for the consumer. You have to be loyal to your consumer by providing him the same stimulations and the same flavors that he loves, and that's probably the most important lesson. Because if you're loyal to your consumers, they are going to be loyal to you.

Nick: What advice would you give a person who is just getting started smoking premium cigars?

Klaas: If there is something that I can tell people that are just getting started, it's to learn to understand why they like the cigars that they like. Because it's very easy to say, oh, I don't like this cigar, it's too strong or not strong enough. Start analyzing your palate. Where are the stimulations? Is it sweet? Is it bitter? Is it acidic? Do you like the cigar because it's sweet? Do you dislike the cigar because it dries your palate or over humidifies your palate? So, one of the most important things is to understand why you like the cigars that you do and that way you can learn how to choose cigars later on.

Nick: Do you feel the ability to detect and identify different taste associations and nuances can enhance a cigar smoker's enjoyment?

Klaas: We all want to enjoy a cigar and we should put that as a priority, but if you are able to enhance it, do whatever you have to do to enhance it. If you're able to understand why you like the cigar, then you're going to be able to enjoy the cigar more. If you're able to understand the tobaccos that are inside the cigar and you're able to understand what the tobaccos do to your palate, then at this moment that is one more level in the whole process, in the whole ritual of enjoying your cigar. So it definitely adds another layer and makes the experience much more complex and, in my opinion, enjoyable.

Chapter 3

Tools of the Trade

*To a man that only has a hammer,
everything he encounters begins to look like a nail.*
– Abraham Maslow

Let's take a look at the pros and cons of tools used by smokers to refine our palate and enhance our smoking pleasure. Before we get down to details, let's answer the most obvious question: Why do people smoke cigars? They

- haven't learned how to vape yet;
- seek another status symbol;
- use it as bait to attract a date;
- have become nicotine "junkies";
- really enjoy the aroma and taste of a fine cigar;
- appreciate how it pairs with their favorite alcoholic beverage;
- believe smoking helps them unwind after dealing with a full day of life's improbabilities;
- relish the cigar smoking ritual and sensorial experience;
- are professional cigar blenders, tasters, or critics.

The aforementioned reasons—except the first few, I trust—strike a familiar chord in aficionados. So then, here is an important question for newbies and veterans alike: Why do *you* smoke cigars? Think about it. Hopefully, you found your motivations in the last half of the list. This book will enrich your cigar experience every time you light up. Regarding the rest, you're on your own.

We probably can agree that the ultimate goal is to enjoy a pleasant sensorial smoking experience. Typically, when a person smokes a cigar, very little mental deliberation goes into the process beyond such thoughts as, *I'm not crazy about this one* or *Excellent cigar–better buy more before they run out*. The bottom line for most folks? Their personal opinion of the cigar.

When evaluating a cigar, however, enjoyment and opinion fade into the background. We move from the emotional right side of the brain to the logical left. Evaluation takes place, not only to enjoy the cigar, but to

- analyze its quality;
- identify specific taste characteristics and nuances;
- determine if the cigar holds true to its style and the tobacco regions it came from;

- decide whether another cigar of its kind merits a place in an already overcrowded humidor;
- settle on whether we deem the cigar worthy of a recommendation to cigar buddies or business associates;
- recommend it to customers if we are in the cigar industry, for example, distributors, shop owners, or online sellers.

You may be wondering, *Why all the fuss about refining the palate?* Bear with me. It will be worth the effort—call it delayed gratification.

Consider some analogies. I'm willing to bet most of you are fans of some kind. You want to know the whole enchilada about your favorite team. You can't wait to find out what teams are home games and when they are on the upcoming schedule, the stats about the new quarterback or wide receiver or the win-loss record of the new head coach, who suffered an injury in the last game, which star rookie the team plans to draft, and who did something foolish and got into trouble with the law off-season.

Music buffs read the liner notes to learn who wrote or composed the music. In the pop and jazz world, they want to know who wrote the song and lyrics; who produced the album and arranged the music; who played piano, bass, percussion, and guitar. In the classical genre, they seek to know the composer, the conductor, the orchestra, and solo or guest artist.

For you wine "snobs," why do you care about the altitude of the appellation where the grape was grown? Or whether the wine was aged in French or American oak barrels and for how many months or years? Was it filtered or unfiltered? As long as you like the taste of the wine and get a nice buzz, it did its job, right? Not so fast. Hold on to your stemware. Common knowledge dictates that *the more you know about a given topic, the more you enjoy it.*

Now that you have noted why you smoke, let's take a look at recent tools of the cigar trade.

Books, Magazines, Websites, Podcasts, and Blogs

There are a few excellent cigar books that address history, brands, and hardware. *History* refers to cigar origins and expansions from the 1500s forward, *brands* refers to box and cigar ring art, and *hardware* refers to the basics of how to store, cut, and light a cigar and so forth. At the end of the chapter, I've listed a few excellent cigar books you might consider adding to your cigar library. After years of researching taste via printed materials, personal interviews, and cyberspace, I was unable to find any books or articles devoted exclusively to the art of tasting our treasured cigars. Currently, a handful of good magazines offer interesting stories and interviews, along with tasting or cigar ratings, and one even throws in a little eye candy. Of the many excellent blogs and podcasts, several are scratching the surface and offering some good advice, but no source offers a comprehensive system to develop your palate.

From the Color Wheel to the Flavor Wheel

Many inventions, including the Flavor Wheel, tend to evolve from the point where someone else left off. Take a look at the following illustration:

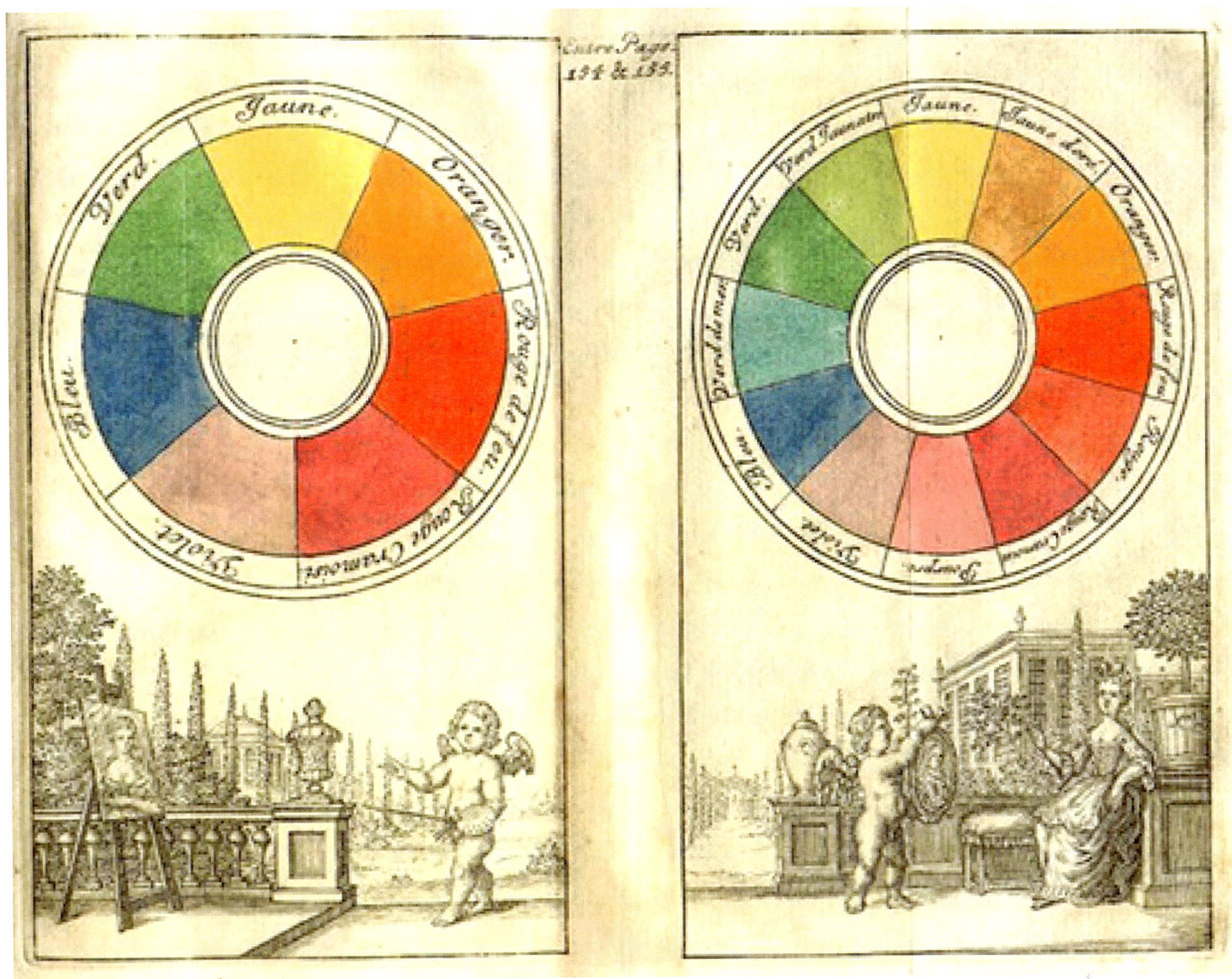

Early 18th Century Color Wheel

Sir Isaac Newton, the father of mechanics and one of the most important scientists who ever lived, changed the standards by which scientists think. Many of us learned about him in grade school for defining gravity, but what most of us didn't learn is that he created the early color wheel which centuries later was adapted by the beer, wine and spirits, and cigar industries.

He designed the early Color Circle by observing light as it passed through a prism. Newton noticed that the light spectrum was composed of different-sized color segments. In 1706, he arranged red, orange, yellow, green, blue, indigo, and violet into a natural progression on a rotating circle. As the disk spins, the colors blur together so rapidly that the human eye sees only see white, proving that white contains small amounts of all the colors in the right proportion.

Tools of the Trade

Newton also transformed the colors into a segmented circle, where the size of each segment differed according to his calculations of the color's wavelength and of its corresponding width in the spectrum. The placement and size of the colored sections of Newton's circle suggested other mathematical and harmonic relationships.

Painters of the day hurried to borrow Newton's color wheel concept to create a guide of their own for mixing colors. It is still used to this day and considered an invaluable tool for artists learning how to mix colors.

Let's fast-forward a couple of hundred years to see how Newton's color wheel has been adapted in other industries. Beer brewing captured a flavor wheel premier in the late 1970s when chemist Dr. Morten C. Meilgaard developed a customized chart for breweries. Then, in the mid-1980s, Ann C. Noble at the University of California developed a flavor wheel for wine. Newton's color wheel concept has also been adapted by the coffee, whiskey, and cigar industries.

Flavor Wheels consist of descriptive words arranged in circular format and color coded. The broad-category nouns located around the "hub" of the wheel indicate the various sources of taste, aroma, and flavor. Following the "spokes" outward, specific references are listed. The wheel offers options that can serve as common ground for tasters and consumers alike. It is probably the best single reference source available.

Before I critique the Cigar Flavor Wheel, let me say that there is not a perfect way to categorize or illustrate something as complex as taste and aroma. My first impression of the Cigar Flavor Wheel was that it was developed by a non-cigar smoker.

The wheel consists of many references that may have a common source, but their aromas are different and, in some cases, unrelated. Citrus, which is listed in the Fruit category, shares no aroma or taste relationship to dried fruit or molasses. The Plants options are all over the map: Grass and hay have very different aroma characteristics along with cedar, tea, tobacco, and vegetable. The Herb and Spices category is probably the most accurate, except that cumin should have been replaced with nutmeg, a very common aroma association found in cigars (whereas cumin is not). If Earth and Minerals were in separate categories, it would make more sense to me: For example, Earth, Barnyard, and Must in one category and Minerals, Lead/Graphite, and Salt in another.

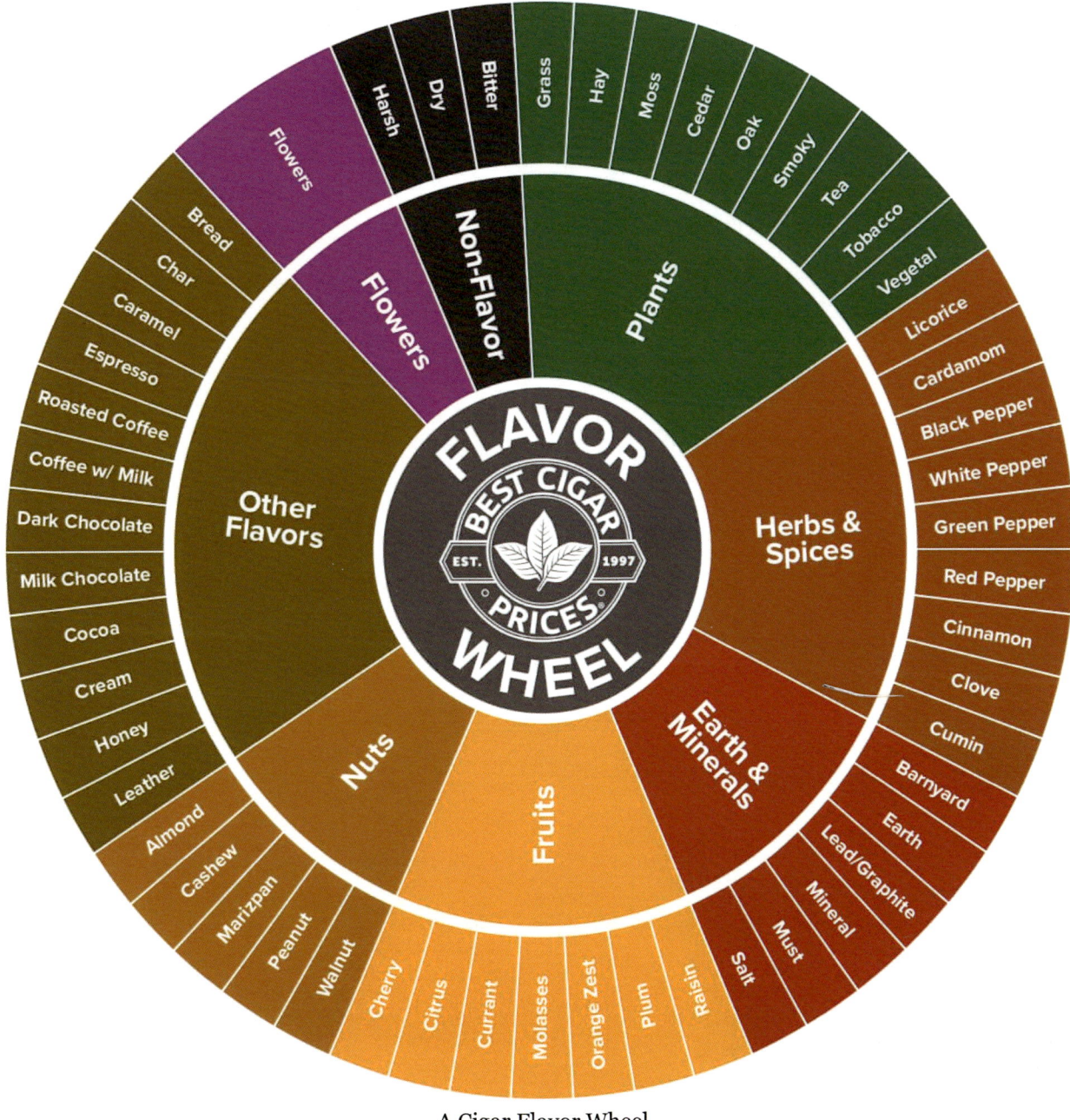

A Cigar Flavor Wheel

Also, the Other Flavors section is almost 25% of the chart. In my opinion, leather, dark chocolate, coffee, and char would fit better in an Earthy subcategory.

Numerous cigar taste models of various quality have sprung up over the years. I'll let you decide which you find most useful, starting with those from Cuba.

Taste Models and Training

Cuban Daily Sensorial Record

In Cuba, professional cigar tasters use these forms to determine quality. The first form has 5 boxes with 5 options and a score of 1 to 4 for each option. The categories are Flavor, Strength, Aroma, Draw, and Combustibility. For flavor and aroma, the choices are subjective and for the other categories, objective. The second form is a summary that is used to score a cigar based the results taken from 5 cigar tasters.

Cuban Model # 2 English Version

EMPRESA DE TABACO TORCIDO-VILLA CLARA
(as appear in Spanish)
Sensory Evaluation Commission
For Export Tobacco, with Blend of Volado y C. Nac. Fza. No 1
Sensor Record

Model No. 2 Factory No. .... Date: ....

Sensor: .... Cigar Band .... Group No. ....

Samples

FLAVOR	1	2	3	4
Pleasant				
Less Pleasant				
Excellent				
Unpleasant				
Very Pleasant				

STRENGH	1	2	3	4
Weak				
Strong				
Normal				
Less Weak				
Very Strong				

AROMA	1	2	3	4
Almost without Aroma				
Imperceptible				
Pleasant Intense				
Unpleasant				
Pleasant				

Draw	1	2	3	4
Excessive				
Insufficient				
Correct				
Insufficient				
Some Excessive				

COMBUSTIBILITY	1	2	3	4
Regular				
Bad				
Very Good				
Terrible				

Cuban Test Evaluation English

EMPRESA DE TABACO TORCIDO V.C (as named in Spanish)	DAILY SENSORIAL EVALUATION SUMMARY	R (MP-05-02)02

Date of production of the sample: _____ Date of Evaluation: _____

Cigar Band: _____ No. Maker: _____

CHARACTERISTICS	TASTER					Total of Points	Average
	A	B	C	D	E		
Draw							
Aroma							
Flavor							
Strength							
Combustibility							
Scent							

Qualification:	Negative aspects:
Evaluation of the general quality of the Cigar band:	

Reported to:			
	Full name and Signature	Full name and Signature	Full name and Signature

Aroma Kits

Aroma kits consist of an assortment of small bottles containing mineral oil and synthetic chemicals that attempt to mimic the flavor profiles of organic substances. Chapter 1 gave you my take on the use of synthetic products. I purchased, but am not a proud owner of, most of the handful of aroma kits on the market. Initially, I was motivated to improve my palate and impress my friends. When the first kit arrived, I eagerly set about testing my palate. Was I ever disappointed in my score—5.7%! In other words, I correctly identified only 5 aromas out of 88 possibilities. Pathetic, I thought.

I tested myself again, since I was a little more familiar with the options. Another awful score of 6.8%. In my desperation to improve, I made one last attempt. Same result, but this time I got a drop of the synthetic liquid on my finger. I could not wash off that eye-irritating smell. Later that evening, as I was relaxing into my smoking ritual, I caught a whiff of my finger. It still reeked of the awful scent, reminding me of the times I've run into "perfume drenchers," people who overuse a treasured fragrance, causing a broad zone of (personal) aroma.

In my case, if I get too close, or worse yet, trapped in their zone of olfactory impact, my eyes and throat burn. Even the Latin cheek-to-cheek air kiss requires extreme caution. In a desire to show affection, someone's cheek may rub against your cheek, depositing a precious fragrance on your skin, leaving behind enough to follow you around for hours or until soapy water comes to the rescue.

Back to the aroma kits. My fate was sealed. I was a palate flop. I might as well give up on the idea of improving my palate and demystifying the art or taste, I figured. Either that or do some "comparison shopping." Was my palate really that bad?

I set out to round up everyone willing to test their palates using the same test. To my surprise, I found it an easy mission to secure taste guinea pigs. Almost all my invitees, especially cigar smokers, wine and whiskey lovers, and foodies, were happy to take a free palate test.

Their glee wore off fast, however, leaving sheer frustration in its wake. They, too, had trouble identifying the reference aromas. Scores ranged from 3% to 7%. Of those who wanted a retest, their scores went down. Aromas they had correctly identified in the first round were missed on the second and third. My diehard tasters eventually experienced eye and throat irritation, and several got mad at me for including them in the experiment.

I contacted several of the companies to ask them what on earth they put in those little bottles. Their replies were "trade secrets" or "synthetic aromas in natural oil." They added that the oils smelled exactly like the reference aromas, insisting that I just needed more practice.

But did I really want to calibrate my palate to a mixture of synthetic chemicals in mineral oil? Not hardly. Fortunately, necessity became the mother of invention, and the idea for the ProPalate® was born.

A New, Effective Approach to Training

I developed the ProPalate® System in response to my unfortunate experience with the aroma kits on the market. My comprehensive approach will help any cigar smoker, from novice to aficionado, improve their palate, and get the most out of every smoking experience.

But don't worry if you lack the discretionary income to buy one of these kits now. You will know how to make your own after reading this book, if you wish to.

The ProPalate® System was designed around the most common aroma, taste, and flavor associations used by cigar magazines, blogs, and personal experiences. I assembled two kits, Level One and Level Two, which in total contain 50 different aroma references. Level One contains 20 of the common taste references and five tobacco wrapper leaves; Level Two contains 20 common and not so common references and 5 compound or multiple aroma references. The 5 compound references will help you learn how to detect and identify layers of aromas or an aroma profile.

All of the aroma references are natural organic substances, such as dried herbs, fruit, spices, nuts, and other foods, in addition to cedar and leather. I've tested people from all walks of life, including cigar smokers, nonsmokers, whiskey and wine drinkers, abstainers, and foodies. You name it: If they had a nose and a notion to participate, I tested them. And not to my surprise, this system helped everyone improve their palate quickly, allowing cigar smokers to apply a newly acquired skill in the next cigar they lit up.

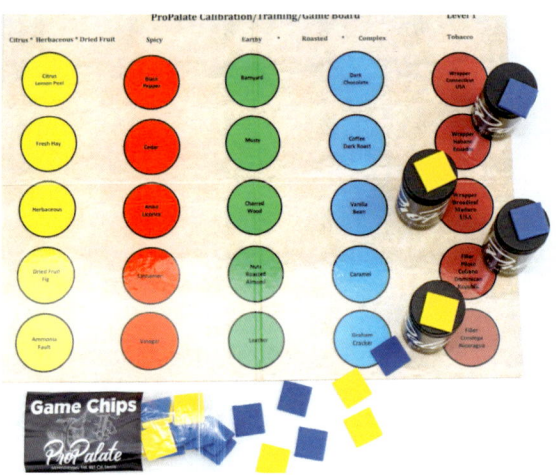

Excerpt from an Interview with Litto Gomez

An Inductee in the Exclusive Cigar Aficionado's Hall of Fame Class of 2016

TABACALERA LA FLOR DOMINICAN, TAMBORIL, DOMINICAN REPUBLIC, FEBRUARY 2020

Nick: Do you feel that having the ability to detect different flavor nuances and taste associations can enhance a cigar smoker's experience?

Litto: It would make it a lot more fun for sure. I don't know if it would make you enjoy it more, but it probably will. It would be a lot more exciting to understand it and pinpoint these flavors. It definitely makes it more fun for me. Okay, I blend cigars, and what you showed me, your kit for understanding flavors, it is going to make it a lot more fun for me.

Nick: Okay, let's talk about that for a moment. Earlier I showed you how the ProPalate® System works. What would you like to share with our viewers about your experience with this system?

Litto: I'm going to get the kit, and I'm going to play with it and challenge myself until I get it perfect, and I will. It makes you focus. It makes you concentrate. That would make a big difference in understanding flavors. Before I approve a blend, I will close my office door and not allow anyone to come in my office. I'll play loud music: Bocelli or some classical music. I'll play it very loud and close my eyes, and I will try to feel the flavors from the cigar. I cannot have any distractions in my head or my thoughts. I just focus on this area here [pointing to his nose]. That's how I'm able to detect things: by focusing and concentrating. I'm just going to concentrate on it and not let anybody distract me until I get it perfect, and I will.

Nick: By looking at the board, we can see which category is represented in this cigar. So, we could say this cigar is a very complex cigar. Some cigars may lean more towards the lighter notes, where other cigars that are blended on the heavy side will lean more towards being darker ones.

Litto: Yes, definitely. That's the principle. That's how it goes. The more oil content in the tobacco leaves and the thicker the leaf, the more intense it will be. Also, as you smoke the cigar, it may go into the heavier aromas and flavors. Once you are an inch into the cigar, it starts to change.

Nick: So, we are into the first third, and this is what we come up with. We could smoke into the second third and start all over again, and then the final third, and if it continues to change throughout the smoking experience, then we could say we have an extraordinary cigar.

Litto: Yes, as the oils go through the leaves, the leaves act as a filter, and they start accumulating these oils all the way down into the last third of the cigar.

Nick: So, we could say it concentrates. I find that a great cigar, an extraordinary cigar, gets better and better until the end. And the only problem with a great cigar is that you have a tendency to burn your lips or your fingers trying to get that last puff of "Cigar Bliss."

Litto: I know, I know that feeling.

Nick: Litto, can we say that we decoded this cigar using the ProPalate® Kit?

Litto: Let me tell you, Nick, it's easy with the kit; it makes it a lot easier. We can think, and we can talk about flavor notes, but with the kit, you can confirm your observations. It's so practical. You can really get to these aromas and flavors as you go through a cigar. I have to congratulate you: This is a great idea.

Nick: Having a compliment from you means a lot to me. You've blended many world class cigars in the last 25 years.

Litto: You're going to make me a better cigar maker with this kit. It's as simple as that. Thank you for sharing your ProPalate® Kit with me today.

Essential Cigar Language:
Subjective versus Objective Descriptions

There are two ways to describe a cigar's flavor profile: Subjective or Objective. Cigar critics often paint a poetic word picture of a cigar's flavor to convey abstract or complex ideas to their audience. Here is an example of a subjective or indirect description:

This is a smooth, straightforward cigar with a beautiful, seamless wrapper leaf, offering ample amounts of smoke and delicate flavors that will pair well with your morning coffee or espresso black or with cream and sugar. It has a nice finish that complements a well-made blend consisting of many enticing and appealing aromas; a very approachable cigar that is easy to enjoy anytime of the day and is recommended for both the novice and the connoisseur.

Here is an example of an objective or direct description:

This is a medium strength cigar. The first third offers notes of citrus and cedar and a hint of cinnamon. In the second third more aromatic notes come forth: anise and nutmeg followed by a touch of leather. As you smoke into the final third, complex notes of dark chocolate, vanilla and a hint of graham cracker come forth. The long finish is creamy with notes of fresh hay, caramel, and vanilla.

Cigar lingo may suffice when enjoying a cigar with a friend on the golf course or at a cigar lounge. But what cigar connoisseurs really want to know is what are the specific taste characteristics and nuances of the cigar. How does one cigar differ from another? Accurately describing taste nuances will challenge a cigar smoker unless they have a baseline or benchmark to work with. When evaluating a cigar, separating personal opinion from facts can be difficult. Your bias about a particular brand, your mood, the environment, and your approach can influence your ability to be objective. The best way to limit these influences is to use a systematic approach. When professionals taste or evaluate a wine, whiskey, or cigar, they always use the same set of criteria, in the same order.

The ProPalate® Evaluation Log is comprehensive way to evaluate a cigar. It consists of four basic categories that will assist you in accurately identifying and describing the taste, aromas, and flavors that you may experience while smoking. This chart will encourage you to focus on the cigar objectively. Once you have a working command of the basic categories, you will be able to correctly evaluate a cigar based on its merits.

Evaluation Log

Pro Palate® — Demystifying the Art of Taste

Section 1

Date	Brand	Size	Cigar Name	Wrapper Type	Binder	Ligero	Viso	Seco
A								
B								
C								

Pre-Smoke Notes

Section 2: Wrapper Aroma — Circle Your Selection

Intensity: Mark with (+) or (−)   Draw Taste: Mark with (d)

	Floral Herbaceous			Citrus			Fruit			Aromatic			Earthy			Roasted			Complex		
Floral/Lavender				A	B	C	A	B	C	Black Pepper	A	B	C	Barnyard	A	B	C	Chocolate	A	B	C
Fresh Hay				A	B	C	A	B	C	Cedar	A	B	C	Musty	A	B	C	Coffee	A	B	C
Herbaceous				A	B	C	A	B	C	Aniseed	A	B	C	Leather	A	B	C	Vanilla	A	B	C
Acidic/Lemon				A	B	C	A	B	C	Cinnamon	A	B	C	Roasted Nuts	A	B	C	Caramel	A	B	C
Dried Fruit				A	B	C	A	B	C	Nutmeg	A	B	C	Smoked Wood	A	B	C	Graham	A	B	C

Section 3: Smoking Notes — Circle Your Selection

Intensity: Mark with (+) or (−)

	Floral Herbaceous			Citrus			Fruit			Aromatic			Earthy			Roasted			Complex		
Floral/Lavender				A	B	C	A	B	C	Black Pepper	A	B	C	Barnyard	A	B	C	Chocolate	A	B	C
Fresh Hay				A	B	C	A	B	C	Cedar	A	B	C	Musty	A	B	C	Coffee	A	B	C
Herbaceous				A	B	C	A	B	C	Anise/Licorice	A	B	C	Leather	A	B	C	Vanilla	A	B	C
Acidic/Lemon				A	B	C	A	B	C	Cinnamon	A	B	C	Roasted Nuts	A	B	C	Caramel	A	B	C
Dried Fruit				A	B	C	A	B	C	Nutmeg	A	B	C	Smoked Wood	A	B	C	Graham	A	B	C

Section 4

Draw				Finish				Balance				Construction/Touch			
Very Tight	A	B	C	Dry	A	B	C	Unbalance	A	B	C	Soft	A	B	C
Tight	A	B	C	Short	A	B	C	Balanced	A	B	C	Soft Spot	A	B	C
Too Easy	A	B	C	Medium	A	B	C	**Complexity**				Hard Spot	A	B	C
Good	A	B	C	Long	A	B	C	Not Complex	A	B	C	Solid	A	B	C
Perfect	A	B	C	Very Long	A	B	C	Complex	A	B	C	Very Solid	A	B	C

Mouth Taste				Smoke Aroma / Ortho Hale				Burn			
Sweet	A	B	C	Pungent	A	B	C	Uneven	A	B	C
Sour	A	B	C	Earthy	A	B	C	Even	A	B	C
Salty	A	B	C	Smoked Wood	A	B	C	**Strength**			
Bitter	A	B	C	Baker's Spice	A	B	C	Mild Body	A	B	C
Creamy	A	B	C	Toasted Bread	A	B	C	Medium Body	A	B	C
								Full Body	A	B	C

Section 5: Cigar Personality

1st Third	75 to 79	A	B	C	80 to 84	A	B	C	85 to 89	A	B	C	90 to 95	A	B	C
2nd Third	75 to 79	A	B	C	80 to 84	A	B	C	85 to 89	A	B	C	90 to 95	A	B	C
3rd Third	75 to 79	A	B	C	80 to 84	A	B	C	85 to 89	A	B	C	90 to 95	A	B	C

Section 6: Overall Rating

75 to 79	A	B	C	80 to 84	A	B	C	85 to 89	A	B	C	90 to 95	A	B	C	96 to 100	A	B	C

Smokable if it's Your Last Cigar in the Humidor	A very Good Everyday Cigar	A Special Occasion Cigar	A Memorable Smoking Experience

Section 7: Rating Instructions

Noted Faults: Burn Issues, Too Humid, Dries mouth, Harsh Notes

Tools of the Trade

Tools to Keep Your Palate Razor Sharp

Below is a list of products to add to your cigar toolbox.

Steam Inhaler

This is an excellent natural way to decongest your nasal cavity when you are experiencing congestion due to allergies, the common cold, or the day after smoking too many cigars. The vaporizer works when you inhaling the vaporized water through your nose, which heats up and softens the mucus in your nasal cavity, allowing you to blow your nose and get rid of the excess mucus.

As an alternative if you don't own a steam inhaler, simply heat up a pot of water, carefully lift the lid of the pot, and breathe in the steam. This takes a little patience and practice, but once you get the hang of it, you can effectively decongest your nasal cavity in your kitchen. Another simple way is to fill a cup three-quarters full of boiling water, place your nose over the top of the cup, and breathe the steam rising from the cup. This works great when you are traveling and want to clear your palate before you enjoy a cigar. In a cigar lounge or shop that serves coffee, just order a cup of hot water. I must warn you: You will get a strange look from the waitstaff and patrons alike, but a few seconds of discomfort from strange looks is well worth an hour-plus of cigar bliss.

If you plan on calibrating your palate and you are a little congested, you will find that any of the techniques above will allow you to smell much better. Most vaporizers come with a packet of eucalyptus which you can add to the water. This works great if you have a cold or flu, but if you are going to calibrate your palate or smoke after your treatment, I highly recommend not adding the packet of eucalyptus to the water. Your palate will reek of eucalyptus if you do.

The Neti Pot

This isn't for the faint-hearted, folks. If you want to rinse your nasal cavity, there is no better and more effective way. There is an improved device based on the same principle, referred to as the "Nasal Wash" Neti Pot 300ml bottle. This device has a *water control valve* on the bottom of the bottle which makes it much easier to use and more effective.

Read the instructions and make sure you add the enclosed packet of salt and baking soda to the water or you will be sorry. The salt and baking soda buffer the water—rinsing your nasal cavity with pure water is painful. Use only unchlorinated water; most tap water is

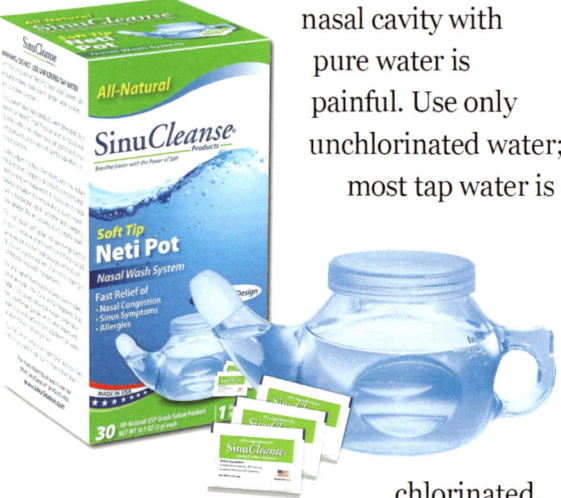

chlorinated. If necessary, use filtered or bottled water, and follow directions carefully.

The Hot Shower

A shower is an easy and effective way to decongest your nasal cavity. It softens the mucus in your nasal cavity as you breathe in and out during a shower. If you live in the city or suburbs, your water is chlorinated, so it is important to add a charcoal filter to your showerhead (see illustration). Chorine is a necessary evil that is added to all municipal water to kill bacteria, but it is definitely not good to breathe hot, chlorinated water vapor since it will irritate your nasal cavity.

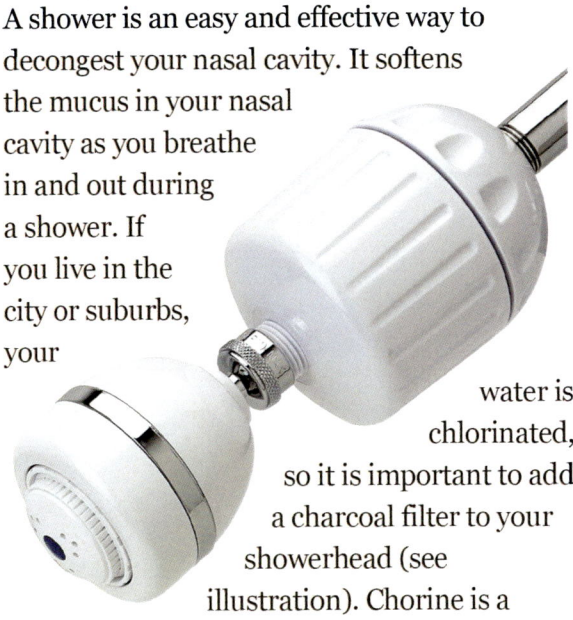

The Humidifier

A humidifier is tool that is useful for those living in a dry climate. You can purchase a portable stand-alone unit that you can put in your bedroom, office, or den. If your nasal cavity is dry, you will not be able to enjoy a cigar to its fullest. To experience the most taste a cigar has to offer, the ideal humidity range for the environment you smoke in is 50% to 70%.

For those living in high humidity climates, a dehumidifier is an effective tool. An air conditioner works by removing humidity from the air, but most smokers don't smoke in their house, so your next best option is to find a cigar shop close to home.

Saline Nasal Spray

Saline nasal spray is a handy tool that can help when your nasal cavity is dry, congested, or stuffy. Some nasal sprays are made with very strong ingredients and will anesthetize your palate for 30 minutes to an hour after using. If you want to light up five to ten minutes after using a nasal spray, make sure you know what you are spraying into your nostrils or you could be sorry. If you are going to use nasal spray, the one I highly recommend is Simply Saline Nasal Mist by Arm & Hammer Daily Care.

If one nostril is uncongested and the other feels congested, that is normal and happens throughout the day (we discussed nasal cycling in Chapter 2). Nasal spray is not a cure-all for a dry, congested, or stuffy nose, so if you are experiencing these symptoms on a regular basis, start looking for the underlying problem: smoking too much; poor or stale indoor air quality, whether at home or the office; breathing too much secondhand smoke; allergies to pollen, medications, or foods.

Hygiene Products

Various hygiene products may not at first seem like appropriate tools, but they are important ones in their own right. Before the average American leaves the bathroom, they have covered their bodies—and inhaled—an array of artificial fragrances, preservatives, and dyes, many of which are known carcinogens. The cosmetic industry is not regulated by the FDA like the food industry is. Many of the allergies we suffer from start in the bathroom.

According to the FDA, the average person uses nine personal-care products daily, containing about 126 chemical ingredients. (See Randall Fitzgerald's *The Hundred Year Lie* for more information.)

When you apply creams, lotions, and deodorant to the largest organ in your body—your skin—you will absorb chemicals from these products throughout the day. Some chemicals are harder to avoid, such as fire retardants used in carpets, drapery, and bedding. Also, many people have become habitual air freshener and fragrance users: their clothes, homes, and cars reek of an artificial odor that for some reason makes them feel fresh and clean. I find these fragrances strong enough to irritate my eyes and throat and suppress my appetite. The more people use them the more they will need to use them due to adaption, which we will discuss at length in Chapter 4. Of course, I am careful when expressing my dislike for their obsessive use of these products and keep extra copies of *The Hundred Year Lie* to give those I care about. If I am successful in motivating them to read even a few pages of this book, they will dispose of all these artificial concoctions immediately.

Sherry A. Rogers, a board certified MD and fellow of the American College of Allergy and Immunology, made an alarming statement in her book *Detoxify or Die* (2002).

> *We are the first generation of people to ever be exposed on a daily basis to such an unprecedented number of chemicals. At no other time have patients, through reading and education, had such an important and crucial role in determining their own wellness.*

To minimize your exposure, you can select products that contain none or at least less of these man-made chemicals.

Let's start with soap and shampoo. You can find hypoallergenic soap and shampoo that have less of the unnecessary chemicals or opt for organic products that have none.

If you read the ingredients in your toothpaste, you may wonder why in God's name do they need to make this stuff with words that you can't pronounce. Again, opt for organic toothpaste or make your own. If you make your own, your palate will be fresh, clean, and ready to enjoy the natural taste of your first sip of coffee or espresso. When your mouth tastes like peppermint or spearmint, your first cup of coffee will never taste good. To make your own natural toothpastes, all you have to do is find or buy a few 1-3-ounce glass jars and prepare the following to create an everyday toothpaste:

One jar of coconut or avocado oil or one of each. If you are a coffee connoisseur, avocado oil is the best choice for a morning toothpaste because it is neutral and will not affect your first sip of your morning brew. Coconut works well for an evening toothpaste. Both of these oils are naturally antibacterial and promote gum health.

Smoking cigars and drinking coffee and red wine will cause tooth stains, so to combat this effect, you can prepare a jar of 3 parts baking soda and 1 part sea salt, and brush with this mixture several times per week. Baking soda and salt are both mild abrasives and antibacterial and promote gum health while balancing your mouth to a neutral pH level. Chapter 4 further discusses the importance of your body's pH and the way it will affect what you taste.

You can also purchase activated coconut charcoal powder, which is an excellent tooth whitener that you can use twice per week—it also comes in a toothpaste, but the powder works much more effectively. Like salt and baking soda, this product is abrasive and if overused can hurt tooth enamel and cause gum irritation. Consult with your dentist before using any new products on your teeth.

Underarm odor is caused by bacteria growing in warm armpits. Commercial deodorants use aluminum to reduce sweating and kill the bacteria, but aluminum is a toxic chemical and is absorbed through your skin into your bloodstream, so it is not a healthy choice. If you don't want to smell like a florist's shop or a perfume shop for half a day and put aluminum in direct contact with your skin, you can choose a fragrance-free organic deodorant or use a Crystal Mineral Deodorant Stick. This product allows you to sweat, which is a natural process, but it will kill the bacteria that causes underarm odor. If you decide to use one of the nonconventional deodorants, you may find that wearing an undershirt will absorb the sweat and keep your outer shirt dry.

Regarding hair spray or hair gel, you can try an organic option that will work as well as a chemically laden conventional product.

Oral Hygiene: What You Need to Know

Everyone should pay attention to their teeth, especially cigar smokers, because teeth and gum problems will surely impact your smoking experience, and not in a good way. You need to ensure that you are doing everything you can to prevent tooth decay, gum irritation, and yellowing teeth. Tobacco contains tar and nicotine which can accumulate on the tooth surface, especially on the back or underside of the tooth. When this happens, it can cause two things. First, it will make your mouth pH more acidic, and second, your mouth will harbor bacteria that can promote tooth and gum problems. Below are some commonsense ways to keep your teeth healthy and in good shape.

Brush and Floss Twice a Day

Most dentists recommend brushing twice a day for two minutes and flossing once a day, and, if possible, twice a day to help keep your teeth and gums healthy. This is a given: Everyone should be doing it, but as a cigar smoker, you really want to make it part of your daily routine.

To help you get the most benefit from your dental hygiene regime, you can purchase an electric toothbrush that will do most of the work for you and let you know when you have brushed for two minutes via a beep. An electric toothbrush is an excellent investment; once you use one, you will quickly realize that you could never brush your teeth as well as this device.

For those who have trouble flossing because their teeth are very close together, you may find that flosser sticks will make the job much easier. If the spaces between your teeth are tight, ask your dentist if you are grinding your teeth while you sleep (teeth grinders typically have razor sharp teeth). If so, your dentist will be happy to make you a night guard, but ask the price first: You might get sticker shock at a price of $500 to $700 or more. If you choose a less expensive option, you can purchase a universal night guard in the price range of $15 to $25, which, though not custom-molded, will do the job in protecting your teeth.

Reducing the Effects of Tooth-staining Beverages and Foods

Tooth staining beverages and foods include coffees, sodas, energy drinks, red wines, marinara sauce, curry sauces, citrus, and berries. When you consume these beverages and foods, make sure you drink some water afterwards, swishing it around in your mouth before you swallow. When it comes to highly acidic beverages and foods, moderation is the key.

Tongue Cleaning

If you notice a white fuzzy buildup on the surface of your tongue, you can scrape it from the back to front or tip of the tongue. If you consume soft drinks, energy drinks, or coffee with sugar, bacteria will accumulate on the tongue's surface, which can lead to bad breath and a decreased ability to taste. You can scrape your tongue from back to front a few times—once or twice a day—with a tongue scraper, teaspoon, or butter knife. You may be surprised how much gunk you are able to gently scrape off the surface of your tongue.

> **TONGUE SENSITIVITY**
> The tongue is 8,000 times more sensitive to bitter tastes then it is to sweet tastes.

Regular Dental Cleanings

Most dentists recommend a dental cleaning at least twice a year. For a cigar smoker who has excess plaque, a dentist may recommend every four months. During a professional cleaning, the dental hygienist will scrape off plaque on the surfaces, in between your teeth, and under your gums. The hygienist will also polish your teeth to soften and remove plaque.

If you have dental insurance, an unscrupulous dentist may tell you that you need a deep cleaning, which is a big deal compared to a standard cleaning. They will charge your insurance company $300 to $400 when a $95 cleaning is all you will receive, and after your co-pay for an expensive "deep cleaning," you will end up on the losing end of the transaction. I fell for this trick for years, until one day I found an honest dentist who told me I needed only regular cleanings. Of all places, I found this dentist in a cigar lounge.

Self-checkups

If you have some issues with your teeth or you are a cigar geek, you may want to examine your teeth once a week or bimonthly to check for plaque buildup behind your teeth and for gum irritation. You can do so by purchasing an inexpensive dental light. Additionally, if you're worried about the yellowing of your teeth, there are toothpaste brands made specifically for smokers, or you can make your own as discussed in the smokers' tools section.

When you smoke cigars, your chances of having issues with your teeth and gums are increased; therefore, I recommend that you take extra care when it comes to protecting them. You get only one set of permanent teeth and only one chance to keep them.

The Smoking Environment and Why It Matters

In Cool Temperatures

Smoking in very cold or very warm weather can have a dramatic effect on your smoking experience. For those who live in southern states or states that never or rarely see snow, 65° degrees may feel cold. Those living in states that experience snow on a regular basis may think that temperatures in the 50° to 70° range as t-shirt weather.

Many smokers may find that they have a tendency to smoke too fast and draw too hard in cold weather and are prone to smoker's nausea, ashtray breath, or reeking of tobacco smoke. It never seems to fail: Around Christmas, a cold front moves through Florida for a couple of days, bringing in what Floridians consider frigid temperatures that drop below 50°. For those of us who aren't allowed to smoke in the house, we brave the cold and usually end up with one or all of the three side effects mentioned above.

When temperatures drop below 50°, we breathe more deeply and our blood vessels narrow, increasing our blood pressure while reducing the blood flow near the body's surface in order to keep our core body temperature as close to 98.6 ° Fahrenheit as possible. What does this mean for a cigar smoker? For some smokers, it's like smoking on steroids. Your heart has to pump harder in order to pump blood through narrower blood vessels, causing you to breathe more deeply, oxygenating your blood, and revving up your respiratory system, similar to how an automobile's turbocharged engine works.

Cigars that you typically experience as medium bodied or medium intensity may now be felt as full bodied or very intense. Full bodied cigars that you usually find pleasing may now be over the top and better saved for another time or place.

With increased oxygen and internal blood flow, the body will absorb more nicotine from the tobacco smoke in your palate (mouth and nasal cavity), affecting you in a positive or negative way. (See the negative effects mentioned above.) On the positive side of this equation, a light or low-intensity cigar smoked in a cold environment may now be felt as medium to medium-plus, and a medium may now be felt as a full bodied cigar. After I made these observations, I started saving light bodied cigars for when I am forced to brave the cold.

In Warm Weather

The temperature your body is acclimated to will determine how smoking in the heat will affect you. When temperatures rise above 78° or when you feel very warm or hot, you will start to perspire, and your blood vessels will expand to increase blood flow near the body's surface in order to cool you down. Your breathing and heart rate will slow, and you will start to feel you are on a slippery slope, headed for the dreaded smoker's nausea.

Acclimatization is the process by which you become physically adjusted to the temperature of your environment. It plays an important role in how well you tolerate the cold or heat. People who spend a lot of time outdoors become "outdoor acclimated." These people are affected less by the cold or heat extremes because their bodies have adjusted to the outdoor environment. I would venture to say that most cigar connoisseurs are "indoor acclimated" and may find braving the cold or heat is a challenge that they would face only if necessary. If a person is in good health, acclimatization usually occurs over a period of about two weeks.

Barometric Pressure

Remember when your grandma used to say that she knew when a storm was coming because she could "feel it in her bones"? It turns out that she may not have been as crazy as you thought. Changes in barometric pressure that accompany storms and shifts in weather patterns do affect our bodies, and some people are more sensitive to those effects than others. Still, many people do experience symptoms when the barometric pressure changes, so it's worth exploring. Let's look at some of the ways that changes in barometric pressure might affect your body and thus your smoking experience.

To help us better understand this effect, let's refer to Sir Isaac Newton's Third Law of Motion, which states that for every action, there is an equal and opposite reaction. Dr. Matthew Fink, neurologist-in-chief at New York-Presbyterian Hospital/Weill Cornell Medical Center, explained that low barometric pressure can cause headaches or migraines by creating a pressure difference between the atmosphere and the air-filled sinuses.

According to biometeorologist Jennifer Vanos, Ph.D., when the barometric pressure drops, so does your blood pressure. "In a low pressure system, which typically brings in rainy weather, your blood thickens along with the fluids surrounding the joints, causing joint inflammation, stiffness, and sometimes pain."

Have you ever noticed a cigar that you know well, and smoke often, sometimes doesn't taste the same? It could be caused by any number of variables, such as

- The cigar was a bad roll (not likely).
- The cigar became dried out or over-humidified due to neglect (likely for some, but not for a cigar connoisseur).
- You were coming down with a cold or in the midst of the flu.
- You were overly excited or emotional, angry, happy, sad, etc.
- The barometric pressure was very high or very low. Depending on how high or low, the pressure can have a mild to a dramatic effect on your smoking experience.

This is phenomenon has perplexed many cigar smokers and even connoisseurs. I used to take my favorite cigars with me when I traveled to share them with comrades, but my eagerness to share my treasured cigars was almost always met with disappointment when a cigar buddy would tell me that one of my favorite cigars tasted, well, just okay. In that moment, I had to agree although I didn't have the faintest idea why the cigar didn't taste like it usually did. Now I take into consideration the temperature and barometric pressure differences between where I stepped onto the plane and where I landed. I remind myself that I am, for example, in a much higher altitude or a very different climate, so that I don't expect a cigar to taste the same way it does in my normal smoking environment.

Atmospheric pressure is generally known as barometric pressure because a barometer is used to measure it. Barometric pressure is simply the weight of the air. It's easier to understand when you think about the concept of water pressure: As you go deeper in the water, the pressure increases. In one foot of water, you have the weight of that foot of water pressing down on you. In two feet of water, you have the weight of an extra foot of water pressing on you. A low pressure system pushes less against the body, allowing tissues to expand; expanding tissues can put pressure on joints, causing stiffness and sometimes pain.

Think of the last time there was a high pressure system moving in. When you woke up in the morning, you and everyone around you, including pets, felt energized, vigorous, excited, and enthusiastic. This is because in a high pressure system, there's more inner pressure on the joints and body, keeping them from expanding, and there are more negative ions in the air (negative ions are a good thing, unlike how it sounds). With each breath of fresh, negatively charged air, you feel energized and notice fewer stiff joints or muscles.

When smoking in a high pressure system, you will have a better chance of a pleasant experience. In a low pressure system, by contrast, you may experience the opposite effect. Low pressure systems are also associated with feelings of moodiness, melancholy, and sadness.

I know this may seem a little extreme to most, but for you cigar geeks, I'm going to give you a little more food for thought. Most people are more comfortable with a barometric pressure range of 29.8 to 30.2 inches of mercury (inHg). The range is small but significant—the higher, the better. So when you check the weather forecast, pay attention to the barometric pressure, and if a high pressure system is moving in, which is signaled by a 30.2 inHg or higher, get your favorite cigars ready to light up.

Many people think that the cool weather is what causes them to feel energized, which is a misconception. Think of the last time you were in someone's home, an office, a hotel room, or even a cigar lounge, and you felt uncomfortably cold. You probably didn't feel any of the positive effects mentioned above. This can happen often in the summer months when temperatures can climb into the 90s outside, and the inside temperature, due to the air conditioning system that removes humidity from the air as it cools it, might be set in the low 70s or, worse, in the upper 60s. In this dry, cool environment, you will probably not feel overjoyed unless someone gives you a belated birthday present consisting of a large box containing all of your favorite cigars and a few that were on your wish list.

So if you are one of the chosen few who notices how the temperature and barometric pressure influence your cigar experience, you are not out of your mind—just a little more sensitive than most cigar smokers.

Tools of the Trade

Temperature and barometric pressure are only two of the many variables that can affect when you might have a pleasant smoking experience. I have a cigar buddy who uses a simpler approach that I've yet to find science to back, but I'll share it with you, nonetheless.

He relies on his astrological chart, looking for the solar phase when his Saturn is transitioning into Capricorn, and Jupiter aligns with Mars; then, and only then, does he take out one of his favorite cigars, knowing he is destined for a memorable smoking experience.

The best response I can offer to his approach is this: To each his own!

Palate Developing Exercises

Exercise 1: Mouth Temperature Versus Cigar Smoke

What to Do

1. Light one cigar.

2. Pour beverage. Alcoholic: a glass of cold beer, scotch, whiskey, or bourbon on the rocks or chilled wine. Non-alcoholic: iced tea, cold water, cold energy drink, iced coffee, etc.

3. Take a drink of your chilled beverage and immediately (within 2 to 3 seconds) take a puff on your cigar.

    What did the cigar taste like? _____

    Did you enjoy the taste?

    no/very slight/slightly/somewhat/a little/a lot/a lot more

4. Take a drink of your chilled beverage and wait 40-60 seconds before you take a puff on your cigar.

    Did the cigar taste different?

    no/very slight/slightly/somewhat/a little/a lot/a lot more

Exercise 2: Adaptation and Refreshing the Palate

What to Do

1. Have one cigar with a light or Claro wrapper and one cigar with a dark or Maduro wrapper.

2. Pour one glass of water at room temperature.

3. Light both cigars, preferably with a touch lighter without drawing on the cigar. Smoke the cigar with the light wrapper first for about 3 minutes or 3 to 4 puffs, then smoke the cigar with the dark wrapper for about 3 minutes or 3 to 4 puffs. Continue to alternate smoking both cigars for 20 to 30 minutes; feel free to take an occasional sip of water.

    As you alternated between the light and dark wrapper cigars, what did you notice in terms of taste?_____

    Did you enjoy each cigar more when smoking them together?
            no/very slight/slightly/somewhat/a little/a lot/a lot more

    After alternating between the cigars a few times did you notice more pronounced taste notes from each cigar each time you alternated?
            no/very slight/slightly/somewhat/a little/a lot/a lot more

Exercise 3: Threshold—Discover Your Levels

You can do this exercise in the morning when you have your first cup of coffee and also in the evening when you are enjoying a drink with your cigar. In Chapter 2, we discussed Threshold and the 1 ppb (one part per billion) concept for aroma. For mouth taste, the threshold is much greater, but if you drink too much at one time, you will overstimulate your palate and taste less. In this exercise, you will experience firsthand what it feels like to cross your threshold. Later, you can use this experience to find your cigar smoke threshold.

What to Do

1. Have one cup of coffee or tea, or one alcoholic drink, such as wine, whiskey, etc.

2. Have one teaspoon and one tablespoon.

3. Use the teaspoon and take a sip of the beverage.

    What mouth taste association did you experienced?

    sweet/sour/salty/bitter/savory

    What palate (retro nasal) taste association category did you identify?
    floral/citrus/dried fruit/aromatic/earthy/roasted/smokey/complex

4. Use the tablespoon and take a sip of the beverage.

    What mouth taste association did you experience?
    sweet/sour/salty/ bitter/savory

    What palate (retro nasal) taste association did you identify?
    floral/citrus/dried fruit/aromatic/earthy/roasted/smokey/complex

5. Wait 40 seconds to 1 minute and repeat the exercise.

    Did you taste more or less flavor with the sip taken with the teaspoon?
    no/very slight/slightly/somewhat/a little/a lot/a lot more

    What are your overall observations? _____

6. Now apply this technique to the amount of smoke you produce and retro hale when smoking a cigar and see if you can increase the amount of flavor you experience.

Recommended Cigar Books for Your Library

The World of the Habano, First edition, February 2012

The Ultimate Cigar Book by Richard Carleton Hacker, 1997

The Cigar Companion by Anwer Bati & Simon Chase, 1995

Cigar Companion by Marvin R. Shanken, 2005

Excerpt from an Interview with Jhonys Diaz

GENERAL CIGAR SANTIAGO, DOMINICAN REPUBLIC, FEBRUARY 2020

Nick: Earlier I showed you the ProPalate® System. Would you like to share your impressions with our readers?

Jhonys: The ProPalate® kit is extremely interesting. I think we have found an approach, a systematic and structured way of, like you said, decoding a cigar by establishing a profile for a cigar both before and after lighting the cigar.

Nick: According to the ProPalate® Calibration Map, this is a complex cigar.

Jhonys: Yes, it's a complex smoke. The ProPalate® Calibration Map got it right.

Nick: Do you have any closing thoughts before we wrap it up today?

Jhonys: Like I was explaining to you in the beginning, the ProPalate® kit is spot-on. Right now, we are going through the process of establishing a procedure for cigar testing. We want to establish a way of mapping and a sensory language, and I think this is right there; it fits in with the type of idea that we have. I feel that we are going to be using this a lot internally, not only with the handmade premium, but also within the other categories of machine-made cigars and smokeless tobaccos. This is a structural way of smoking and actually calibrating your palate and defining the profile of a cigar.

Nick: I appreciate you taking the time to sit down with me and offer your comments. Thanks again for having me.

Jhonys: It's been a pleasure.

Chapter 4

The Psychology Behind the Art, Part 1

All truths are easy to understand once they are discovered; the point is to discover them. You cannot teach a man anything, you can only help him find it within himself.
—Galileo

We've all heard the expression, "He's a born athlete/musician/writer/salesman, etc." But I've yet to meet a man or woman who is a born cigar connoisseur, someone who clipped and lit their first cigar correctly and, after taking a few puffs, exclaimed,

This medium-plus intensity cigar offers a dense opulent smoke flavor profile, consisting of delicate floral, fresh hay, cedar, and citrus notes in the first third. In the second third, it opens up offering a rainbow of aromatic notes of black pepper, paprika, and cinnamon with hints of aniseed and nutmeg. The final third transitions nicely from dominant aromatic notes to more complex notes of espresso, dark chocolate, vanilla, and black licorice. The cigar's finish is exceptionally long, echoing all the previous taste notes in a symphony of flavors that dance on the palate. The wrapper leaf imparts a silky, oiliness that coats the palate and the lips for what seems like hours after the cigar was left to die with dignity in the ashtray.

We've all known people who were gifted early in a given discipline, art form, or sport. At the time, it seemed unfair that they didn't need to study for endless hours like the rest of us just to get a grade above a D, nor did they have to work out or watch what they ate in the off-season to get in shape for spring training, or practice a musical instrument every day to be considered a good musician, let alone a great one. With some exceptions, most of us ended up at the same finish line via different paths, some a little sooner and others a little later, rather like the fable of the tortoise and hare.

We are all naturally inclined to do some things better than others. Having the right mindset in any discipline is crucial if you what to excel. But in order to excel in any given field, it takes a concerted effort, and that is why I recommend you make a serious commitment to study, practice, and internalize the information presented in this and the remaining chapters.

By now, you have a better handle on the reasons for past confusion about how we perceive aroma, taste, and flavor, and how we develop taste associations. Let's do a quick review of the first three chapters.

In Chapter 1, we learned how we acquired flawed taste references and associations and, in some cases, no references. From an early age, most of us consumed processed foods, spiked with synthetic flavors, dyes, and preservatives. Those inaccurate food footprints kept us from developing accurate taste references and associations found in premium cigars, wines, spirits, and coffees, raising the question of whether we really are in charge of our palates.

In Chapter 2, we learned the importance of sensory perception and how it enables us to experience aroma, taste, and flavor. We delved into technical aspects of the two senses most critical to a cigar smoker: *mouth taste* and *smell*.

In Chapter 3, we looked at palate-related tools available on the market: the tongue map, flavor wheel, taste and evaluation charts, aroma kits, books, magazines, blogs, and podcasts. Although they offer some good advice regarding brands, hardware, and cigar reviews, none offer a comprehensive approach to develop or improve your palate.

Taste References and Associations

There are many examples of young kids who learned a second language by the ripe old age of five without ever studying vocabulary or grammar. The brain of a young person is like a sponge, ready to absorb everything without questioning or analyzing the why and how. You may find that you will be able to identify taste and flavors that you were exposed to as a youth very easily and may have to work a little or, in some cases, a lot harder to identify the ones that you became familiar with as an adult.

Our first exposure to an aroma or taste resembles a social first impression. We find it hard to erase that initial response, be it good or bad. This leads us further into the critical topic of *taste associations,* as they relate to cigars. Once you have a working command of this most important concept, you'll exclaim, "Aha!" Mid-stogie, you may note a hint of dried lemon peel, followed by a touch of aniseed, with notes of cedar, dark chocolate, and aged leather. Epiphany!

Taste Associations: References Required

As we discussed in Chapter 1, many Baby Boomers and Millennials had diets consisting of mainly processed foods along with limited life experience. Life experiences could include walking into a barn and experiencing smells and aromas of fresh hay, sweet feed, and horse sweat; or sinking your hands into dark, rich, earthy humus; or walking in a forest; or eating a variety of fresh and dried fruits; or dining on a gourmet meal either in a highly rated restaurant or at home prepared by you or your gourmet home chef; or trying different wines, bourbons, whiskeys, coffees, etc. Of course, there are different degrees of life experiences, ranging from very limited to normal to extraordinary.

Unhealthy diets might include sugarcoated cereal and Pop Tarts for breakfast, baloney sandwich and bag of potato chips for lunch, and a hamburger and fries for dinner. Beverages might include coffee with enough cream, milk, or sugar to turn it into a dessert beverage; sodas; and energy drinks. And to make matters worse, those who grew up on those foods have references of only synthetic flavors and have never tasted or smelled many of the true taste associations used in cigar lingo, such as dried lemon peel, herbaceous, dried fig, aniseed, nutmeg, dark chocolate, real vanilla, caramel, and graham cracker.

The ability to make taste associations is not instinctive, so if you want to learn how to make them you will need to practice. It would also help if you have the opportunity to engage with others who either are interested in developing their palates or already have a developed palate. Also expanding your dietary footprint to include a broad range of foods, herbs, and spices will help you in your quest.

It is human nature to want to share feelings of joy, elation, sadness, and disappointment. In order to do so, people use words to express these emotions—that is, unless they are an accomplished artist, in which case they may use a paint brush, a quill or pen, a musical instrument, or their body in some form of a dance.

Cigars that are simple need few words to convey how they taste; however, at the other end of the spectrum, the finest cigars are so full of taste characteristics and nuances that they demand our full attention in order to accurately and fully appreciate and describe them. It's similar to the challenge of finding the right words to describe the emotion felt when standing in front of a masterpiece such as Rembrandt's *Night Watch* or Michelangelo's *David*. Or when Pavarotti or Bocelli hits a high C at the climax of the opera. Or when your favorite sports team comes from behind to win the Super Bowl in overtime.

However, cigar language, while at times challenging, shouldn't be ambiguous. Using words to describe a sensory experience— beyond describing basic aromas and tastes— requires imagination, creativity, and a solid command of your palate. This doesn't mean the language has to be extravagant.

The Psychology Behind the Art, Part I

The French use a peacock's body and tail as a reference in describing the finish of a great wine. In describing a cigar, the peacock's radiant blue breast might be viewed as the cigar's core tastes and its dazzling tail feathers as the cigar's delicate, expansive, exotic, and complex tastes experienced in the cigar's finish: the lingering flavors that resonate in your palate after you exhale.

Identifying different taste associations is just the beginning and can be accomplished by repetition. After that, what distinguishes a sophisticated connoisseur is that he can describe the dynamic interplay between the individual elements. Putting a sensory experience into words requires the utmost awareness, attention, and training.

Often there is more than one accurate association, but a sophisticated cigar, wine, whiskey, or coffee connoisseur will use the most appropriate or verbally pleasing descriptor. Let's look at what happens when someone chooses to use less pleasing descriptors. Someone may describe an earthy note as musty, even though most people associate musty as an unappealing aroma. More extreme examples could be a smelly dog, a sweaty horse, and horse manure, when *barnyard* would serve as an accurate descriptor; yet more extreme, *body odor, and smelly socks*, are just over the top. I have a cigar buddy who has a discerning palate and an impressive humidor; however, he has a hard time finding someone to join him when he smokes, even when he's providing the cigars. I've tried to explain to him the reason no one wants to sit down and enjoy a cigar with him because of his use of distasteful descriptors, such as *stinky cheese, smelly dog*, and horse *manure.*

Examples of Descriptors

Accurate/Common/Appealing	Accurate/Uncommon/Unappealing
Dried lemon peel	Sour, acidic, sour dish rag
Dried fruit	Sour or rotten fruit
Piney, resinous Woody Bitter almond	Turpentine, fresh paint, paint solvent Cardboard box, sawdust Marzipan, Grandma's Christmas cookies
Roasted nuts and caramel	Nougat
Barnyard	Manure, sweaty horse
Leather	Horse saddle, baseball glove, hidey
Musty	Attic or basement smell, Grandma's house
Shiitake mushroom, malt, yeast Savory, delicious	Cheesy, smelly socks, body odor Umami

> Let's check out how food found its way into a cigar smoker's life. Javier, an old friend, tells the tale his first association with a particular flavor occurred one Saturday morning when his grandmother returned from a trip from Pinar del Rio, Cuba. She made pancakes, using fresh vanilla bean and cinnamon and smothered the pancakes with black molasses that she had brought from her homeland. Every time he smells or tastes vanilla, cinnamon, or molasses, he thinks of pancakes. The only problem crops up at the cigar lounge. When his buddies ask him what the cigar tastes like, he says, "Pancakes." They all have a good laugh at his expense and threaten to ban him from their inner circle and games of dominos.
>
> Bear with me while I share another anecdote as a study in cigar-palate development. This one spotlights two brothers. We'll call the older boy, "Agusto" and the younger, "Juanito." Their father loved horses and built a stable in back of his cigar factory. The boys' father taught them that the tobacco plant will tell you what it needs in terms of water and fertilizer. Every morning and late afternoon during the tobacco-growing season, Dad and Agusto saddled up their horses and trotted through the fields for inspection. Juanito, who was left behind, loved horses, too, until one fateful day when a large stallion bucked him into a pile of manure used to fertilize the garden. Worse yet, he broke his foot in three places when it caught in the stirrup. From that day on, Juanito hated everything about horses, especially the way they smelled. He still had to clean the stable, both as part of his basic chores and as punishment for disobeying one of his father's rules: No mounting spirited horses alone.
>
> Both Agusto and Juanito followed in their father's footsteps and became cigar blenders. Agusto pursued the style his father was known for: bold and earthy. A typical description of one of his cigars might sound something like this: A powerhouse, full-bodied, with strong notes of wood smoke, barnyard, dark coffee, and aged leather and licorice in the finish. Juanito's blends, on the other hand, steered clear of bold and earthy. His cigars resonated with dominant notes of floral, dried fruit, black pepper, aniseed, nutmeg, cedar, and roasted nuts. He wanted nothing to do with anything that would remind him of a barn.

A Surprising Lesson Learned During a Training Session

Here is one last example of a cigar taste association setup, this one experienced firsthand while conducting a private palate training session with John, a seasoned cigar blender. The guy exudes talent. He has blended several cigars, which, in my opinion, are as superb as any I've ever smoked. And I would like to think that I've had my fair share of great cigars over the last 45 years of lighting up on a daily basis.

The session always starts with confirming aroma references to make sure the trainee is in charge of his taste and then calibrating the palate to those aromas, the first of which is dried lemon peel. John smelled the aroma bottle, smiled, and asked what it was. "Just tell me what it reminds you of," I replied. "There is no right or wrong answer; it's your association." He hesitated and finally said it reminded him of shrimp. *Shrimp?* I thought to myself. *This will be a long session.*

As we moved through the calibration process, I felt embarrassed for prejudging an industry guru. John aced 18 out of 20 aromas, thanks to a highly developed palate. His off-the-wall shrimp response nagged at the back of my mind, but I didn't let it hinder our momentum. We breezed through a four-hour workshop in three hours. John was on top of his game.

He invited me to dinner that evening at his favorite seafood restaurant. I ordered stuffed, wild-caught sea bass, topped with a gently spiced marinara sauce. John ordered grilled shrimp, with extra lemon on the side. When the entrées arrived, the server greeted him by his first name and placed a large bowl of lemon juice next to his plate. I glanced down at my friend's dinner before I took my first bite. He was swirling his shrimp in the lemon bath, as if he were taking the crustaceans for a night swim. A light bulb came on! At that moment, I understood why in his training session lemon peel smelled like shrimp.

To have an association, you must first have a reference, whether from cleaning a horse stable or dipping shrimp in lemon juice.

Neuro-Linguistic Programming (NLP)

In the pancake, barnyard, and shrimp stories, were the main characters correct about what they tasted? Based on their life experiences, yes. However, it behooves us to clarify the two types of taste associations: accurate and flawed. Theirs were the latter. What can one do to reset the palate once it has run amok? I recommend practicing a method called Neuro-Linguistic Programming or NLP. This sounds heavy in theory, but it is quite simple in practice, and we all do it whether we realize it or not. Let me introduce you to Anthony Robbins, a specialist in NLP.

Some readers may recognize Robbins as a popular motivational speaker. He gained fame in the 1980s and 1990s for his training workshops, books, and recordings in the field of neuro-linguistic programming. The need for NLP evolved from the premise that a sensory experience while in an emotionally charged state leaves a lasting impression on the psyche. Everywhere, but hopefully not in our bathroom mirror, we see people stuck in the quicksand of limiting, unproductive behaviors.

For example, a grown man may be deathly afraid of dogs because a Chihuahua bit him when he was a child. Or a woman almost jumps through a sliding glass door at first sight of a mouse or a snake. Could it be because a mouse ran across her bare feet in the kitchen late one night when she was raiding the cookie jar, or her brother put his pet snake in her bed just for kicks and giggles. Or a cigar smoker who refuses to smoke a gifted, super-premium Maduro cigar because the first and last Maduro he smoked years ago made him turn green— *before* he knew how to smoke a heavy, full bodied, full flavor, intense cigar.

So how can you use neuro-linguistic programming to correct flawed taste associations and instill new, authentic references, for example, to rare spices such as nutmeg or cardamom? Simple. You mindfully smell the aroma and repeat to yourself or out loud, several times, a brief sentence with the correct name. Our pancake-man-turned-dominos-outcast would say, "This is cinnamon," while smelling that spice. You can find books galore on neurolinguistic programming, but now you have the essence in a nutshell.

Calibration

This leads us to calibration. When you *consciously* smell an aroma or taste a food, you are first establishing a reference and then calibrating your palate to that aroma or taste reference. The more you do so, the better you will be able to recognize and identify the broad range of taste characteristics and nuances a great cigar has to offer. In Chapter 5, we will learn what you can do every day to calibrate and improve your palate.

It is important to develop a strong foundation for basic aromas, tastes, and flavors. Once you have a working knowledge of the basic references, you can start to detect subtle nuances. Many substances share common characteristics, such as herbaceous, which has grassy, herbal, and earthy notes. Fresh hay has a sweet and floral aroma note. Black pepper has a bright, spicy, top note with a touch of fruitiness. White pepper has a bright top note, but also a pungent mid-palate note. Dark chocolate is extremely complex, offering notes of earthiness, along with acidic (sour), dried fruit, barnyard, and various aromatic notes depending on the region in which the cacao was grown.

Below, I've listed a few of the most commonly used taste associations. Along with those, you'll find explanations as to what gives them their unique taste/aroma characteristics.

Let's start by breaking down a few individual flavor associations to understand *why* they smell or taste the way they do. Once you have a working knowledge of this approach, you will no longer have to ask someone else to tell you what a cigar tastes like. You will be able to formulate your own objective opinion. This doesn't mean you will ignore others' judgments—quite the contrary. You will find cigar reviewers, shop owners, salesmen, and cigar buddies whose palates resonate with yours.

Before we get started, I'd like to share a personal story of my experience with the aroma, or *odor* as many refer to it, of ammonia.

Ammonia odor emanates as a by-product of fermentation. When tobacco leaves begin to ferment, the smell of ammonia can knock you over.

My initiation took place in the early 1990s at a factory called General Cigar. Back then, GC welcomed and offered a tour of its operation to any cigar-smoking tourists brave enough to travel to an undeveloped country and show up at the factory's front door. (Boy, have things changed!) A small group of cigar buddies and I trudged through the pre-aging room. To this day, I recall the pungent smell and burning sensation. My eyes, nose, throat rebelled in pain.

This pungent odor comes from moistened wrapper leaf (the wrapper is moistened to make it elastic before it is rolled over the cigar bunch) which gives off a little ammonia aroma, or odor, call it what you like. Many of the fresh cigars, taken right off the cigar maker's table, have this pungent aroma. Many cigar smokers and even connoisseurs haven't had the opportunity to smoke a fresh cigar, right off the cigar maker's table. If you are one of them, don't despair, I can almost guarantee you that you will enjoy smoking cigars out of the humidor much more than off the cigar maker's table.

After the freshly made cigars go through quality control, the manufacturers put them in a pre-aging room with humidity and temperature control. In this room, the excess moisture in the different filler leaves evaporates and balances out, as they become one, or "marry," as it is referred to in the industry. During the process, the cigars will off-gas ammonia. Depending on the number of cigars placed in this room, the room may be aired out several times per day until the off-gassing ammonia subsides, which could take several days to a few weeks, depending on the size of the pre-aging room, the number of cigars, and the ventilation system. Then the cigars are transferred to the aging room where they are allowed to rest, undisturbed, for several months and in some cases a year or two.

The blenders test the cigars at various intervals, and when they determine that the tobaccos have married, the aging process is complete, and the cigars are ready to be smoked. Their decision is based on several factors: the style of the cigar, the cigar blend, and their particular palate preference and sensitivity. By the time the cigars hit the brick-and-mortar shops' shelves or online retailers' warehouses, they are waiting to be enjoyed.

Depending on your palate sensitivity, when you remove the cello of a cigar, you may still sense a rather faint vinegar or ammonia smell on the wrapper leaf. Most cigar smokers tolerate this aroma. It wakes up and stimulates the palate when it is accompanied by other aromas, such as fresh hay, herbaceous, dried fruit, cedar, barnyard, or dark chocolate. On the other hand, too much ammonia can turn off even an eager smoker. In most cases, once you light up the cigar, the vinegarish or ammonia aroma dissipates, but a cigar displaying too much ammonia in the pre-light smell was probably made with tobaccos that were not fully cured and will always taste green, harsh, or bitter no matter how long you age it.

A premium cigar that has been maintained in a controlled environment remains alive, which is why it will continue to off-gas less and less. Have you ever seen a yellow cello? If not, ask one of your seasoned cigar buddies to dig deep into his humidor and find a cigar that has rested in cello for a few years. Remember: Unless a cigar is totally dried out, it continues to live as its ages, waiting for you to ignite it, turning mere matter into an intoxicating exotic and seductive aroma. Or until it "dies." Once the microorganisms residing in the tobacco's leaves expire, the cigar no longer tastes like a premium cigar—it will have little or no flavor other than dried-out hay.

Most Common Taste Associations and Their Unique Characteristics

Allspice

Even though its name implies a blend of spices, allspice is actually one spice that comes from a dried, unripe berry of the Pimenta tree. It has a sweet taste that's reminiscent of a number of different spices, including cloves, cinnamon, and nutmeg; hence its name–Allspice.

Anise Seed

One of the oldest known spices, anise has a unique licorice-like flavor and is commonly used in making licorice to enhance the licorice flavor.

Cardamom

Of all the spices, few have as complex and enticing an aroma as cardamom. Cardamom is a dried seed pod that comes from several plants in the ginger family. It has a strong, sweet aroma and a flavor that is often described as a combination of ginger, cinnamon, and mint, with hints of lemon and floral notes. Cardamom is a great breath freshener: Just pop one tiny seed in your mouth, bite into it, and you will experience a flavor burst like none other. Cardamom is the third most expensive spice, surpassed in price by only vanilla and saffron.

Dark Sweet Cherry

Most cigar smokers don't talk much about a dark cherry taste note. In fact, most adults have a strong and often negative reference to the taste of cherry due to their first exposure of this reference in medicines they were forced to take in their childhood by their parents. It is not uncommon for someone to describe a strong cherry taste or aroma as medicine-like, because their reference dates back to their first and sometimes only association to that flavor. In the NLP section in Chapter 3, we discussed what happens when you are in an emotionally charged state of mind: Listening to music, watching a movie, or eating or smelling something will have a lasting impression that is branded in your brain, whether good or bad, positive or negative.

But dried dark sweet cherry actually has a delicious aroma and taste, similar to dried fig, plum, raisin, black currents, and raspberry. In the wine and coffee worlds, dark cherry is commonly used as a taste reference. Let's look at cherry's history to better understand how the situation came about.

According to Nadia Berenstein, a researcher at the University of Pennsylvania,

"The synthetic flavor industry goes back to the middle of the 19th century, which a lot of people don't realize. Artificial cherry flavors mainly came from esters, which back in the day had some pretty dubious origins. Esters were generally produced from either by-product of alcohol distillation or sometimes chemicals that were produced as by-products of the coal industry."

The most recognized cough medicine in the United States was once Robitussin's cherry-flavored formula. I asked a cigar connoisseur with an exceptional palate to describe the taste for me: "In a nutshell, it tastes like cherry kosher wine mixed with a hefty dose of saccharine. Disgusting—I'd rather take two aspirins, drink two or three shots of whiskey with honey, and light up a cigar and suffer through it."

Here is the takeaway: Purchase some fresh, frozen, and especially dried dark sweet cherries and get familiar with this taste. And then add it to your cigar vocabulary options.

Dark Chocolate

The aroma and flavor of dark chocolate is an important flavor association for a cigar smoker to become familiar with. It offers a broad range of flavor characteristics and nuances. Let's take an in-depth look at dark chocolate, starting with its origin. It is made from the seed pod of a cacao tree (the scientific name is *Theobroma*, which translates as *Food of the Gods*. The cacao tree produces a fruit called a cacao pod that averages 1.1 pounds when ripe and ready to harvest. In its raw form, the fruit is too bitter to eat, but once the fruit is fermented and the beans are separated from the pulp and lightly roasted and mixed with sugar, voila: synergistic magic!

During the roasting process, the Maillard Reaction takes place when the oils in the form of amino acids combine with reducing or melting sugars, creating new flavor molecules and compounds, producing a complex flavor profile. Dark chocolate has a mouth taste that is sweet and creamy and slightly acidic and bitter. On the palate, it can offer a wide range of flavors, consisting of many of the following flavor associations depending on what region it is grown: floral, dried fruits, earthy, aromatic, nutmeg, roasted nuts, caramel, coffee, and cardamom.

Milk Chocolate

This is a commonly used descriptor. Milk chocolate has some of the aroma of dark chocolate and creaminess, but in my opinion falls short for an accurate cigar taste association for cigars. Here's why: All chocolate is not created equal, just as all cigars are not made with the same quality of tobaccos and blended to perfection. Lower-grade cocoa—and far less of it—barely makes it into milk chocolate. This type contains as little as 10% cocoa and copious amounts of milk or cream, sugar, and a vegetable oil as an emulsifier and imitation vanilla as a flavor enhancer. An 8-ounce milk chocolate bar is comprised of only 0.8 ounces of cocoa, whereas a 70% dark chocolate bar has 5.6 oz of high-quality cocoa. The bottom line: Milk chocolate can boast of little more than a sweet, creamy taste with a hint of cocoa. When used to describe a cigar's flavor note, one can assume that the taster is sensing a little cocoa accompanied by a sweet creaminess. I have yet to smoke a cigar that had the sweetness or overall taste of milk chocolate, but to each his own.

100% Chocolate

> I encourage you to purchase a bar of premium 70% dark chocolate and smell the chocolate before you taste it. Then taste it using the pinched nose calibration technique discussed at the end of Chapter 2 in the exercises section. This will allow you to experience the intense range of flavor characteristics and nuances dark chocolate has to offer.

This is commonly referred to as *Baker's unsweetened chocolate bar* or *bitter chocolate*. It is referred to as bitter chocolate for good reason: In this form, it is not appetizing and has very little to no aroma. The reason it works in baked products is due to the considerable amount of sugar that is used as part of the recipes. The sugar, along with the heat in the oven, creates the Millard reaction as mentioned above.

The bitterness blends into the background, and the chocolate flavors we are all familiar with and enjoy comes forth.

Coffee

This is often mistaken for the taste and aroma of dark chocolate. When used as a taste association, try to be specific. Do you mean an espresso coffee black, with no added sugar? Or a sweet espresso with so much sugar that it tastes like a sweet, liquid coffee dessert? Or are you referring to a cup of American style coffee made with premium Arabica coffee beans?

Let's take a look at where coffee's flavor comes from. Similar to chocolate that comes from the cacao fruit seed pod, coffee starts out as a red cherry fruit that is fermented to remove the pulp, then the beans (which are really seeds) are dried and roasted, undergoing the Maillard reaction, which increases its flavor molecule from a mere 100 to as many as 800. Many cigar smokers drink coffee with their cigar, thinking that it will cleanse their palate, but this a misconception: If you want to accurately evaluate a cigar, the best beverage is unchlorinated, flat water at room temperature.

If you are smoking for pure enjoyment and like to have a cup of coffee or a shot of espresso with your cigar, that's fine—they pair well together. I would venture to say that someone who finds coffee flavor in every cigar he smokes is enjoying his cigar with a cup of coffee or shot of espresso—but that is just my unproven hypothesis.

Earthy (Musty)

A cigar made with aged tobacco leaf and rested in an aging room or humidor with high levels of humidity for several months to a year may have a light, earthy aroma notes. This earthiness is desirable for most seasoned smokers. Like drinking scotch, it is an acquired taste or aroma. I've yet to meet a teenager who cut his teeth drinking a well-aged, peaty, single malt Islay scotch.

Dried Fruit

This is a very appealing, complex flavor. Dried fruits all share elements of sweet and sour notes, along with their individual characteristics. The most common dried fruit aroma associations found in cigar are fig, plum, raisin, dark sweet cherry, and, less commonly, black currant and apricot. I refer to dried fig and plum as taste twins because it hard to discern the difference between the two, whereas raisin, cherry, black currant, and apricot can each be detected by a person with a trained palate.

Hay

There are two distinct types: fresh hay or sweet hay and dried-out hay or old hay. Fresh hay has a sweet aroma and is commonly found in most premium cigars. Dried out hay has lost its sweet aroma notes and may be found in cigars that have dried out due to poor storage or a cigar blend that was made with low quality seco and volado tobacco leaves. And if too much of these leaves is used in the blend, the cigar will cause your mouth to feel dried out, commonly referred to as "cotton mouth."

Licorice

Like chocolate and coffee beans, licorice root is bitter, lacking an appealing flavor in its raw form. But when heated and combined with anise, wheat, molasses or cane sugar, the licorice flavor we are familiar with comes forward. Licorice has a rich, creamy mouth taste with a top note of anise, which is experienced in the retro or ortho hale. Most dark-wrapper Maduro and Oscuro cigars have a strong licorice note, so I recommend that you become familiar with this taste association so you can find it in your favorite dark-wrapper cigars, but with one caveat: Some cigar blends with a light or natural wrapper may also offer notes of licorice, which comes from a blend of rich, extraordinary filler leaves. When purchasing licorice, a word of caution: The majority of licorice is made with imitation licorice and loads of high fructose corn syrup, so if you want to calibrate your palate to true licorice, make sure to read the ingredients on the package before you buy it.

Nutmeg

This spice is a warm and aromatic herb with hints of clove, pine, and resin and is a common taste association found in cigars, especially those blended with Olor tobaccos from the Dominican Republic.

Peppers

Black Pepper: The most popular pepper is black peppercorn. It grows on a woody, climbing vine and is harvested before fully ripened. Then the green peppercorns are in soaked in warm water causing the skins to float to the top. The peppercorn is then aired dried. This process allows its volatile oils and aroma compounds to develop, giving the peppercorn its bright, spicy aroma.

White Pepper: This pepper is less aromatic than black pepper and has a slightly pungent or musty aroma. White pepper is made from fully ripened berries. After the berries are harvested, they are soaked in water and then fermented for about ten days. After the berry is air-dried, it is ground into a powder or sold as whole peppercorn. White pepper is less aromatic than black pepper and is commonly used in Brazilian, Asian, and Cajun soups and dishes.

Paprika: This vibrant complex and aromatic spice has a sweet, slightly fruity and earthy aroma. It is made from grinding sweet chili pepper pods. When ground without the seeds, it is a mild spice with a big aroma. You may find the taste of paprika in cigars made with rich robust filler tobaccos.

Chili Pepper: Also referred to as cayenne pepper, it has a sharp top note and a bold, pungent, mid-palate taste that leaves a pleasantly biting heat on the tongue—if not used in excess.

Sassafras

Sassafras was one of America's first export crops that was a bigger seller than tobacco in the 17th century. American colonists and Europeans used it to treat a long list of ailments, including arthritis, gout, fevers, blood pressure, urinary problems, kidney stones, eczema and other skin disorders, and intestinal problems. When research showed that astronomical quantities of safrole, a compound found in the sassafras plant, caused cancer in rats, in 1960 the FDA banned the sale of sassafras in America putting an end to a long tradition that started 1875 in making old-fashioned root beer. However, Americans and Europeans have enjoyed sassafras tea and root beer with no ill effects for centuries. It has taste notes of anise and lemon, along with its unique flavor characteristics.

Vinegar

This falls into the category of acidic or sour. You may note this aroma when smelling a cigar's wrapper in the pre-smoke. Like ammonia, the vinegar aroma is a by-product of fermentation and has an appeal if balanced with other aromas, such as fresh hay, nutmeg, leather, or graham cracker. The vinegar-like bite in the right proportion excites the palate. The aroma dissipates in a lit cigar.

Like ammonia, vinegar is not a flavor typically used in describing a cigar, but it is present in most cigars that have not been aged for an extended period of time. Many taste associations, such as vanilla, chocolate, and dried fruit, have a light sour or vinegarish note. Foodies who watch cooking shows have probably noticed this when the chef squeezes a dash of lemon juice over an appetizer or entrée, right before serving. The same acidic benefit applies to vinegar. Coffee connoisseurs always start out describing a coffee's quality in terms of the balance between acidity and bitterness, such as, "This medium roast coffee bean displays a good balance of acidity" or "has low acidity" or "has high acidity."

Now that you see how an aroma or flavor can be broken down, you can apply this method to any taste association. In Chapter 5, we will put all the common taste association in categories that will enable you to easily identify them when you are evaluating a cigar.

Defining the Cigar Connoisseur

Many cigar newbies or non-connoisseurs may find my definition of a cigar connoisseur exaggerated or over the top, but I beg your indulgence for moment while I try to prove my point.

Cigar connoisseurs are some of the most highly taste-sensitive individuals on the planet. They have been known to drive across town in rush hour traffic or board a plane and travel hundreds, even thousands of miles to undeveloped countries in pursuit of a cigar that can offer them only fleeting seconds of intoxicating palate stimulation derived from mere smoke. They can detect and appreciate a broad range of palate stimulation and minute differences in tobacco characteristics and nuances. They are people who treat their cigars as sensorial taste vessels that are capable of transporting them back in time or forward into the future.

The cigar connoisseurs is so in tune with their palate that they find great pleasure in smelling the provocative aroma of the smoke wafting from the foot of their own lit cigar or someone else's.

I would venture to say most cigar connoisseurs, and those aspiring to become one, are some sort of maverick. The word was coined back in the 1800s to describe Sam Maverick (1803-1870), a prominent Texas landowner who refused to brand and confine his cattle, allowing them to roam freely. Maverick became synonymous with unbranded cattle and later a term to describe a stubborn streak of independence or a person of unorthodox views.

Let's look at some common attributes that mavericks share and see if you, too, are a maverick.

Six Maverick Traits

- They are authentic.
- They challenge the status quo.
- They have strong convictions.
- They believe in themselves and their own vision of the world.
- They always find a time and a place to light up their favorite cigar.
- Mavericks come in all shapes and sizes. What makes them special is the power of their spirit and desire to make a positive impact on whatever they pursue.

Understanding Your Primary Frame of Reference

All humans have a primary frame of reference in terms of the way they perceive the world around them and process information. When you know your primary frame of reference, you will have a better understanding of how you perceive and express your thoughts and ideas. This awareness will make you a more sensitive smoker and allow you to better express your impressions of a cigar's characteristics and nuances. People who have mastered the art of sales use this technique, whether acquired through training or intuition, to connect with potential buyers, and you, too, can use it to better communicate your point of view to your cigar buddies, significant other, and friends and family.

Below is a simple question: Your answer will identify your primary frame of reference.

How would you describe what it is like when you take a walk on the beach? _____
_____

After you have read about the three ways that we perceive and process information, come back and check off your primary frame of reference:

- Visual
- Auditory
- Kinesthetic

There are three primary ways humans perceive and process information. Most of us have a dominant sensory reference followed by secondary references. In your answer to the question above, did you describe your walk on the beach using only visual cues or did you use a few visual cues followed by an auditory and a kinesthetic cue?

We all know people who are heavily weighted to one frame of reference over the others.

Visual

People whose primary frame of reference is visual typically describe people, places, or things in the following manner: I *see*, or I *saw*. Do you *see* what I'm saying? She (or he) *looks* great. It's not uncommon for them to have an artistic flair and like to dress well, enjoys decorating and redecorating their house and covers their walls with pictures with nice frame and the best quality artwork they can afford. They like nice cars and frequent car washes and detail shops.

Auditory

People whose primarily primary frame of reference is auditory typically describe people, places or things in the following manner: I *hear* what you are *saying*. If only she would *hear* what I am *telling* her. Can you *hear* the faint *sound* of the train in the distance? Listen to the mourning doves: They are sing in harmony. This type of person gravitates to music in every form: a musician, a wannabe musician, a music teacher, a speaker, a news reporter, and so on. When in their personal space, they usually have some form of music playing in the background or foreground. They may not be overly concerned with the way they dress, preferring comfort over the latest style. They typically have a lot of friends because they are good listeners and offer their undivided attention when listening.

Kinesthetic, Tactile, or Feeling

People whose primary frame of reference is kinesthetic typically describe people, places, or things in the following manner: I *feel* sorry for him. I *felt* awful when I heard the news. It *seems* to me. I can't *wrap* my head around this situation. They like to internalize information before they respond or make a decision. This type of person is the hardest type of person to convince or sell something to—just ask any car salesman who is the hardest type person to "close," and they will likely say the *engineer type*.

How Our Brains Influence Our Taste Perception

When you smell or taste something, you may assume that you experience it in your mouth or palate, but in reality, we experience taste in our brain. Our taste buds and olfactory bulb are only the receiver of stimuli: They send a coded message to our brain, and our brain processes the input and searches for the appropriate associations.

Here's how this relates to identifying taste associations. Aroma is not tangible in the same way that a cigar, cigar cutter, or cigar match is tangible. We can't see or touch it with our hands.

An aroma is first perceived in the right hemisphere of our brain. Then the left hemisphere has to describe the aroma association using words. When we first sense an aroma, the right hemisphere of the brain uses imagination to take us back in time to find a reference point, going through a library of options similar to a computer that has stored information. Then it has a conversation with the left hemisphere, which in turn comes up with the words to describe it. There's always a conversation going on between the left and right hemisphere. If you used only your right hemisphere, you might describe a cinnamon aroma as pancakes. If you don't have a reference, then the chances of making an accurate taste association is zero. If your reference is weak, your left brain may not offer a word to describe the aroma, but your right brain recognizes the aroma, which may lead to an argument between the left and right hemispheres, and frustration will set in. The harder you try to identify the aroma, the further it eludes you.

The scientific community once believed that creative people live in the right hemisphere of their brain, and logical people lived in the left hemisphere; however, this is now considered a misconception. A healthy, productive person uses both the right and left hemispheres of their brain. A person who spends too much time in the left hemisphere of their brain would be considered a dysfunctional person lacking emotion and the ability to express themselves. On the contrary, a person who spends too much time in the right hemisphere would be considered overly emotional or impractical, or a dreamer who will never amount to much.

A good example of a person who spent too much time in the right brain is no other than Vincent van Gogh, the French Impressionist painter who, unfortunately, lived and died a pauper, selling only one painting in his lifetime. One hundred years later, his *Portrait of Dr. Gachet* sold for $82.5 million in the opening three minutes of the auction at Christie's Auction House in New York. According to some scholars (for example, Judy-Arin Krupp in *The Journal of Education*, vol. 169, 1987), he displayed symptoms consistent with borderline disorder, impulsivity, self-destructive behavior, fear of abandonment, an unbalanced self-image, authority conflicts, and other complicated relationships. I'd like to think of him as just a genius, born way ahead of his time.

Not all geniuses display an unbalanced use of right- and left-brain function. Einstein is a perfect example of someone who was able to utilize both spheres of his brain equally well. His creative right side developed theories that changed conventional wisdom, while his left side used words, graphs, and charts to demonstrate his hypotheses.

Adults learn new things very differently from children. When an adult is confronted with new information, they filter it through past experiences, attempting to make a connection, whereas a child just accepts it.

Before adolescence, your brain is like a sponge and readily absorbs all input without questioning it. As we age, our ability to accept new input is reduced due to the filters we have developed to process information.

In our adolescence, references to taste and aromas are readily ingrained in our brain and are easily accessed. As we age, this process becomes slower and more difficult, similar to the process of learning a second language as a youth versus learning as an adult.

In Europe, it is not unusual for a child living in multicultural neighborhoods to speak three languages without ever studying grammar or vocabulary. In America, we have many examples of children who learn a second language from their parents, grandparents, or caregivers, again without ever cracking a book or studying.

So if you are an adult, which I trust you are, you may have to work a little harder to establish a taste association that was not developed in your youth. The good news is you *can* teach an old dog new tricks—it just takes a little more time and effort. When learning a new aroma association, don't question it; instead, accept it as a child does when learning a language. Take it at face value and don't overanalyze it. Think, *It is what it is*. For instance, if you're learning a new association to nutmeg, just tell yourself, *This is nutmeg—* don't relate it to anything else.

> I have a friend I'll call "Joe" who was obsessed with gaining control of his palate, and one day we were scheduled to meet at a cigar lounge to relax and puff away the problems of the world. When I drove into the large shopping plaza, I noticed he had parked his car in the farthest parking spot from the cigar shop, so I pulled in next to him and asked if he was having car trouble. He looked at me with a smirk and said that he was going to get his daily exercise before he spent an afternoon in a leather sofa chair.
>
> I parked, and we started to walk towards the shop. I couldn't help but notice a clacking sound coming from his pants pocket. I asked, "What in God's name do you have in your pocket?" He reached in and pulled out a spice jar with fresh hay, then another with aniseed, and a third with roasted nuts.
>
> It didn't take long before Joe was in charge of his palate.

When you start to train, or calibrate, your palate, you may notice that you are able to make some associations easily while others seem difficult, and then there are those that, for the life of you, you just can't make an association. The previous section identified three frames of reference: visual, auditory, and kinesthetic. In the following exercise, we will stimulate the visual and kinesthetic frames, so if your primary frame of reference is auditory, you may have to work a bit harder.

The average adult forgets about 25% of what they learn within one hour and 85% within one week, so repetition and multiple exposures are key to success and eventual mastery.

An Exercise for Stubborn Associations

Let's use nutmeg as the referenced aromatic association. First, find a quiet spot in your home without any distractions, including your cell phone. Take the sifter cap off the bottle, pour a few pieces of nutmeg into the palm of your hand, and look at the spice. Then smell the spice and tell yourself, *This is nutmeg*. Smell it again and repeat, *This is nutmeg*.

Do this once or twice a day for several days, and you will establish a strong reference. After that, you can calibrate from time to time to keep your palate tuned up to the aroma of nutmeg.

When doing this exercise, don't analyze it with the left hemisphere of your brain, trying to compare it to something else—for example, *It reminds me a little of allspice and black pepper, with a touch of resin and earthiness*. Instead, think of it as a spice that is very aromatic, and it is nutmeg, period. If you have an ongoing problem with a particular aroma, you can use trigger words as discussed in the next section.

Taste Triggers

Taste Triggers are metaphors that you can use to find those taste associations that are elusive and next to impossible to accurately identify. We all have our strengths and weaknesses, similar to a baseball hitter who can hit any ball out of the park, except an inside curve; for some unknown reason, this pitch will send him back to the dugout every time. For cigar smokers, we may have a mental block for certain taste associations that may be difficult to identify for several reasons:

- Your first impression was not strong or noteworthy.
- Your first impression was a negative one, one you don't care to remember.
- It is not a common taste association or aroma.
- You have not calibrated your palate to that aroma for a long time.
- You recently encountered an aroma that was very similar to a previous aroma.
- You are suffering from palate fatigue.

There is nothing more frustrating than smelling an aroma that you recognize and were able to identify previously, but for some reason the name now eludes you. There are several ways to find a useful taste trigger, which are similar to the process of remembering a person's name by associating it with something else. For instance, if you are at a party and are introduced to John Churchill, the president of a company you would like to do business with and you don't want to forget his name, you may say to yourself, "He is named after two historical leaders (John F. Kennedy and Winston Churchill) who both enjoyed fine cigars, and a popular cigar size, Churchill, was named after one of them. For people who smell cedar and instantly think of their grandma's closet (due to the cedar rings she put in there to ward off moths), they will use that association as their trigger. The same would apply to a baseball glove.

Both cedar and leather are very common aroma and taste associations found in cigars. Can you imagine how you would sound at a cigar lounge surrounded by a group of cigar connoisseurs if you boldly announced, "This cigar has dominant taste notes of my Grandma's closet and an old baseball glove"?

VISUAL CUES	
Light Tone Colors	light brown, beige, yellow, turquoise,
Images	floral arrangement, perfume shop, wheat field, haystacks
Association	lavender, fresh hay, dried fruit, citrus, menthol
Mid Tone Colors	red, sienna, green, brown, orange
Images	bakery shop, fresh baked desserts, Brandy Alexander drink
Association	aromatic: black pepper, cedar, aniseed, cinnamon, nutmeg, paprika, sassafras, cardamom
Dark Tone Colors	burgundy, walnut, burnt amber, black
Images	peacock feathers, Monet painting, abstract painting
Association	complex: earthy, leather, barnyard, dried mushroom, dark chocolate, espresso, vanilla, licorice, molasses
AUDITORY CUES	
Light Sounds	acoustic music, string quartet, birds chirping, running water
Association	lavender, fresh hay, dried fruit, citrus, menthol
Mid Sounds	easy listening, folk, jazz, smooth jazz music
Association	aromatic: black pepper, cedar, aniseed, cinnamon, nutmeg, paprika, sassafras, cardamom
Heavy Sounds	hard rock concert, large symphony, sporting event, waterfall
Association	complex: earthy, leather, barnyard, dried mushroom, dark chocolate, espresso, vanilla, licorice, molasses
KINESTHETIC CUES	
Light Feeling	light-headedness after running, fresh breath of mountain air
Association	lavender, fresh hay, dried fruit, citrus
Mid Feeling	throat stimulation, feelings felt in the heart
Association	aromatic: black pepper, cedar, aniseed, cinnamon, nutmeg, paprika, sassafras, cardamom
Heavy Feeling	feelings felt in your gut or throughout your body, confused, perplexed, fascinated
Association	complex: earthy, leather, barnyard, dried mushroom, dark chocolate, espresso, vanilla, licorice, molasses

Adaptation

Commonly known as "palate fatigue," adaption is something we experience throughout the day. Palate fatigue is the way our sense of smell gets used to or *adapts* to what it is smelling, and as a result it becomes less and less sensitive to that aroma, taste, or flavor until we no longer can perceive it.

Think of the last time you went to your favorite restaurant, walked in off the street and how the aromas of fresh-baked sour dough rolls, shrimp scampi sautéing in a garlic, butter, and olive oil, and a charred sirloin steak made your mouth water with anticipation of your forthcoming meal. After a few minutes, your palate adapted, and those bold, delicious aromas went unnoticed.

I know a foodie who will ask his waiter to let him know about five minutes before his entrée will be brought to the table, and when he receives the cue, he walks outside for a few minutes, taking breaths of fresh air, and returns to his table with a fresh palate. The same holds true for a *home chef* who, after spending the afternoon preparing a gourmet meal, rarely enjoys the meal as much as the guest who waltzes in and sits down with a fresh palate, lost in the moment, savoring every bite of the delicious meal. If you are one of these *home chefs* and want to enjoy the fruits of your labor as much as your family or guests will, simply go outside just before serving the meal and enjoy a few minutes of fresh air, and return with a refreshed palate. You will be amazed at the aromas and flavors you created.

This adaptation also occurs with bad odors. If you have ever driven through a town with a paper mill or sewage treatment plant, you couldn't help but notice the pungent smell of sulfur; but after a few minutes, the awful smell goes unnoticed. Our sense of smell tires rapidly, but it also recovers rapidly.

> I never smoke in excess. That is, I smoke in moderation, only one cigar at a time.
> –Mark Twain

Cigar smokers, from connoisseurs to novices, experience palate fatigue from time to time. Have you ever noticed when you are smoking too fast for whatever reason (dinner will be served in five minutes or the playoff game is going to start in ten minutes), as you puff away seeking too many sensorial highs, the cigar seems to lose its taste? These are classic examples of palate fatigue.

This may sound strange to some of you, but people working in the cigar industry are most prone to palate fatigue. Too much of *any* good thing rarely results in a good outcome. For instance, consider the impact of one or two glasses of your favorite wine versus one or two bottles; two or three whiskeys versus a half to a full bottle; one appetizer, one entrée, and one dessert versus two appetizers, extra rolls, two entrées, plus four sides and two desserts. Burning through a Double Corona in fifteen minutes and lighting up another will give you similar results.

What does palate fatigue *taste* like? Like *nothing*, actually. You lose your ability to taste. In the early stages, you notice less and less flavor. The natural reaction is to smoke harder and harder, which worsens the condition until you can't taste anything. If you haven't learned *when to say when* and continue to push the envelope, you will end up with *smoker's nausea*.

If you have never succumbed to these conditions and feel compelled to see for yourself if they're really that bad, try this exercise. Next time you light up, take a puff every 5 to 10 seconds for 3 to 5 minutes, without breaking the puff frequency. In less than 5 minutes, you will have a firsthand experience you won't want to repeat. Fortunately, the autonomic nervous system, acting in the unconscious realm, steps in to protect us when we're too careless to watch out for ourselves. Bodily functions such as heart rate, blood pressure, and respiration rev into high gear to make us feel awful. "Don't do that again," they whisper.

> In this high tech, high def, in-your-face world, we often disregard obvious solutions. Let me recommend one tiny ounce of prevention that is worth pounds of cure. Slow Down! Take your time.
>
> Mastering this simple approach will pay huge dividends, starting with the next cigar you smoke and everyone thereafter.

Smoker's Nausea

If you smoke cigars, you may at one time or another experience smoker's nausea, which we will address in more detail. Below are the major causes and remedies.

COMMON CAUSES	REMEDIES
Smoking too fast	Smoke more slowly, time your draw frequency, aim for 40- to 60-second intervals.
Smoking a cigar with a tight draw (When a cigar has a tight draw, you are forced to draw too hard to keep it lit.)	Put it in the ash tray or return it to the supplier.
Smoking a full bodied, intense cigar on an empty stomach	Eat a snack: dry roasted nuts, dark chocolate, or saltine crackers before you light up.
Consuming too much alcohol before or while you are smoking	Know your alcohol limit and adhere to it.
Smoking when you are dehydrated	Drink water at room temperature before and while you smoke.
Smoking a blend cigar that doesn't agree with you	Some tobaccos may not agree with you. Put it down and grab another cigar. If you can't stomach throwing away an unfinished cigar, cut a half inch off the cigar head and offer it to a comrade. See if it affects him the same way.
Sitting in a big, fat leather chair for too long while you puff away	Get up and walk outside, if weather permits.
Your body's pH being off: too acidic or too alkaline	Test your pH at home or at your doctor's office.

Of all the remedies listed above, getting up from your chair and moving your body will often give you the quickest relief. An ounce of prevention is worth a pound of cure, so at the onset of smoker's nausea, put your cigar in the ashtray and move your body.

When I am in a cigar lounge and start to feel a little uncomfortable, I simply tell my friends that I left something in the car or I have to make a phone call and go outside and walk around the parking lot. If I'm at a friend's house and we are sitting on the porch smoking, I might say that I need to make a personal phone call and walk away from our sitting area. While you're walking outside, take long, deep breaths, and after a few minutes, you should feel better and ready to go back to your cigar. When you return, drink water instead of alcohol until you feel back to normal. For temporary relief in severe cases, you can try the following:

- Put a teaspoon of sugar in your mouth and let it dissolve slowly.
- Drink a non-diet soda or fruit juice.
- Eat a candy bar.
- Eat anything available.
- If you are perspiring a lot, rinse your face with cold water and put a cold washcloth on your neck.
- Lie down and while you wait for your God to have mercy on you, analyze what you did or didn't do to get in this state and make a mental note to never do that again. Repeat to yourself, "I will never do that again."

Nicotine: What You Should Know

It's tough to talk about nicotine. It is both politically and emotionally charged. Academics and lawmakers have difficulty separating it from well documented negative side effects of smoking cigarettes. However, when nicotine is studied or talked about without the word *cigarettes* casting a dark cloud over the topic, surprising findings come to light.

In March 2014, *Harvard Health* published an interesting and in-depth article, "Nicotine: It May Have a Good Side":

> *Nicotine is rightly reviled because of its associations with smoking and addiction. But the rogue substance has a wide range of effects on the brain, which may include some healing properties. Researchers are testing nicotine and related compounds as treatments for Alzheimer's disease, Parkinson's disease, attention deficit/hyperactivity disorder (ADHD), and other conditions.*

The psychological effects of nicotine at first seem contradictory: increasing alertness while providing a sense of relaxation and calm. One possible explanation is that the effect varies with the user's initial state. For someone who's agitated, nicotine has a calming effect. For someone who isn't, it heightens alertness. Epidemiological studies have hinted at nicotine's therapeutic potential. During the 1980s, several found that smokers had lower rates of Parkinson's disease than nonsmokers.

In another study conducted in 2007, researchers demonstrated clearly that smoking protects subjects from Parkinson's disease. This is due to the effects of nicotine on dopamine neurons (Parkinson's disease is caused by the increasing loss of these neurons), both stimulating motor function and protecting the neurons from dying (Villafane, G. et al., "Chronic High Dose Transdermal Nicotine in Parkinson's Disease: An Open Trial," *European Journal of Neurology*, 2007, 14, 1313-1316).

When nicotine enters the body, it releases dopamine in the pleasure and motivation areas in the brain. Therefore, the user experiences a pleasurable sensation. Dopamine affects our emotions, movements, and sensations of pleasure and pain. The higher the dopamine in the brain, the higher the feeling of contentment. This probably explains why a person smoking a cigar is usually not angry, agitated, or confrontational. Quite the contrary: He or she is typically relaxed, poised, thinking of pleasant things, and acting like a true gentleman or lady. Cigars seem to bring out the best in most of us.

Nobody wants people to associate cigarettes with any health benefits, so for many, anything containing tobacco is taboo, and unfortunately cigars are carelessly thrown into most discussions regarding tobacco. There are several reasons cigarettes should not be compared to cigars. First, cigars are consumed differently; there are very few cigar chain-smokers. The vast majority of cigar smokers smoke for pleasure, not to satisfy an addiction to nicotine. Second, cigar tobacco is extremely rich and robust, and even a so-called tough guy can't inhale cigar smoke into his lungs without coughing and feeling nauseous. Many of us have accidently inhaled cigar smoke into our lungs and felt that awful burning feeling.

The reason cigar tobacco is so rich, robust, and flavorful is the way it is cured. Cigar tobacco is hung in well ventilated barns and allowed to dry over a period of four to eight weeks, a process referred to as "air cured."

> If I had taken my doctor's advice and quit smoking when he advised me to, I wouldn't have lived to go to his funeral.
> —George Burns

Cigarette tobacco is "flue cured," a process in which the tobacco is cured over flues (pipes) that are heated by externally fed fire boxes for about a week. Cigarettes are made with flue-cured tobacco because the smoke from this tobacco is milder and inhalable. Cigarette tobacco is also sprayed with the manufacturers' secret recipes or formulas that give them slightly different tastes.

In 1999, a controversial movie, *The Insider*, shed some light on this industry fact. The flue-curing process allows cigarette smokers to inhale the smoke into their lungs, which is why the tobaccos used to make cigarettes versus those used in cigars are very different, and one should never use the word *cigarettes* and *cigars* in the same sentence, unless a sensible example is being made that distinguishes one from the other.

Interesting Facts

- Nicotine is the major alkaloid found in tobacco and can be found in lower concentrations in plants of the same family such as potatoes, tomatoes, and eggplants.
- From centuries before Columbus arrived to present day, tobacco has been used in North, South, and Central America for magico-religious, medicinal, and recreational purposes.
- Tobacco has been used as medicine and stimulant for at least 2,000 years.
- Ritual tobacco use in shamanism is probably as old as the beginning of horticulture, some 8,000 years ago.
- American Indians recognized tobacco as a powerful medicine.
- Tobacco used as a form of currency between colonists in the Thirteen Colonies when gold and silver were scarce.

Like caffeine, nicotine can have a mild laxative effect in some people, particularly from some filler tobaccos, especially a filler leaf called *medio tiempo* (the top two leaves of a tobacco plant) sometimes used in full body cigars, special blends, and limited editions.

Nicotine may one day be considered a potential weapon to fight against neurological disorders such as Alzheimer's disease. If there's one thing we've learned about the history of medicine, it is that sometimes a solution is often found in the most unlikely places: In our case, it just might be in our humidor. I can only muse about the day when a doctor's office gives out cigars instead of lollipops to adult patients.

All these positive aspects of nicotine use have been studied and reviewed for over two decades (Le Houezec, J., "Nicotine: Abused Substance and Therapeutic Agent," *Journal of Psychiatry and Neuroscience*, 1998, 23, 95-108), but little progress has been made to further explore these potential beneficial effects of nicotine. One can only assume the main reason lies in the association with nicotine and cigarettes. Rest assured there are maverick scientists out there who will continue to explore the benefits of nicotine.

In the 1960s David A. Boska, MD, a maverick doctor, endorsed cigar smoking. He was the cigar smoker's doctor and his patients were celebrities from all walks of life: from sports and entertainment figures to government officials, including John F. Kennedy. Here is what the doc had to say:

"Cigar smoking is a very pleasurable thing. It's mental health, there's no doubt about it. You don't get hooked on it like you do with some relaxant drugs, which usually don't last very long anyway. It takes a while to smoke a cigar and gratification is instantaneous. I also happen to think that group therapy is very beneficial if you happen to have a few friends that you like to smoke a cigar with."

In 2015 the FDA published a **systematic review** in *BMC Public Health* open access, peer-reviewed journal. Their findings state, "Cancer risks nearly nil for 1-2 cigars per day."

Secondhand Cigar Smoke: What You Should Know

Secondhand smoke combines smoke from a burning cigar and smoke exhaled by one or more smokers. This is a topic that every cigar smoker should pay attention to: This will affect your smoking experience and possibly your health.

When smoking, the smoker has the ability to control how much smoke he produces and where the smoke will travel. By drawing lightly on a cigar, the smoker can produce less smoke, and conversely by drawing harder, he produces more smoke—he is in control. Also, a smoker will control how long to leave the smoke in his mouth before releasing it, how much he allows to travel up through his nasal cavity, and, most important, how to not allow the smoke to go into his lungs, which would make him feel very uncomfortable.

The problem with secondhand smoke is that it is hard to avoid. The smoker will consequently inhale secondhand smoke into his lungs—although only a small amount—but with every breath he takes, it will add up quickly, especially in a smoke-filled room.

Most cigar shops and lounges pay close attention to the ambient air in their shops and lounges and use effective filtering systems to clean the air and to exhaust excessive secondhand smoke. If you live in a small town with only one cigar shop or lounge that doesn't have a good filtering system, you may consider working with the owner of the establishment and patrons to do what is necessary to install an effective filtering system.

Virgin Palate

Let's examine the most intense sensorial experience. Virgin palate involves the first taste of a cigar—or for that matter, a glass of wine, a snifter of whiskey, a cup of coffee, or any food or snack. By smoking, drinking or eating slowly, you allow the palate to refresh or recover from prior sensory stimuli. Even the finest cigar will not impart its subtle or even its bold taste nuances if you're smoking too fast or your palate is already shot from smoking too many cigars in a given day.

There are a few commonly shared methods among cigar smokers to help restore palate fatigue, but most are counterproductive and temporary at best. They include drinking a glass of coke or a shot of espresso, eating a candy bar, or putting a teaspoon of sugar in your mouth. Though these may help relieve temporary nausea, in order to cleanse the palate, I have found none as effective as dry crackers and water. This is commonly used in the wine and spirits industry and for good reason: It works. You can use this method, for example, if (1) you have a bad taste in your mouth from a cigar you are not enjoying and want to smoke something else, or (2) if you ate a gourmet meal consisting, of an appetizer of escargot in a heavy garlic butter sauce, followed by a bowl of pasta smothered in a spicy Sicilian red sauce, topped with a blend of well-aged imported cheeses. Don't let the simplicity of the dry crackers and water method fool you. I'll explain the science in a minute.

Palate Cleanse and Your Body's pH Level

To conduct a palate cleanse, you will need Saltine crackers with unsalted tops, typically labeled "Premium Unsalted Tops" or any plain, dry cracker *without* spices and herbs.

Drinking Water: Filtered water, odor-free well water, tap water filtered through activated charcoal, or bottled water, all at room temperature. When possible, a*void* unfiltered tap water; water filtered through a softener; stale bottled water with a plastic taste, sparkling water, or flavored waters, also referred to as seltzer or tonic water.

To conduct the palate cleanse,

1. place ½ to 1 cracker in your mouth and chew it slowly,
2. allow it to move around the inside of your mouth and swallow,
3. rinse with a few sips of drinking water.

If you want to get more enjoyment out of your cigars, and your meals for that matter, try sipping water at room temperature throughout a smoking session and during a meal. Keep in mind that the temperature inside your mouth is around 98.6°, and the temperature of ice water, iced sweet tea, or soda with ice is 38° to 48°. You can only imagine how your sensory taste receptors feel when you take a gulp of an iced beverage: anesthetized.

Back to the soda cracker routine. Why does this simple palate cleanse work so well? It helps neutralize the pH in your mouth. A healthy person's saliva is around 7.0 pH; someone with a serious disease, the flu, a fever, or taking a lot of meds will typically have pH 6.5 or lower. It is important to understand that the difference in pH numbers is exponential: for example, the difference between 7.0 and 6.5 is not 0.5% but 5 times as acidic. Vegetarians who don't consume enough protein or starch may have an above average pH level of 7.25+. Also, some medications may cause your pH to go too high or low, which in both cases will cause your cigar to taste off. When your pH is off—too high or too low—it can affect your taste sensitivity. Some things you may not taste at all, while others may taste too bitter or sour, too sweet or salty.

Why saltines crackers? The key ingredients are unbleached flour, salt, malted barley flour and baking soda. Flour, salt, and baking soda absorb flavor molecules in your mouth which helps to neutralize the previous flavors from a cigar, wine, whiskey, coffee, or food. Another benefit is that salt and baking soda are both alkaline, so they work together to balance the pH in your mouth.

If your diet consists of foods and beverages with a low pH value, such as processed foods, sodas, and large amounts of starch and protein, your pH may be on the acidic side of the scale. Also, most medications are acidic and will lower your pH. With that said, if your pH becomes too acidic, most cigars will taste off: they will taste bitter or have little to no taste. Interestingly, if your pH is in the upper end of the scale at 7.5+, most cigars will taste off: They, too, will taste bitter or have little to no taste. In addition, you may be more prone to smoker's nausea.

Think about the last time you had a cold and tried to smoke your favorite cigar:
It probably didn't taste right. This is caused by two things: Your nasal cavity was coated

with excess mucus, and your pH was acidic. I've talked to aficionados who tell me their "cigars just don't taste like they used to," as if they suspect the industry has cut corners. When I probe further, I discover they just started a new medication. Or they admit they have been suffering from a chronic health condition. Here's the bottom line: Memorable smoking experiences occur when we're in optimal health, feeling good, and on top of our game.

A Cigar Taste Dilemma

I have a friend who has a very refined palate, whom I will refer to as "Tom." One day in confidence he shared with me his cigar taste dilemma. His compulsive, excessive, fanatical behavioral traits are best described as a type-A personality. We have all met these types of people: They are usually very successful at whatever they pursue and are often referred to as high achievers or workaholics. When they decide to do something, it is all or nothing.

Tom invited me over to show me some of the vintage cigars he had recently purchased at an auction. After showing me the vintage cigars, he asked if I would mind smoking two of his "go-to" cigars, comparing taste notes as we smoked. Before I could answer, he added that he would send me home with one of them. He had already selected two highly rated cigars for us to smoke: One cigar was medium bodied with a Habano Rosado wrapper grown in Ecuador, and the second was a full bodied cigar with a San Andres wrapper from Mexico. Since I had shared with him the concept of adaptation (that our palate adapts to given stimuli, and the longer we smell or taste something the weaker and weaker the stimuli become), he usually smokes two or three cigars at the same time. Nice luxury if one can afford it.

As we were toasting the foot of our cigars with long, wood matches, he shared his dilemma with me. Tom told me he was losing his taste: Cigars that were once his favorite no longer tasted as good. He went as far as to say that all of his cigars had started tasting bitter a few months before, and he was experiencing smoker's nausea when he smoked. As he told me of his dilemma, he had a sad, hopeless look on his face. I asked him if he was taking any new meds. With a smirk, he responded, "You know I don't take any meds."

This middle-aged guy was in perfect shape, not for his age, but for any age. His hobbies were CrossFit training and participating in marathons and triathlons. He was also fanatic about his diet, and I'd yet to see him eat a dessert or even one of his wife's famous Christmas cookies, which she prepares from scratch using only the best ingredients. I continued to probe, asking him if he had made any significant changes in his diet. He thought for a few seconds and said no. I followed with, "Are you sure—nothing?"

He replied, "Well, the only thing that is different is a special drink that I prepare and take three time a day to dissolve my kidney stones." A dim light came on in the back of my mind. I asked him what was in the drink that would dissolve kidney stones. He gave me the answer that I expected: vinegar. I played dumb and asked him how vinegar dissolves kidney stones. He went on to tell me vinegar dissolves kidney stones in our body the same way vinegar dissolves mineral or calcium deposits in a coffeemaker. He was also adding a teaspoon of baking soda to make the concoction even stronger. The light in the back of my mind was getting brighter.

Tom had been drinking this concoction for about three months, but the lower back pain and spasms kept coming back. I asked him if he knew his body's pH level. Clearly surprised, he fired back, "What does my body's pH have to do with the price of a pre-embargo Cuban cigar?" I shared with him what I knew about pH levels and taste, and before I could finish talking, he exclaimed, "I'm ready to take a pH test to see if it will shed some light on my dilemma—how can I do it?"

I told him that he would have to wait until his stomach was empty and he wasn't smoking and drinking scotch. I suggested the morning as the best time to get an accurate reading. He followed me home to get a few test strips. Midnight was approaching, and the drive from his home to mine was about 45 minutes.

The next morning, a Sunday, I was awakened by someone banging on my front door. I looked at the clock: It was 5:15. I live on a dirt road, miles from the nearest town, and the only person I knew who would have the audacity show up at that hour was Tom. As I opened the door, Tom was rambling away that he had tried to call me several times but I hadn't answered, so he thought something might be wrong, and thus he came right over. As I started to complain about the early hour, he interrupted to show me the two test strips I had given him a few hours before: "Look, my pH is way off; this might explain why I've lost my taste."

I agreed with him and suggested that he see a doctor to first confirm that he had kidney stones and second to discuss treatment options. A few days later, he called me to tell me the doctor confirmed that he didn't have kidney stones, but instead was suffering from lower-back cramps due to his excessive and strenuous exercise routine. The moral of this story is to always seek a professional opinion when things don't seem right. In Tom's case, he sought the advice of a doctor who was licensed to practice both in holistic and conventional medicine.

The moral of this story: Pay attention to your health and consider adding pH strips to your toolbox.

Barrel Aging Tobacco: How It Influences a Cigar

It is universally accepted that aging mellows and improves the taste of freshly distilled spirits and wines. While the spirits and wine rest in oak barrels, the alcohol acts as a solvent, extracting tannins and esters out of the wood, which will give a spirit or wine a slight vanilla and sometimes coconut flavor, along with a smoky oak aroma—all this while smoothing out and balancing the overall flavor footprint. Whiskey, cognac, rum, port, and wine makers have long known the importance of the vessel in which their precious liquid is laid to rest. Likewise, cigar manufacturers understand the importance of allowing freshly rolled cigars to rest in a cedar lined humidor.

> Like all types of fermentation, be it whiskey, wine, food, or tobacco leaf, barrel aging tobacco is a type of enhanced fermentation which has become more and more popular over the two last decades.

Oak barrels, sometimes referred to casks, are made by joining raw wood staves (wood planks) made from American and French white oak without adhesives or nails. After the barrel is constructed the interior of the barrel is toasted or charred. Toasting is achieved by gently heating the interior of the barrel staves, while charring is achieved by using intense heat to burn the interior, producing a thick layer of burned wood. The charred oak staves act as a filter, absorbing the by-products of fermentation while smoothing out the overall flavor footprint. As the distilled spirit or wine rests in an oak barrel, the wood staves become saturated with the spirit it contains, causing the wood to swell which keeps the barrels from leaking. The oak barrel's wood staves will interact and influence the liquid by imparting exotic aromas and taste notes typically not found in the liquid alone. Each time an oak barrel is *reused*, a variety of flavors from the wood and liquid combine, creating new flavors and causing the barrel to take on a character all its own.

The same holds true for cigars. The freshly made cigars, which are hand rolled with aged tobacco leaves, are typically placed in large walk-in cedar lined humidors to rest, allowing the filler, binder and wrapper leaves to marry, as mentioned in the previous chapter.

It is important not to look at this process as a flavor additive. The oak barrels don't artificially flavor tobacco, cigars, or liquids: It is all about how the tobacco, cigars, spirits, and wines interact with the barrel. It is a pure, natural organic process.

Barrel aging tobacco has deep roots, dating back to the late 1700s. You may have noticed a Native American Statue prominently placed at the entrance or inside a cigar shop or lounge: The shop owner or company is giving credit where credit is due. We have to thank the Native Americans, not only for sharing their precious tobacco with Columbus, but also later showing settlers how they stored and aged their tobacco leaves. This process can be traced back to the Louisiana Territory to the local Choctaw Indians who stored their tobacco leaves in hollowed out tree stumps. I would venture to say, after a few settlers smoked some of the tobacco stored in a hollowed-out tree stumps, they knew the Choctaws were onto something. Borrowing this way of storing tobacco, the settlers substituted tree stumps with used bourbon or whiskey barrels and the art of aging or *enhanced fermentation* was born. The process has changed very little since its inception.

Most of the barrels used in the cigar industry are used rum barrels; however, it is not uncommon for bourbon barrels to find their way into a cigar factory. To call a spirit bourbon, the distiller must use a new oak barrel by law; however, to make a whiskey, the distiller can allow its spirit to rest in previously used barrels. The preferred vessel for of aging whiskey is used bourbon or sherry barrels.

> Over the last two decades, cigar manufactures have increasingly explored the use of barrels to age tobacco leaves and, in some cases, finished cigars. This enhanced fermentation process will influence the aroma, tastes, and flavor of the cigar.

Let's take an in-depth look at how oak barrels find their way into a cigar factory. New oak barrels are made to age bourbon, wine, and sherry. Then after one or more uses, they are sold in a secondary market, primarily to the whiskey, scotch, cognac, port, rum, and tequila distillers. (See The Life Cycle of an Oak Barrel below.) After a long journey, they may find a new home in a cigar factory.

By the time a cigar factory acquires a used oak barrel, the oak staves in most cases have been saturated with bourbon, whiskey, or rum and in many cases all three. When the conditions are right, these barrels can impart exotic aromas and flavors—subtle to bold—in the tobacco leaf. After aging tobacco leaves in the oak barrels, a master blender with an exceptional palate creates a blend with just the right amount of barrel-aged tobaccos.

A word of caution: If a cigar is made with barrel-aged tobacco, it doesn't mean you will go bonkers over the cigar. Most of us have come to realize that all cigars are not enjoyed by all smokers to the same degree. They may not impress everyone in the same way. It depends on the cigar, your palate sensitivity, and your willingness to be open to a new sensorial experience. I know smokers who love these cigars and others who would gladly put them in their giveaway box.

If you decide to try one of these cigars, plan on spending a little extra money for a cigar that was made with barrel-aged tobaccos. The process is labor intensive and can take many months and even up to a year or more to achieve a desired result. The tobacco leaves have to be constantly rotated from the center to the outside, so each leaf spends equal time in close proximity with the charred oak staves.

For those of you who have already decided to smoke one of these cigars, remember to go into the experience with an open mind. If you find the taste notes over the top for your palate, try drinking a strong beverage, such as espresso, cappuccino, bourbon, cognac, port, or dark heavy stout beer that can stand up to the robust aroma and tastes of a cigar made with barrel-aged tobaccos. Take your time and take sips of water or your selected beverage while you explore what these cigars have to offer. If you still find it over the top, let it rest in the ashtray, light up another cigar, and come back to it later. Then alternate between cigars.

The Life Cycle of an Oak Barrel

Wine Barrels: New oak barrels are used from 1 to 3 times, then sold to the whiskey industry.

- Bourbon barrels: By law, for a spirit to be called bourbon, it must be aged in new oak barrels. Therefore, they are used only once and then typically sold to the whiskey industry.
- Whiskey: Whiskey barrels can be used as many times as the distiller chooses, but typically 4 times, and then sold to the rum, tequila, beer, tabasco sauce, or cigar industries.
- Rum: Barrels are typically purchased from the whiskey industry and used up to 7 times, then sold to the tequila, tabasco sauce, or cigar industries.
- Tequila: Barrels are typically purchased from the whiskey or rum industry and used up to 10 times, then sold to the tabasco sauce or furniture industries.
- Cigar Industry: Barrels are purchased from the bourbon, whiskey, and rum industries, and the number of uses is a well kept secret.
- Only two barrels can be made from a mature oak tree that takes several decades to grow.

Depending on what alcohol was aged in the barrel, the cigar manufacturer uses to age the tobaccos, you many find subtle to robust taste notes associated with the following references:

- Rum
- Dried fruit
- Vanilla
- Caramel
- Molasses
- Wood smoke
- Charred wood
- Roasted coconut
- Anise
- Licorice
- Allspice
- Bitter almond
- Black currents
- Menthol
- Ginger

Average Cost per New Barrel

- America white oak, $600 to $1,200 per barrel
- French white oak, $900 to $2,000 per barrel

Although the origins and use of the first oak barrel are cloudy, many historians would credit the Celts as the first to construct and use an oak barrel—dating from around 350 BC. For over 2,000 years, up to the 1900s, oak barrels were the most popular container in the world and the preeminent vessel for transporting small goods and liquids: Steel barrels and containers would eventually replace oak barrels.

Below are some of the many products that were transported locally and across oceans in oak barrels for centuries:

- Fruits and vegetables
- Clothes and shoes
- Whiskey
- Grains
- Porcelain and china
- Brandy

- Meat
- Building supplies
- Wine, sherry, port
- Oil
- Hardware
- Balsamic vinegar
- Honey
- Guns
- Beer
- Water
- Gun powder
- Tabasco sauce

Value versus Cost

> A well stocked humidor of great cigars always has room for something different. The connoisseur is always seeking a new, exotic, and elusive aroma and flavor.

Have you ever wondered why some spices such as saffron, cardamom, vanilla, and nutmeg all carry sticker prices that seem to defy logic? The least expensive of these herbs is nutmeg at $29.00 per pound, and the most expensive is saffron at $30.00 per ounce or $2,000.00 per pound. Does limited supply cause things to have appeal, or is it nature's way of not spoiling us? Another way to say this is that most prized and delicious luxuries typically come in small quantities. Nature is funny that way: The best tobaccos typically come from smaller regions and in limited quantities, which adds to their allure. The most expensive spices require intensive agricultural practices, are grown in a limited region, and are more susceptible to fungal diseases, bugs, and climatic conditions.

If they were common and found in abundance, would they lose their attractiveness? I have noticed that when I haven't eaten a given fruit such as a tangerine for a long time, the first one I eat tastes absolutely delicious, and if I continue to eat one or two every day, they become less and less spectacular. So I would argue that limited exposure to a given fruit, spice, or cigar will enhance its appeal, but with two caveats: First, you must first enjoy the taste of the given food, herb, spice, or cigar, and, second, it must be of superb quality.

Expensive cigars do not have a monopoly on good quality. There are many cigars that are easy on the wallet and are very enjoyable to smoke. On the other hand, there are some cigars that don't seem to live up to their sticker price. If you are a connoisseur, you have probably smoked your fair share of expensive cigars that left you wondering. The reason we are perplexed is that we intuitively use different criteria to judge different cigars. Simple cigars come with modest expectations and should be judged by those standards, whereas expensive cigars that make claims of higher quality should be judged accordingly.

Our expectations typically adjust to the cost of the experience or pleasure, such as paying $10 for a high school football game with free parking versus paying anywhere from $7,000 to $60,000 for NFL Superbowl game ticket and $300 for parking. Or buying a Johnny Walker Red Label drink for $15.00 versus an ounce of Louis XIII de Remy Martin Cognac for $250.00+.

If you compare a number of different cigars of the same type and at the same price points, it will not be difficult to judge which one is the best value. This type of comparison is simple because it has very few variables. We make these types of comparisons every day, whether it's purchasing one wine, scotch, or cigar brand over another. The same holds true when purchasing any commodity: a pair of shoes, a car, or a home. When cost is not a consideration, scarcity and fashion, rather than quality, often guide and determine the final decision. Some vintage, limited editions and specialty cigars are now sold at prices that seem out of proportion to the pleasure they give.

The Cigar's Finish

The cigar's finish is the lingering taste that resonates in your palate after you exhale the smoke. A mediocre cigar's finish is short and will fade almost immediately after you exhale, whereas a great cigar will offer a lingering finish that displays an array of flavor nuances and taste characteristics that seem to coat the palate with a lavish and delicious aftertaste. A great finish will hold your attention while it teases your palate. In the wine industry, the quality of a wine is often determined by its finish. A cigar smoker may find it enjoyable and rewarding to relish the cigar's finish, whether smoking for enjoyment or evaluating a cigar.

A Great Finish

Let's refer back to the peacock here as a reference: an intense, dynamic array of taste and flavor sensations that linger long after the smoke is exhaled. The finest cigars have the intensity and inner energy to hold your attention as their personality unfolds, offering a rich array of flavors and complex aromatic nuances.

Before we get into comparing the value of various cigars, let's compare the value of a cigar over other luxuries. Below is a chart that I developed that is based on the duration of pleasure versus the cost of that pleasure, which I call the Pleasure Value Rating (PVR)™.

PD ÷ C = PVR

PD = Pleasure Duration (number of minutes)

C = National Average Cost of the Pleasure

PVR = Pleasure Value Rating

The Psychology Behind the Art, Part I

Premium Cigar Value versus Other Indulgences			
INDULGENCE	C	PD	PVR
Standard/Common			
Coffee/espresso	$3.00	5 minutes	1.6
Mixed drink	$10.00	15 minutes	1.5
House wine	$10.00	15 minutes	1.5
Whiskey	$10.00	15 minutes	1.5
Cognac	$15.00	15 minutes	1.0
Premium Cigar	$8.00	80 minutes	10.00
Specialty/Name Brands			
Specialty coffee	$5.00	5 minutes	1.0
Mixed drink	$12.00	15 minutes	1.25
High-end wine	$15.00	15 minutes	1.0
Whiskey	$18.00	15 minutes	0.83
Cognac	$20.00	15 minutes	0.75
High-end Cigar	$20.00	80 minutes	4.0
Luxury/Exclusive/Rare/High-end			
Wine by the glass	$30.00	15 minutes	0.5
Whiskey by the snifter	$40.00	15 minutes	0.375
Cognac by the snifter	$125.00	15 minutes	0.12
Ultra-premium (Reserve, Vintage, Small Batch) Cigar	$50.00	80 minutes	1.60

As the chart demonstrates, nothing comes close to the value of a premium cigar. Let's summarize the results:

A Premium Cigar scored 10.0, or 670%, higher than its peers.

A High-end Cigar scored 4.0, or 400%, higher than its peers.

An Ultra-premium Cigar scored 1.6, or 500%, higher than its peers.

Talk about value for your money. If your partner complains about what he or she perceives is an expensive cigar hobby and is hooked on lattes, fancy cocktails, and wines, copy this chart and post it on the bathroom mirror, kitchen cabinet, and refrigerator.

What Affects Cigar Costs

There are many factors that determine the cost of a cigar, whether it is very expensive, expensive, modestly priced, or a bargain. Understanding the variables can lead to some great cigar deals. Would you rather spend a couple of hundred dollars to half fill your humidor with excellent cigars or that same dollar amount to fill it up? Let's explore some of the most common influences on the cost and see how they relate to taste.

Bargain Price

- The cigar is less expensive to produce.
- There is an oversupply.
- The manufacturer is making room for new releases.
- The manufacturer is introducing the consumer to a new brand or blend.
- The manufacturer or retailer is going out of business.

Full Retail

- The manufacturer used the finest, most expensive tobaccos.
- The manufacturer romanced the process with extended aging, extraordinary packaging, and an expensive marketing campaign.
- The manufacturer produced a limited edition which inevitably affects the supply and demand dynamics.

Spending more money on a cigar doesn't guarantee that you will enjoy it more than a cigar half the sticker price. And furthermore, it may bias or skew your expectation, which may lean too far to one side of the scale, causing a positive or negative result.

When you willingly spend two or three times what you would normally spend on a cigar, you want to enjoy it so much that you love the taste of the cigar before you light it up and take your first puff. However, when you are "forced" to spend twice as much of your discretionary income on a cigar due to peer pressure, you'll expect it to taste at least twice as good as a cigar half the price.

I grew up in a household with modest means, so many would consider me frugal by today's standards. When a dear friend returns from a cruise to the Caribbean Islands or a trip to Cuba and brings me a box of Cuban cigars, the first thing I ask is where they purchased the beautiful cigars. When they tell me *in the back room of a super mercado* or *from a taxi driver*, I thank them for thinking of me and buying such a generous gift. I also add, "Please don't buy me any more cigars because I'm trying to quit smoking. I'm continuing to drink, however, so if you ever feel inclined to buy me a gift, any single malt scotch will do just fine."

I immediately label these cigars as "giveaways" and put them in the freezer for three days before the tobacco weevil eggs hatch and the insects raid my humidor. The next thing I do is call a few good friends who love Cuban cigars and tell them about my problem: My humidor is overflowing, and I need to find a home for some Cubans that were gifted to me. Their first question is, "Do they have original bands with the new hologram imprint?" When I answer yes, they tell me they are on their way.

> Grandpa had five daughters and was trying to get the last two married off so he didn't have to work on Saturday. Feeding and clothing teenage girls was not only expensive but emotionally challenging. If a daughter had a date, the first question he would ask was, "Do you really like this guy, and does he have a job?" If the answer was yes, he would tell his daughter to invite the potential suitor for dinner. He was a great cook.
>
> One evening after a big Christmas party, I saw Grandpa rinsing out a few fancy wine bottles, and when I started to ask him why he was doing that, he put his index finger over his lips, which was one of the signals commonly used in our family. The meaning could be Quiet, Don't talk back, or, in this case, It's a secret—don't tell anyone. Several weeks later, one of his daughters invited her suitor over for dinner, and a fancy bottle of wine appeared on the table before he arrived. When everyone sat for dinner, the suitor asked Grandpa if he could pour some of the wine for himself and Grandpa. As he was pouring the wine, acting rather pretentious, he asked Grandpa where he had purchased such a fine vintage bottle of French wine. Grandpa replied that it was a gift. The young gentleman lifted his glass, made a toast to the chef, and took a sip of the wine, proclaiming, "This is real wine. This is what wine should taste like." Unknowingly, he was drinking the cheap jug wine that my grandpa poured into the expensive bottle before the dinner guest arrived. Later that evening in private, Grandpa told me that the suitor drank the label on the wine bottle, not the wine!

In my early smoking days, I would often succumb to the power of suggestion to the point of becoming physically ill. If someone gave me a cigar with a Cuban band, I would treat that cigar like was gold. I would put it gently in the humidor and check it every day, waiting for a special occasion to smoke it. With all that fanfare, how could I not love this cigar? Well, as most connoisseurs know, most Cuban cigars that find their way to the United States are fakes, meaning that they may contain 100% Cuban tobacco, but were not made in a Cuban cigar factory. The majority of the fakes do not draw well, causing the smoker to draw on the cigar like a vacuum cleaner to keep it lit and get an adequate volume of smoke out of the cigar. This excessive drawing may quickly lead to the dreaded smoker's nausea.

Many Cuban fakes are cigars made outside of Cuba and are dressed up with an original or counterfeit cigar band. If the cigar was purchased in Cuba, then it was made with Cuban tobacco that is inherently rich, so when a cigar maker gets his hands on a bunch of ligero or viso leaves, he makes a cigar in his home with what he has to work with in hopes of selling it on the street to make a week's worth of income with just one cigar, and the poor soul who paid $20.00 for a cigar with a blend consisting primarily of strong tobacco leaf will probably turn green trying to get his money's worth out of the cigar. Don't feel bad if this has happened to you: Most of us have fallen victim to this at one point in our cigar journey.

It has never been more challenging to shop for cigars than in the last two decades due to the overwhelming number of brands, blends, limited editions, reserva, small batches, and so on. The options in a large retail store's humidor or catalog can confuse and sometimes paralyze even a savvy cigar smoker. When I enter a humidor with over 800 cigar options, I can become so overwhelmed that I have to sit in the corner facing the wall and instruct the salesman to pick out his favorite cigar, cut it with my guillotine cutter, light it with three matches, and bring it to me. As I sit in the corner puffing away my paralysis, I take out my notepad and study my taste notes from previous purchases.

The moral of this story is to make a list and remember to take it with you. Refer to it as you peruse the humidor. Here are some suggestions when preparing your Buy List:

- Determine your budget limit.
- Determine the form of payment: cash or credit card.
- If it is credit card, get preapproval from your partner.
- If, by some stroke of luck, you find some extra, unaccounted for cash in your wallet, plan on spending all of it before your partner finds out.
- Have a Game Plan or a specific Buy List.
- Study Puros: cigars made with tobaccos from one country.
- Study one type of wrapper leaf: U.S. Conn. or Ecuador Conn.; Ecuador Habano or Nicaraguan Habano; Mexican San Andres Maduro or U.S. Broadleaf.
- Study the same blend in different cigar sizes (ring gauges).
- Study the same blends with different types of wrapper.
- Do a vertical study: the same brand of different vintages, 2010, 2012, etc.
- Do a horizontal study: different brands from the same region.
- Try a Wild Card (cigars on the discount table): Select a few blends or brands you haven't smoked.
- Leave room on your Buy List to make notes for future purchase options.
- If possible, shop when the store isn't busy: during the week or early in the day, on the weekends.

Once you have a plan of action, the trip through a large humidor will be an enlightening and enjoyable experience.

Luxury products are typically those things that the wealthy indulge in often and the rest of us rarely or never get a chance to experience, except maybe on a special occasion. Some premium cigars, fine wines, scotches, bourbons, and cognacs have earned a reputation as luxury products, but you don't have to break the bank to smoke or drink well. Even cigar insiders and connoisseurs don't smoke the luxury and collectable cigars every day. Two things make a luxury product special: First, it must be of the highest quality, and second, it must be enjoyed from time to time and not overindulged in.

Try different price points and make notes of your impressions when you smoke the cigar. Study reviews and ratings, and find reviewers whose palates resonate with yours.

Seek advice. If a shop owner or sales rep spends eight hours a day around cigars and cigar smokers, chances are he will learn something about cigars by talking with his customers. Tell him what you are looking for in in terms of styles and intensity with a few examples of cigars you enjoyed in the past and ones you didn't and, most important, your budget. If you are honest, a good salesman can be an excellent resource. If you purchase cigars through online catalogs, you will find that many of the sales reps are very knowledgeable and willing to guide you in the right direction: Happy customers make repeat customers.

When you talk to a sales rep, don't feel like you have to tell him how much you think you know; if he is experienced, he will know right away by your comments that you are not a seasoned smoker. One of the biggest mistakes I hear from non-seasoned cigar smokers is their desire to sound like a connoisseur by dropping big names when the sales rep asked them what they usually enjoy smoking: "Well, last night I smoked a couple of Padron 1926s, and just the other day, I smoked a few Opus X new releases while I was shooting par at a PGA course." Unless you have a pocket full of money or a large positive balance on your credit card, you will find it a lot cheaper to tell the truth and get the best value with the budget you are working with.

If you have a cigar shopping list and share it with a sales rep, he will respect you for being forthright, and he will gladly assist you in accomplishing your mission. Years ago, I showed my shopping list I titled "Cigar Mission" to a veteran sales rep, and he was so impressed that he threw in a few extra cigars and a lighter and invited me to join him in smoking two of his private stock cigars while he shared cigar stories that spanned several decades. I learned more in that cold winter afternoon about the cigar industry than I had previously known up to that point in my cigar journey.

Here is the bottom line:
- Be honest.
- Be receptive and continue to learn.
- Strive to be in charge of your palate.

Remember that your perception of what you experience is what makes it special.

Thinking in Thirds

The following concept that I am going to share with you is something I became consciously aware of the in the mid-1990s at the onset of the cigar boom. As I mentioned before, in the beginning of the cigar boom, a cigar was typically described as a *light*, *medium*, or *full bodied cigar* (an objective opinion) and as a *bad*, *good*, or *great cigar* (a subjective opinion). I have come to realize that most of us perceive things in simple terms. Fewer complications help us cope in our complex, technological world. The movie was bad, good, or great. We dined in a bad, good, or great restaurant. In other words, *I don't care for it; I like it; I like it a lot*. You get my point.

However, when a person is knowledgeable in a given subject, they will often expand their observations to fifths (or five levels):

Let's see how the chart would look when describing a cigar strength or intensity in thirds and fifths.

THIRDS		
1	2	3
Very light	Average	Very strong

FIFTHS				
1	2	3	4	5
Very light	Light	Medium	Strong	Very strong

Taking it a step further, an expert in a given field or a very smart person will have a description scale that uses sevenths or even ninths:

SEVENTHS						
1	2	3	4	5	6	7
Super light	Very light	Light	Medium	Medium strong	Very strong	Super strong

NINTHS								
1	2	3	4	5	6	7	8	9
Super light	Very light	Light	Medium light	Medium	Medium strong	Strong	Very strong	Super strong

How does all this apply to cigars? When you sense a stimulation, think of its intensity using one of the charts above, and remember that if you use the Thirds chart, you will sound like a newbie, and if you use the Seventh or Ninths chart, you will sound like a connoisseur.

Get ready to start applying your newfound knowledge in further developing and improving your cigar palate!

Palate Development Exercises

Exercise 1: Adaptation/Palate Fatigue

What you will need:
- One lit cigar
- Watch, clock, stopwatch or smart phone
- Note pad and pen

1st Interval: Take two short puffs followed by one normal puff every minute, for 3 cycles totaling 3 minutes.

2nd Interval: Then take two short puffs followed by one normal puff every 40 seconds, for 3 cycles totaling 2 minutes.

3rd Interval: Then take two short puffs followed by one normal puff every 20 seconds, for 3 cycles totaling 1 minutes.

At what interval did you experience the most flavor?
- ○ 1st
- ○ 2nd
- ○ 3rd

At what interval did you experience palate fatigue?
- ○ 1st
- ○ 2nd
- ○ 3rd

What interval best suits your palate?
- ○ 1st
- ○ 2nd
- ○ 3rd

Take a break, then repeat the exercise and see if your experience changes.

Exercise 2: Palate Fine Tuning

Next time you conduct a pre-light test of the wrapper aroma, use your left nostril first, then your right nostril.

> Did you notice different aromas in the left nostril versus the right nostril?
> no/very slight/slightly/somewhat/a little/a lot/a lot more

> Was the aroma's intensity in the left nostril more than the right nostril?
> no/very slight/slightly/somewhat/a little/a lot/a lot more

Exercise 3: A Hidden Aroma Delight

Next time you are in the final third of a cigar, gently remove the cigar band and smell the underside of the band. The smell of a cigar band from a high-quality cigar will offer an exquisite and delicious aroma.

Excerpt from an Interview with Eric Newman

President J.C. Newman Cigar Company

YBOR CITY, TAMPA, FLORIDA, SEPTEMBER 2020

Nick: Early today we used the ProPalate® Kit to calibrate your palate, test your DNA for taste sensitivity, and evaluate one of your well-known cigars, the Julius Ceasar Diamond Crown. What would you like to share with our readers regarding the ProPalate® System?

Eric: I've been in this industry 48 years and I am still learning about cigars. Like I mentioned earlier, I know what I like and what I don't like, but I never knew why I liked or disliked a cigar. The ProPalate® Kit helps you stay focused and prepares you to start asking yourself what you are sincerely enjoying about a cigar: What tastes, what flavors, what nuances—they all contribute to your enjoyment of a cigar.

When I enjoyed a cigar, I didn't know exactly why—now I do. So I thank you for opening my mind and help me discover my palate. This is a learned behavior and you have to practice if you want to master it. I am looking forward to smoking more cigars while remembering my experience here with you today and also to applying this knowledge to crafting new blends that other cigar smokers will like and enjoy smoking. So thank you for sharing your new training system with me today.

Excerpt from an Interview with Manolo Quesada

An Inductee in the Exclusive Cigar Aficionado's Hall of Fame Class of 2012

Quesada Cigar Factory, Medio Licey, Dominican Republic, November 2019

Manolo: I have to ask; Whose idea was it to have a game on the other side of Calibration Board?

Nick: I must confess, I'm guilty of coming up with the idea of a *Tobacco Belt Game*. The inspiration came from my desire to memorize the different tobacco-growing regions, and what better way to learn something than when you are playing a game and having a good time.

Manolo: Cigar smokers today are a lot more informed and a lot more interested in finding things out, and the game is a great way for them to do so: Five cigar smokers playing this game, they're going to have a ball—I am awed by what you've come up with!

Nick: After reviewing the ProPalate® Kit and calibrating your palate using this method, do you have any final thoughts that you would you like to share with our readers about your experience with the ProPalate® Training System?

Manolo: First and foremost, it's fun, it's amazing, because there are 20 aroma references, different possible stimuli that you can find from going through the board, and these are all things that we experience in life at one time or another. We have all smelled black pepper, we have tasted salt, you have smelled a barn, you have smelled and eaten cinnamon rolls.

All of these are things that you have experienced in different situations. When smoking a cigar, you may not find all 20 aromas references, but it will definitely bring a host of the ones that are on the board, and this is where it's enjoyable, because first, these are things that you like and you're amenable to, and second, to have the power to say, "I can feel, I can detect, I can perceive this particular sensation.

Also, the kit functions as a tool that could enhance your experience when you taste things by having little points of references and combinations thereof. This will enhance and multiply the experience that you're having with whatever sensorial product you enjoy. So, I tip my hat to you, Mr. Cutro: It took a lot of courage and a lot of knowledge and a lot of experience and experimentation to come to what you have created, and it really is a magnificent way of going about enhancing and bettering your taste experiences. Congratulations!

Chapter 5

The Psychology Behind the Art, Part 2

*A true master is someone adept in a discipline,
realizing what they know is always less than there is to know.
They start out as a student of their discipline and forever remain a student.*
——Nick Cutro

> Every meal or snack provides an opportunity to establish a reference, or to calibrate, your palate. Once we identify sought after cigar aromas and flavors, we should identify a healthy diet with as many of them as possible. In other words, a cigar aficionado may resolve to regularly dine on select foods and beverages as they seek to refine and keep their palate razor sharp.

You may think that broadening your food footprint sounds interesting, but you might also be concerned that it will broaden your waistline. On the contrary: New and improved habits come with surprising side effects, like better health and pounds shed. Consuming natural, nutrient-dense foods will make you feel more satisfied after a meal and less apt to overeat and indulge in sweet desserts. When you consume foods full of empty calories and lacking nutrients, your body's autonomic nervous system responds by making you feel hunger in hopes that you might consume something containing the nutrients it is lacking. Unfortunately, it doesn't tell you what to eat, and often we continue to consume foods or snacks full of empty calories, lacking the nutrients we need.

I find it ironic that the United States, a country that spends at least twice as much money on healthcare as all the other developed countries combined, has an alarming number of people in poor health. Americans also spend half as much of their disposable income on food, which might explain the problem: inexpensive, tasty foods full of empty calories, additives, and preservatives. It is no longer a secret that many Americans have developed weak immune systems, creating a host of health issues that their ancestors rarely experienced. Another way to explain this phenomenon might be to say many Americans are undernourished on a full stomach.

> I want to remind you of important points from Chapter 4 regarding associations that share similar or secondary characteristics. "Many substances share common aroma characteristics, such as herbaceous, which has dried grassy herbal notes along with notes of earthiness. Dried fruit, dark chocolate, coffee, and vanilla also have an earthy and sour or acidic note along with their individual aroma characteristics.

Ortho Hale and Retro Hale

Ortho Hale

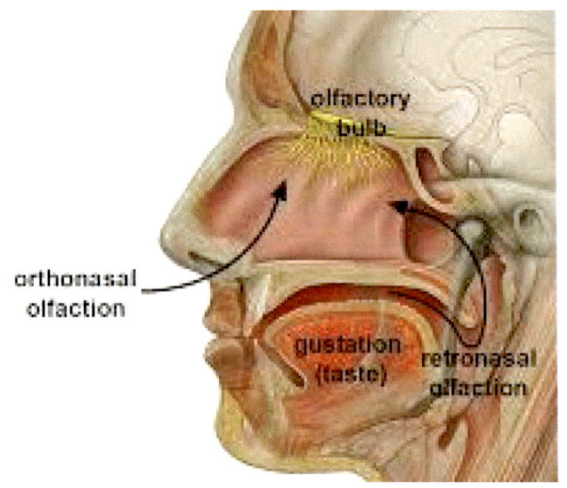

The aromas that can be felt in an extraordinary cigar in the ortho hale are often the most seductive, complex, and intoxicating aromas you will ever experience.

When smelling the smoke wafting off the foot of a cigar, you are bypassing the influence of mouth taste (sweet, sour, salty, bitter, and savory) and, in essence, experiencing pure aroma.

Many times, these aromas are hard to describe, short of saying, "It smells delicious!" Cardamom is one spice that I feel captures this exquisite aroma. Most cigar smokers are not familiar with cardamom, so it's not possible for them to make this taste association in either the orthro or the retro hale, so in this case, the best description just might be *delicious*.

Before we address what to eat, first let's brush up on taste associations not to eat. That means ortho hale (smell only). Here are examples:

Fresh hay	Woody	Barnyard
Lavender	Charred wood	Leather
Cedar	Wood smoke	Pencil lead
Musty	Earthy	Road tar

No doubt, with a quick glance at the aforementioned list, you managed to figure out the *Do not ingest* advice. I beg the indulgence of smart readers, but one cannot be too careful these days.

In order to develop accurate taste associations, you first need a *reference*. After that, you should *calibrate* your palate until you can identify taste associations quickly and accurately. Only then will you know that you are in charge of your palate.

Retro Hale

Now let's discuss retro hale, the aroma associations for flavor.

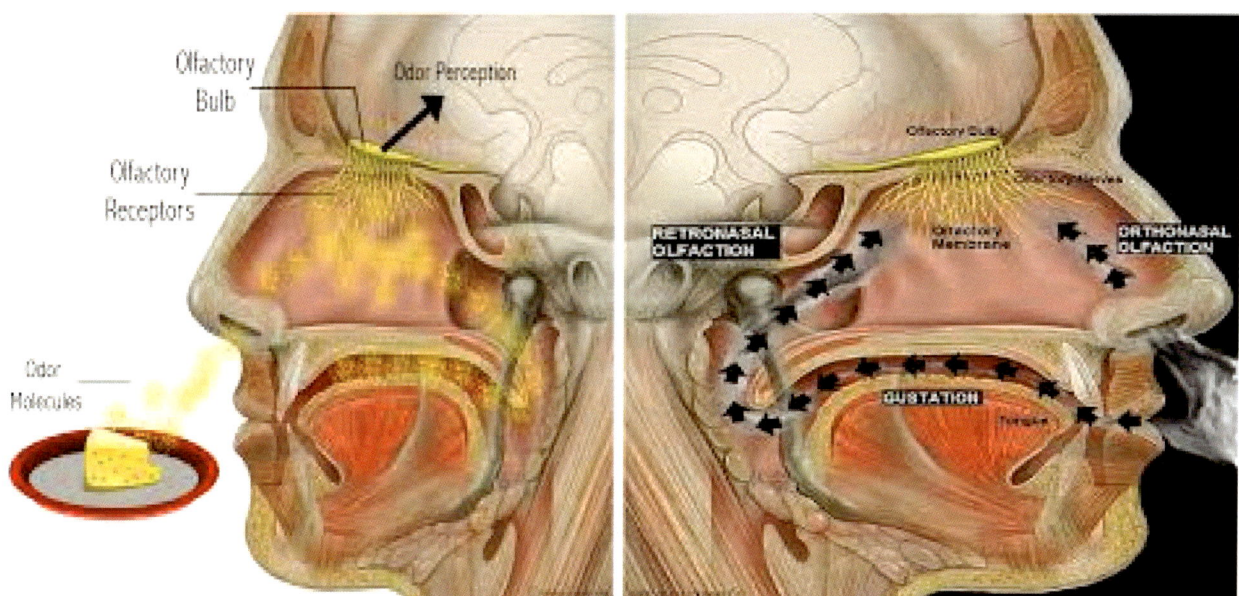

Main Categories	Most Common	Not as Common
Floral	Lavender	Hibiscus, rose, violet, honey suckle
Citrus	Dried lemon peel	Dried orange peel
Herbaceous	Fresh hay, dried dill, dried nettle	Chamomile
Dried Fruit	Fig, plum, raisin, cherry, black current, apricot	Mango, blueberry, raspberry
Aromatic	Black/white/red pepper, Paprika, cedar, nutmeg, anise, cinnamon, bitter almond	Allspice, cardamom, sassafras, menthol, eucalyptus
Earthy	Barnyard, musty, leather, bread yeast, shiitake mushroom, malted barley	Aged cheese
Roasted/Smokey	Roasted almonds, hazel, pistachio and cashew nuts, Smoked wood	N/A
Complex	Dark chocolate, coffee, vanilla, caramel, graham cracker, licorice, molasses	N/A

If you are serious about developing your palate, you may want to consider making an aroma kit or investing in the ProPalate® Training System, where years of research and testing have been done for you. All bias aside, ProPalate® far outperforms aroma kits comprised of synthetic chemicals mixed with mineral oil.

I first created the system to improve my own palate and was surprised at how quickly my palate developed. My cigar buddies wanted to borrow the kit, but I wasn't letting it out of my sight, so I put together a handful of kits for my closest cigar comrades. When word got out, I was overwhelmed with requests for training kits.

A cigar connoisseur who is able to detect, identify, and describe various levels of taste nuances is like a painter who has mastered the art of seeing—and using—color. When a lay person or untrained artist sees one of the three primary colors—red, yellow, or blue—or one of the secondary colors—orange, green, or violet—they will describe that color in simple terms such as, "I see red/green/violet." However, a trained or gifted artist will see a more precise hue, such as venetian red or cobalt blue.

Taking Control of Your Palate

The concept I am going to share with you is how to use a visual approach or method to accurately identify and describe a cigar's taste associations and flavor profile. Even if your primary frame of reference is auditory or kinesthetic, this method may resonate with you, especially if you have an artistic bent.

You can think of this concept as a new or different way of looking at taste and flavor and of expressing the stimulation you experience while smoking. Once you are in charge of your palate, you will be able to expand your taste vocabulary to make a more accurate taste association which will enhance every cigar you smoke and everything you eat and drink. Aroma and taste will come alive, expanding the possibilities. If you don't get this concept on the first read, don't worry: You won't be alone. It took me 20 minutes to write the story and 45 years to know what to write.

> This story is about my dabbling in fine art. It will set the tone and help put you in the right mindset for learning a different way to perceive aroma, taste, and flavor. If you grasp this concept, your sensorial world may expand exponentially.
>
> I consider myself a Jack of All Disciplines and a master of none. After the cigar boom flattened out, I had a lot of free time on my hands and I decided to try painting. No, not painting houses—painting the sort of fine art that hangs in museums. Thirty minutes from my home, world-class painter Christopher Still offered a drawing and painting workshop on Wednesday evenings for young, aspiring artists and artist wannabes.
>
> I clearly was in the latter category, but surrounded by students in the first, many half my age, who planned to earn university degrees in fine arts and graphic design. Teaching in a local art center on Wednesday nights was Still's way of giving back and sharing what other master teachers had taught him on his journey to become a great artist. True artists, like true cigar tobacco farmers and blenders, for example, are driven by their passion, not money or fame.
>
> The style of painting Mr. Still taught is best described as creating a 3D image on a 2D surface using layers of translucent color. His teacher lineage could be traced back to the Renaissance. The rule was that before you were allowed to dip your paint brush in paint and touch a canvas, you were required to take his drawing classes: And you had to draw and draw and draw. Many

of the students in the drawing class had been there for years, never able to advance to the elite painting class.

One day I showed up early and caught Still during a quiet moment and asked him how long he thought it would take before I could start painting. "Based on your most recent drawings, probably never, but you'll enjoy the drawing class nonetheless and learn to see like an artist." All my drawings of the human figure looked like something Modigliani would have drawn or painted: elongated necks and distorted faces. The only difference between Modigliani and me was that I was trying to draw the figure in correct proportion, hoping to one day advance to the painting class.

A year after beginning the drawing class, I was invited to join the painting class. I felt like a child the week before Christmas, brimming with anticipation. I arrived early on the first day, bringing three canvasses and two boxes of paint, with 18 tubes of different colors in each box. When class began, Still told everyone to squeeze out a little paint from the tubes of the three primary colors—red, yellow, and blue—and white. Most of the time we painted live models, which I really enjoyed, especially when he was able to find a female model willing to pose in front of twenty painters in her birthday suit for three hours.

As we painted, Still walked around the room and looked at each painting, asking questions regarding what the student saw in the model, the foreground, and background. I was the last painter he addressed in the first hour before the break. He looked at my painting, then the model, and again at my painting and asked me, "What is the dominant color scheme of the model, the foreground, and the background?" This seemed like an easy question, so I quickly responded, "The model is white, the foreground is blue, and the background is black."

He looked at my painting and the model again and told me to pack up my paints, go sit in the corner, and pay full attention for the rest of the class. I felt as if someone had just punched me in the gut, knocking the air of excitement out of me. Later I learned from other students that they, too, were initiated into the class in the same manner. It was Still's way of putting you in the right mindset and letting you know that to paint well would require your full, undivided attention and the ability to think outside the box.

Here is the way I used the lesson "how to see like an artist" in the painting class to help me "taste like a connoisseur." I started to think about taste and aromas in an abstract way, using colors as visual clues to identify the stimulations I was experiencing when smoking. I started by using primary colors as cues to identify broad taste references. The first step is to gain a working command of the broad categories, then zero in on specific notes, then step back and look, listen, or feel for the overall quality of the stimuli.

Paint (Broad Categories)	Cigar Association (Broad Categories)
Yellow	Sweet, sour, and bitter, floral, citrus, herbaceous
Red	Aromatic, smoky, roasted
Blue	Complex
Individual	Individual
Paint (Specific Colors)	**Cigar Association (Specific Tastes)**
Crimson red	Cedar, black pepper, paprika, cinnamon, aniseed, nutmeg
Ultramarine blue	Barnyard, smoked wood, roasted nuts, leather chocolate, coffee, vanilla, caramel, dried mushroom
Color Intensity	**Cigar Intensity**
Very low, low, somewhat low, medium low, medium, medium-plus, very, extreme	Light bodied, medium bodied, medium bodied plus, full bodied, too strong
Overall Impression of the Picture	**Overall Impression of the Cigar**
Basic primary color scheme Impressionistic Abstract Kaleidoscope of colors	Simple, singular Interesting mix of flavors Different or unusual taste notes Over the top, not rounded or balanced

It's important to keep in mind that many associations can have a dominant taste note accompanied by secondary, subtle, or underlying taste notes as mentioned above.

Herbaceous, dried fruit, cinnamon, all dried peppers and nutmeg, and most of the earthy, roasted, and complex references in the list below have an earthy quality underneath their dominant taste note.

Below is a chart with some of the most common taste associations found in cigars. Check off all of the taste associations that you have identified or sensed when smoking a cigar, and circle the ones that you have not, but would like to experience from your favorite cigars. The categories are arranged in the same order as in the Evaluation Log in Chapter 3.

Floral Citrus	Herbaceous Dried Fruit	Aromatic	Earthy Roasted	Complex
Yes | Floral lavender	Yes | Black pepper		Yes | Barnyard	Yes | Dark chocolate
Yes | Fresh hay	Yes | Cedar		Yes | Musty	Yes | Coffee/dark roast
Yes | herbaceous	Yes | Anise		Yes | Leather	Yes | Vanilla
Yes | Dried lemon peel	Yes | Cinnamon		Yes | Roasted nuts	Yes | Caramel/toffee
Yes | Dried fruit/fig	Yes | Nutmeg		Yes | Charred wood	Yes | Graham cracker

The sky's the limit in a creative dietary regime for a sophisticated cigar palate. In the following, you'll find a few ideas to help you integrate both goals. I have included one taste association from each of the main categories. I and my loyal subjects have tested these "recipes" over the years, but I urge you to draw from your own well of ingenuity. Yours may be deeper than ours.

Taste Associations

Citrus: Lemon

On a hot day, nothing refreshes like fresh squeezed lemonade made with only tart juice and raw sugar. Also, use lemons as a gourmet garnish for both food and drink. Whether dining out or at home, squeeze some lemon on your food to enhance the flavor, the way a chef does.

You also can add dried lemon peel to your herb collection and sprinkle it over chicken, beef, pork, or fish before you bake or grill.

Dried Fruit: Fig

You should become intimately familiar with this association. When I showed the ProPalate® Kit to tobacco icon Pepin Garcia and asked him to smell the aroma jar with the dried fruit sample, he couldn't help but feel nostalgic. "Every cigar blender," he mused, "dreams of having this aroma in his cigars." He went on to tell the story of how, as a young boy in Cuba, he and his friends would chase the oxcart, full of figs, on its way to market with high hopes of picking up a few that fell on the ground.

Several dried fruits share very similar aroma notes with fig, such as dried plums, raisins, dark sweet cherry, black currants, and apricots. Simply buy a bag of each organic fruit labeled "unsulfured" and "no preservatives" for an easy way to establish an accurate reference and calibrate to these appealing tastes and aromas.

Herbaceous: Dried Dill or Dried Nettle

These two herbs both have similar aroma characteristics, with notes of herbaceous and earthiness. They are unlike several popular herbs used in Italian and Mediterranean cooking, such as oregano, basil, rosemary, and tarragon, that do not serve as good descriptors due to their overwhelming aroma characteristics. Both herbs pair well with seafood and chicken and can also be used to flavor sauces.

Herbaceous: Chamomile

Of all the herbs I've tested, the warm, sweet, floral aroma of chamomile with hints of apple represents an element found in mild intensity and medium intensity cigars with light wrappers, a very popular style in the 1990s. Several Dominican manufacturers still specialize in cigars with this delicate yet complex flavor.

You can store chamomile teabags in a spice jar and drink healthy, caffeine-free tea anytime. This is an excellent alternative for the person who consumes too much coffee and nicotine. Try it as a soothing after-dinner drink to aid digestion and relaxation. If you are an S or US DNA type, try adding a little raw sugar (1-2 teaspoons per 8-10 ounces of liquid). This will bring out the natural chamomile flavor by offsetting the slight bitterness found in teas.

Aromatic: Cinnamon and Nutmeg

If you are bored with your daily routine of eating a bowl of oatmeal, quinoa, or yogurt, here are two quick and easy ways to spice up your breakfast and calibrate your palate. Add a pinch of cinnamon or nutmeg while you are cooking your oatmeal or just before serving. Notice I said one or the other, not both at the same time! You can also add a pinch of either spice over your toast or cottage cheese.

Cinnamon has a warm, woody, sweet aroma, while nutmeg is an intense spice with a strong nutty, sweet, resinous aroma. You don't have to limit your use of these two spices to only breakfast: They both pair well with baked winter squash or a steamed veggie medley. Cinnamon and nutmeg are great spices, but they are very powerful, so use them with care—a little goes a long way. You will also find these spices in custards and dessert sauces along with holiday cookies and cakes, so if you are going to splurge before your New Year's Resolution diet starts, you might as well get the benefit of calibrating your palate to these commonly found, aroma-taste associations. If you are one of the fortunate ones who has someone prepare your meals, ask them to test your palate by alternating between cinnamon and nutmeg and occasionally a combination of both spices and see if you can identify the spice or spice combination.

Earthy: Dried Shitake Mushrooms

Ortho hale, or smell only, applies to most aromas in this family, but dried shitake mushrooms are the exception. Not too many veggies can ramp up the flavor dial in a soup or over a grilled steak like dried shitake mushrooms. These mushrooms have both a strong aroma and a strong taste. When smelling the dried mushrooms, you will notice an earthy, barnyard aroma and strong note of bread yeast or malted barley. When I trial tested this rich association, I found that most testers had trouble distinguishing the difference between the dried mushrooms and bread yeast. When eating dried mushrooms after they are cooked, you will notice a rich, savory mouth taste. Add them to your herb and spice cabinet so you have them ready the next time you are making a soup or grilling a steak.

As a side note, many well-aged dark wrappers from the Dominican, Ecuador, Honduras, Mexico, and U.S. (Broadleaf) display this earthy aroma.

Complex: Dark Chocolate

In Chapter 4, we discussed how dark chocolate is made and why it is so complex. Let's examine it in more detail since it is one of the most misunderstood associations.

First, let's first identify the various forms of chocolate. The FDA does not have a standard to identify dark chocolate other than "a food which bears no artificial chocolate flavor or natural flavor derived from a source other than cacao bean." Dark chocolate typically contains at least 60% cocoa with no added milk solids, while unsweetened chocolate is made with 100% cocoa bean with nothing else added. It is used primarily for baking and is generally considered too bitter, harsh, and chalky tasting for eating. Bittersweet chocolate comes in a broad range of 35% to 70% unsweetened cacao and is used for baking.

All of these chocolates have an inherent bitterness, but as sugar is added, reducing the percentage of cacao, the bitterness fades into the background. I find that, for most people, 70% dark chocolate best represents the broadest aroma and taste characteristics that can be easily detected.

But not all 70% chocolate is the same. Each manufacturer has what they refer to as their secret recipe that they usually boast about on the labeling. If you are the inquisitive type and want to know their secret recipe, that's simple: Just read the ingredients on the back of the wrapper.

It still gets a little tricky, since most of us have been eating chocolate with the addition of imitation or natural vanilla flavoring. Recall that vanilla is one of the most widely used flavor enhancements, including in so-called secret chocolate recipes. Now there is nothing wrong per se with using vanilla extract to enhance flavor, especially if it is made with natural instead of imitation vanilla. But it is not the best chocolate to use if you are trying to calibrate your palate to the true or pure taste of dark chocolate.

Dark chocolate has a broad range of flavors. In the mouth taste, you will find a touch of bitterness, a little more acidity or sourness, along with sweetness and creaminess. In the nose, you will experience a broad range of taste notes depending on where the cacao was grown and how it was processed. Some of these taste notes may include sweet, sour, bitter, and savory; dried fruit (fig, plum, dark red cherry, apricot, black currents); aromatic (aniseed, cinnamon, nutmeg, allspice, cardamom); dried nuts (almonds, cashews, hazelnuts); earthy; coffee; and molasses.

I've yet to meet a cigar smoker, or anyone for that matter, who didn't enjoy chocolate. Most stores carry an assortment of chocolates, so treat yourself to a healthy snack while calibrating your palate. Try chocolates from different regions and percentages such as 60%, 70%, 80%, and 90%, but you might want to stay away from the ones that infuse the chocolate with mint, raspberry, coffee, and other flavors if you are calibrating your palate. You can also use the pinched nose technique discussed in Chapter 2 to intensify the aroma you will experience with a virgin palate (your first bite).

Next Steps in Calibrating Your Palate

Now that you have an extensive list of cigar taste and aroma references, continue to integrate them into your palate calibration routine. Sensing aromas and tastes requires concentration. If your mind is preoccupied, you will have a hard time identifying the taste or aroma. While you eat, do so mindfully. In order to launch into this attentive mindset, you can ask yourself questions:

- What aromas do I smell? (Potentially hundreds)
- What is the mouth taste I am experiencing in this food? (Sweet, sour, salty, bitter, or savory)
- What is the mouth texture? (Spongy, soft, chewy, crunchy, creamy, astringent, or burning cayenne pepper)

- What is the temperature of the food or drink? (extremely hot, hot, warm, lukewarm, room temperature, cool, cold, very cold, or freezing cold)
- What is the dominant flavor note?
- What are the secondary and subtle flavor notes?
- What herbs and spices do I detect?
- What would I do differently if I prepared this dish or asked someone to prepare it for me? (Less garlic, less cayenne pepper, more olive oil, less or more cumin, etc.)

Aspiring musicians constantly listen to recordings of style masters to expand their personal melodic and harmonic repertoire. Aspiring writers read countless famous books to enhance personal command of the language. And a cigar connoisseur constantly explores new frontiers of aroma and flavor beyond light, medium, medium-plus, and full bodied cigars or smoking cigars with only light, natural, or dark wrappers.

Be adventurous with sampling food and beverages when you dine out, especially if someone else is picking up the tab! If you normally drink a Jack and Coke, order a single malt scotch, neat. Don't focus exclusively on the right column of the menu, as I was taught as a youth. Stay focused on the left side while searching for interesting, gourmet options. No fried anything, no matter how appetizing the fried calamari or fried green tomatoes seem at the moment. Don't even think about humdrum french fries, no matter how tempting. Instead, go for something exotic: Baked brie topped with wild raspberries and truffle sauce.

When dining out with an adventurous mindset, you may encounter a few obstacles. The first may happen when it is your turn to tell the waiter what you would like to order. If I'm not sure how to pronounce the name of a dish, I simply tell the waiter, "I'll have #8." In a swanky place, I might comment about the dim lighting or the animated guests, while I angle the menu toward the waiter and point at the desired entrée. She usually pronounces the foreign name, to which I respond, "Yes, I'd like to try that tonight." Don't be afraid to allow waiters to earn a generous tip. Encourage them to tell you about the different dishes—how they are prepared, what flavors to expect. I have found that waiters delight in sharing the info they had to commit to memory. When I take a suggestion from a top-notch waiter on a novel item, I enjoy a welcomed surprise—and my ambitious palate thanks me.

Excerpt from an Interview with Joselito Dominguez

TABACALERA VICTOR SINCLAIR IN GURABO, DOMINICAN REPUBLIC, NOVEMBER 2019

Nick: What tips or techniques can you offer a cigar smoker to help them improve their palate.

Joselito: First of all, start to look for the taste characteristics that they would like to sense in a cigar; they really exist. I didn't know they existed until you showed me with your ProPalate® Kit. To me a cigar was either bad, good, very good or extraordinary—nothing more than that. I could not describe a cigar as nutty, chocolatey, fruity, or having hints of leather until I started learning how to find those characteristics and identify them using the ProPalate® Kit.

Nick: What advice would you give a cigar smoker who wants to get the most enjoyment out of his cigar?

Joselito: I would suggest for them to start to look for and learn how to find the taste associations you promote in your ProPalate® Kit. Not only will new smokers really get a kick out of your kit, but seasoned cigar smokers will find that they will enjoy their cigars even more.

Nick: Do you have any closing thoughts before we end the interview?

Joselito: Yes, I would like to share with your viewers that your training method has been quite an eye-opening experience for me. There haven't been a lot of new things in the cigar industry in the last decade, except for creativity in packaging. To me, the ProPalate® is the newest thing in the industry that can really teach you something about cigars. The ProPalate® gives you an idea of how to smoke and think about the cigar in a different way.

It shows you how to smoke differently and pay attention to a cigar: not to just smoke it mechanically. The majority of cigar smokers smoke mechanically. I feel strongly that the ProPalate® is beneficial to the whole industry. Nick, I must say that you are definitely an innovator in developing such a practical and useful method to help cigar smokers develop their palate.

Cigar Ritual: Getting in the Zone

Let's talk about the cigar ritual. If you don't have one, it's time to develop one. Are you a sports fan? I bet you have a ritual in that domain. No doubt, you and your friends arrive at the stadium early for a tailgate party or to scout out refreshments while the teams warm up, performing their rituals. This all transpires long before the kickoff or the first pitch. Did Babe Ruth or Hank Arron really have to step into the batter's box, tap his bat three times on the plate, point the tip of his bat at center field, then cock the bat while rocking back and forth several times before he stood still, signaling to the pitcher that he was ready for the pitch? If baseball rules didn't allow for such theatrics, would they still have broken home run records? I am sure they would have found a ritual that got them in the "zone" prior to stepping into the batter's box.

The same holds true with your cigar routine: A ritual will put you in the right mindset, in the *zone* to get the most out of your smoking experience. If the environment permits, light your cigar with wooden matches rather than cedar spills. Spills make a mess, and the first third of your cigar will taste like cedar. Most cigars can be properly lit with three long cigar matches.

Instead of taking a puff when you think the cigar is fully lit, gently blow air through the cigar. This will reveal the burning stage and exhaust the excess carbon buildup. Your first draw with a virgin palate on a fully lit cigar may be felt throughout your body, like a shot of espresso or a good whiskey.

Lighting your cigar with a match invites you into the zone and prepares you for a relaxing and pleasurable smoking experience. Torching the end of a cigar with a 5-flame lighter, while you draw on it like a vacuum cleaner, is a good way to blow out your palate before you begin. Smoking too fast can happen to experienced smokers in many common circumstances: after refraining from smoking due to a bout with the flu, a hefty delay in an airport, cross-country travel to a big smoke event, a factory tour in Nicaragua, or the IPCPR (the International Premium Cigar & Pipe Retailer show—a yearly international convention for manufacturers and retailers, not the general consumer). Talk about an interruption of routine.

Finally, we light up our first cigar in what seems like ages and draw on it like an exhaust fan. The last time I took a shortcut and skipped my ritual and just fired up and started smoking like there was no tomorrow was when a good friend shared one of his treasured pre-embargo Cuban vintage cigars thirty minutes before Super Bowl kick-off. Won't do that again.

When you find yourself smoking too fast, simply put the cigar in the ashtray once in a while and evaluate your smoking rate. How often do you puff on a cigar? The ideal rate for most, if not all, smokers is a minimum of 40 seconds to one minute or more between puffs. The palate is not a muscle; it is more like a high-speed dual processor running at the speed of light, responding to sensory stimuli. There is a limit to how much or how hard you can push it.

Forget about the "no pain, no gain" mantra from the fitness club. Apply this to your palate and you may damage palate sensitivity forever. There are many hard rock and acid rock fans who can attest to hearing loss caused by listening to their favorite music at high volume. The same applies to your palate. Many cigar aficionados who have smoked hard for years need to continue to smoke hard to get any flavor out of their cigars.

> **PURGING YOUR CIGAR**
>
> To purge your cigar, lightly blow air through the barrel of the cigar every few minutes before you draw, this will relieve the excess carbon buildup caused by tobacco that was not fully combusted, preparing it to deliver pure aroma on your next puff.

If your cigar goes out a few times during a smoking session, great! That's an indication that you're not smoking too fast. If it goes out, just touch it up and continue to enjoy. Also, if you find that your cigars seem to get bitter in the second or final third, you are probably smoking too hard or too fast. You may find that blowing air through the cigar every few minutes before you draw will relieve the excess carbon buildup caused by tobacco that was not fully combusted while you were heating up the foot of the cigar, preparing it to deliver pure aroma.

The Importance of Exercise

Any form of exercise will help improve your palate: jogging or swimming at the beach, taking a hike on a mountain trail, playing tennis or racket ball, or engaging in any type of aerobic exercise that got your heart rate up. Remember that feeling of exhilaration when you breathed long and deep? Even a daily brisk walk for 10 to 15 minutes can offer hidden benefits that you will realize over time.

If you are in good shape, you will experience more pleasure from every cigar you smoke. But I caution you: Cigar smokers vary in their stages of age and health. Whether you're young and super fit or young and out of shape or whether you're older and healthy or older and out of shape, ask your doctor how much you should exercise. But don't tell him why—unless he is a cigar smoker!

Mucus-inducing Foods

You may find it useful to get familiar with mucus-inducing foods so you don't overindulge in them right before a long-awaited cigar event or a long weekend earmarked for tasting several new blends. Keep in mind, however, that what affects one person may not affect another.

Through our autonomic nervous system, our body produces the necessary amount of mucus, on average 1 to 1.5 quarts per day to keep us healthy. When fighting a cold or flu, we can crank it up to twice that amount. Mucus keeps the nasal cavity from drying out and collects aroma molecules for identification. It also traps unwanted airborne particulates like dust particles, pollen, and bacteria to protect our lungs.

Some foods can cause our bodies to produce more mucus than necessary for normal bodily function. Below is a list of mucus-causing or mucus-thickening foods to consider reducing or removing from your diet if you are experiencing an excessive amount of mucus or trying to get over a cold or flu. They are listed from the worst to the least:

- Dairy: milk, including condensed and evaporated, cheese, yogurt, ice cream, butter
- Starch: bread, white pasta, cereals, potatoes, corn, and soy products
- Sugar: sweet desserts, candy, sodas
- Alcoholic beverages: sweet wine and mixed drinks
- Miscellaneous: processed meats and foods

Let's talk a little further about dairy, the #1 mucus-forming food. Humans are the only species on the planet who continue to consume milk after weaning. Milk is produced by a cow for her calf, weighing an average of 86 pounds at birth. The calf typically weans at 6.5 months, weighing in at over 500 pounds. Milk enables the calf to gain 2.5 pounds per day, every day for 6.5 months. Makes you wonder: Moderation or elimination? To make matters even worse, dairy cows are given rBGH, a growth hormone that helps them produce 1 to 2 gallons of extra milk per day. This growth hormone may be implicated in premature body changes for both girls and boys.

- Milk: This applies especially to condensed and evaporated milk.
- Cheese: A super-rich, nutrient-dense food; depending on the type of cheese, it takes an average of one gallon of milk to make 8 ounces of cheese. Real cheese goes through an aging process similar to the fermentation process of tobacco, grapes, and grain and is healthy in moderation.
- Yogurt: Most commercial yogurts are loaded with sugar. If you enjoy yogurt and it agrees with you, you might want to consider unsweetened organic yogurt.

I can hear what many of you are thinking, *What's left to eat?* The following are examples of foods that cause the least amount of mucus:

- Protein: lean beef, chicken, and pork in moderation. *Wild-caught* fish: salmon, tuna, sardines, flounder, grouper, red fish, sea bass, cod, etc. Avoid farmed-raised fish at all costs. They are fed a starchy diet made with GMO corn along with antibiotics, hormones, steroids, and orange dye. (Ronald Hites, et al., "Global Assessment of Organic Contaminants in Farmed Salmon," Science, Jan. 2004 (303):9).
- Fruit: all citrus, blackberries, blueberries, raspberries, pineapple, bananas, papaya, etc. Whole fruit is best; juice is too concentrated and often contains added sugar
- Herbs: garlic, ginger, cayenne, pepper, herbal teas

- Veggies: broccoli, kale, cabbage, spinach, romaine, carrots, celery, watercress, onion, pickles
- Miscellaneous: all dried, roasted nuts and seeds, honey, avocado, olive and coconut oils

Mucus-inducing Environments

It is estimated that up to 40% of Americans can have mild to severe allergic reactions to cats. Cat dander can be one of your palate's worst enemies. If you are allergic or even sensitive to cats, you are not alone. You will know it when you enter a person's home, even if you don't spot that furry, allergen-producing creature running around. Your eyes and throat will start to feel scratchy, and your sinuses will become congested. The reason is a protein called FelD1 found in a cat's urine, sebaceous glands, and saliva. A cat grooms itself by licking its fur, and when the saliva dries, watch out: This enzyme turns into a microscopic powder that floats in the air. The powder can linger in the air or settle on your bedding, sofa, curtains, and flooring, and even attach itself to your clothing, so you can take it everywhere you go. Inhalation or physical contact with this allergen can trigger an allergic reaction. The effects can include watery eyes runny nose, sneezing, congestion, itching, rashes, hives, and even asthma.

> Be wary of air freshener sprays, hanging air fresheners, or plug-in fragrance devices: They can wreak havoc on your respiratory system and palate.

Like some people love their dogs, others are devoted to their cats equally as much. My first and last experience with a cat lover happened many years ago when I was dating a woman I thought was "the one." The minute I walked into my fiancé's apartment, my nose felt stuffy, and my eyes and throat felt scratchy. On a bitterly cold winter night, I was in a deep sleep and was startled by strange furry thing covering my face. I instinctively grabbed it and threw it across the room. When I was fully awake, I realized it was a cat, one of the four my fiancé had living in her apartment. At the time I was traveling back and forth to the DR, so I spent only the weekends there. I suspected that, during the week, the cat slept on the pillow where I laid my head on the weekends, and that night I was in his spot.

In a state of desperation, I told my fiancé that either the cats had to go, or I would. To my surprise, she made me well aware that the cats lived there, not me. I thought I'd be a sport and show a little flexibility and issue a new ultimatum: When I was sleeping in the bedroom, the cats had to sleep in the other room with the bedroom door shut. She said no can do—wouldn't be fair to the cats to lock them out of their bedroom. After my traumatic experience of being awakened with a cat on my face, there was no way I could sleep in the same room.

I tried to sleep on the couch, but the cats had free range of the apartment, and there were cats in the living room, too. I couldn't go back to sleep in that apartment, so I took a thick blanket and went to my car to try to get a few more hours sleep. At the crack of dawn, I was awakened

> by the bright sunlight shining through the car windshield. I decided to make coffee and breakfast, so when my sweetheart woke up we could have an adult conversation.
>
> But she reminded me that the cats were there before me, so I was just going to have to get used to it. What's the big deal? She asked. I gave her back the key to the apartment. I wish I had said, *C'est la vie*, but what I actually said I still am trying to erase from my memory.
>
> If your partner is a cat lover—and you aren't—here are a few suggestions to help mitigate problem:

- Invest in a high-quality HEPA portable air purifier for the bedroom.
- Make your bedroom a cat-free zone. If this is not possible, then wash your bedding often.
- Limit the kitty's domain. Establish designated areas where your cat can travel within your house. Keep your cat away from your workstations by closing doors, for example. Make sure to supply plenty of cozy, warm places in kitty-approved areas.
- Decorate wisely. Minimizing rugs or carpeting can vastly reduce the amount of allergen buildup in your home. Carpeting, in particular, can accumulate 100 times as many allergens as hardwood floors.
- Brush your cat—outside! This way, allergen-laden dander can disperse and blow away, rather than accumulating in your home.
- Vacuum the floor and furniture once or twice per week and install a HEPA vacuum cleaner bag in your vacuum cleaner.
- Install a high-quality HEPA filter in your HVAC system and change the filter as instructed.
- Bathe the cat as often as your vet recommends.
- Remember that taking pills or getting shots may compromise your palate and your immune system.

Cats love to explore, so leave the back door open when your partner is away, and your kitty problem will be solved. Just kidding.

Medicines and Their Effect on Taste

Hopefully, this section doesn't apply to you. But even if it doesn't, I urge you to read it for two reasons. First, you can advise a cigar buddy who has recently lost the pleasure he once found in a fine cigar. Second, the day may come when your doctor suggests that you should start taking meds which may decrease palate sensitivity. Once you fully understand the positive benefits and risky side effects, you can make an informed decision. Should you take the meds or find an alternative? Know which drugs can affect your palate in a negative way.

Below is a list of the most common drugs. If you are taking any of these and have noticed that your sense of smell isn't what it used to be, you may want to consult with your doctor. Share with him or her that three of your greatest pleasures are dining out, feasting on a six-course, healthy meal with a glass of wine or single-malt scotch, and an occasional cigar.

Your physician may be one of those narrow-minded docs who insist that, in order to be healthy, you have to take pharmaceuticals and not smoke or drink anything. If so, you might want to interview other doctors who have a more open-minded approach—especially those who enjoy an occasional or daily cigar. They are out there, and the best place to find one is at a cigar shop or lounge. Simply ask the salespeople and patrons at the shop; they will gladly share the information if they know one. If you are given the name of a doc who is a specialist and you need a generalist, ask for a recommendation. Cigar-smoking doctors are an elite group and, like birds of a feather, they tend to flock together.

Drugs that May Cause Smell Disorders	
Phenylephrine, Pseudoephedrine	Nasal decongestant
Oxymetazoline	Nasal decongestant
Zicam	Nasal decongestant
Phenytoin	Antiepileptic
Amitriptyline, Clomipramine	Antidepressant
Desipramine, Doxepin, Imipramine	Antidepressant
Codeine, Morphine, Cocaine	Opiate
Carbimazole	Antithyroid
Streptomycin, Doxycycline, Terbinafine	Antibiotic/antifungal
Cholestyramine, Clofibrate, Statins	Lipid-lowering
Nifedipine, Amlodipine, Diltiazem	Calcium channel blocker

Common Sense about Scents

If you want to allow your cigar to take center stage, you will need to keep the air around you as neutral as possible. When possible, avoid strong fragrances found in colognes, lotions, hair products, and aftershave. And air fresheners. Depending on how your partner feels about your new quest for a sophisticated palate, ask them to do the same. Remember that all of these products, with few exceptions, are made with synthetic fragrances, preservatives, and dyes. You can purchase fragrance-free or hypo-allergenic hygiene products. Some of these products are also made with natural fragrances, and if used in moderation may not cause any palate interference.

Most partners probably will understand if you explain the reasons for what they may feel is a strange request. Just drop a few obscure phrases like "Olfactory Sensory Overload" or "Aroma Threshold." Then share the Olympic-size pool example you read about in Chapter 2 that illustrated what one part per billion (1 ppb) would look like—1 tablespoon per 650,000 gallons—and they should get the message or at least act as if they do to appease your strange request.

You may also choose to be a sport and stop at a health food store on your way to or from the cigar lounge and purchase some new products for both you and your partner to try. If you do all your shopping with your fingers, then while at the cigar lounge you can do a Google search and find fragrance-free products. You may have to do a little digging around, but once you find a source, the problem is solved.

On a hot summer day a few years ago, I invited a close friend to meet me at a local cigar lounge to enjoy one of my vintage Cubans, an H. Upmann Churchill. We went through our cigar ritual, smelling the wrapper and taking a pre-light draw, then calling out the aromas we could detect. Then we toasted the cigars with several long wood matches until they were fully lit and the cigars were ready for the first puff. The first third of the vintage cigar still had those famous "Cubano" flavors: earthy, herbaceous, woody, leather, and vanilla, with hints of anise and chocolate.

A strange thing occurred when I returned to my stogie after a restroom break. I picked up a strong lavender-floral note. It is not uncommon for cigars with a light or natural wrapper to have a floral note, but this was the first time I experienced lavender as the dominant taste note in a cigar. Sharing this observation with my smoking buddy was no help. He suggested I have another double espresso. I had already had enough caffeine for the day, so I opted for another plan.

From my briefcase, I took out a resealable bag. You can probably guess what it contained: saltine crackers, of course, for a palate cleanse! Afterwards, the lavender aroma still prevailed. I shrugged it off and continued to while away the hour with my friend and my cigar. As I was smoking into the end of the final third, my smoking buddy returned from the restroom.

"Taste Master!" he exclaimed. (He had coined my nickname, as it assured him of an endless supply of free cigars.) "Now I'm picking up that lavender aroma note." I wiped the grin off my face and headed to the restroom to find the strange aroma culprit. There it was: a fancy glass

> bottle of French lavender hand soap. Of course, I had to read the ingredients, eventually finding the answer I was looking for: artificial lavender fragrance. Why it takes 26 ingredients to make a hand soap is beyond my ability to comprehend.
>
> If you don't want to avoid scented hygiene products altogether, at least exercise restraint. Your cigar palate and cigar comrades will thank you.

Alcohol and Cigars

Don't worry. No admonition here to turn teetotaler—I wouldn't do that to you or to me. Let's put things in perspective, though. Just as the right meds in the right dosage can foster healing and save lives, too much of the wrong prescription can harm or kill.

> If alcohol is queen, then tobacco is her consort. It's a fond companion for all occasions, a loyal friend through fair weather and foul. People smoke to celebrate a happy moment, or to hide a bitter regret. Whether you're alone or with friends, it's a joy for all the senses.
>
> —Luis Buñuel

I used to wonder how different drink choices stack up, not only in taste, which I had experienced, but as health defenders. I was pleased to learn that some alcoholic beverages can actually be healthy. Like premium cigars, fine wine, whiskey, and craft beer, all come from agricultural products (tobacco leaves, grapes, and grain) that undergo fermenting, blending, and aging. During fermentation, yeast feeds on the inherent sugars, resulting in by-products of alcohol and antioxidants. Alcohol has a calming effect on the central nervous system and lowers blood pressure. Antioxidants, of course, support a strong immune system that keeps one healthy.

After a drink or two or three, how does your sense of smell fare? Quite well, it turns out. A modest amount of alcohol may boost the olfactory organ (the palate), according to research published by **Yaara Endevelt** ("Disinhibition of Olfaction," *Behavioral Brain Research*, Vol. 272, Oct. 2014, pp. 66-74).

A few drinks = heightened palate sensitivity. A few too many = the reverse.

The verdict is still out on exactly how this works, but we do know that alcohol increases circulation, heightens sensitivity, and lowers our inhibitions, allowing the smoker to relax and think outside the box.

The key is moderation. Most would agree that we can improve our sense of smell through practice not consumption of alcohol only.

Pairing Your Cigar with a Beverage: Two Distinct Approaches

Pairing your favorite cigar with a drink is probably one of the most misunderstood concepts, second only to retro hale. There is a lot of artistic flare around pairing a wine with food. For years, I naively followed the recommendations of waiters and sommeliers, not truly understanding the science behind the concept.

One evening, while enjoying my nightly ritual of savoring one of my favorite full bodied cigars, I was out of the recommended liquors to pair with this cigar and had to resort to what I had available. The recommended drink to pair with this cigar was a heavy cognac or peaty, single malt scotch. In my desperation to have something alcoholic to accompany my cigar, I poured what I had available: a single malt scotch from the Highland region in Scotland. Most Highland scotch is known for a delicate and fruity quality, which is due to the scotch makers' method of drying the fermented barley. Most scotch from the Islay region has a smoky, peaty, menthol aroma and flavor. This is due to their use of dried peat moss as a heat source when drying the sprouted barley grain.

Back to my paradigm shift. As I smoked the full bodied cigar, I noticed pronounced tastes, flavor characteristics, and nuances that I typically didn't experience when pairing with a heavy drink. As a bonus, the Highland scotch tasted better than ever—its sweet fruity flavor notes were particularly evident. As I sipped on the scotch, my palate was cleansed of the heavy, dark, earthy, smoky taste notes from the cigar and vice versa.

To make sure this wasn't some kind of fluke, the next night I selected the same cigar, and this time paired it with an Islay single malt scotch I had purchased earlier that day. My observations from the previous night were confirmed: The cigar didn't have the same complex flavor profile as the night before, and the scotch's distinct smoky, peaty, menthol aroma and taste were subdued or muted. So, on the third night, I selected a Davidoff Signature known for a delicate flavor profile and paired it with the heavy, peaty Islay scotch. The result was the same as the first night: The cigar and the scotch tasted better than ever. On the fourth night, I paired the Davidoff Signature with the fruity, light Highland scotch, and neither the cigar nor the scotch tasted as good as the previous night.

This led me to dig deep into my taste library to find supporting documentation. I started with a book written by Elin McCoy about Robert Parker, titled *The Emperor of Wine*. If you like fine wine and are not familiar with Robert Parker, you owe it to yourself to get a copy of this book. Parker is one of the main reasons millions of wine connoisseurs and novices alike drink wines from Simona and Napa Valley, California.

In the 1980s, Parker published a wine magazine called *The Wine Advocate* that offered brutally honest taste notes and scored wines with a 100-point rating system that he had created. He based his scoring system on the grading scale from his earlier days in school. It is commonly considered that 70 points or better on a test is a passing grade, 80 to 89 is a good to above average, and 90-plus is "A" quality. Initially, most wine writers and publications scorned Parker for trivializing wine, but within two years they were all using Parker's 100-point scale. *The Wine Advocate, Wine Spectator, Wine Enthusiast,* and *Wine & Spirits* are among the highly respected wine publications that publish ratings based on the 100-point scale.

During the legendary 1987 Pairs Convention, Parker was the unexpected star, turning the wine world upside down. Prior to this event, the most sought-after wines were of Europe origin, but the tables turned and California wines were on the map. By now you are probably wondering what this has to do with pairing your cigar. Let me explain. Fine European wines were typically blended to pair with gourmet foods. Parker's approach was to evaluate a wine's taste characteristics based on its merits alone, not how well it paired with foods, which brings us to two distinct approaches.

As just noted, European wines are traditionally designed to balance a meal, creating a harmonious experience. Heavy reds with strong tannins are paired with roasted lamb, beef, pork or wild game. The heavy reds tone down the robust meat taste and vice versa via *adaptation* (discussed in Chapter 4). Chardonnay wines, on the other hand, offer pear, peach, citrus, pineapple, apricot, and melon flavor notes that tone down the taste of chicken and fish via adaptation. Light, semi-sweet wines such as Sauvignon Blanc and Pinot Grigios are paired with appetizers such as cheeses, salads and fruits.

It's important to understand the different approaches and how one showcases the cigar's flavor characteristics and the other tones it down. Another way to look at pairing is to borrow a term used in music called *counterpoint*, which means *point against point,* or the relationship between voices that are both interdependent and independent of each other. Johann Sebastian Bach was a master of counterpoint and composed a famous work, Concerto in D minor for Two Violins, BWV. It can serve as excellent example of counterpoint that will transport you into a state of "Auditory Bliss." YouTube has several excellent recordings of this masterpiece. This technique has been used in music for over 300 years. Even today you will hear it used in classical, jazz, and pop music; listeners find the contrast pleasing to the ear.

Similar to refreshing the palate in tasting, counterpoint in music refreshes the ear, making the music more interesting and appealing. A counterpoint line is still harmonious, meaning it doesn't clash with the opposing line. In taste, the same holds true: The opposing beverage must still complement the cigar; just pairing with something different may not always work, such as drinking a Bloody Mary or a Long Island Iced Tea with any cigar blend. The tomato juice is too rich and acidic, while the Long Island contains too many ingredients and is too sweet for most sensible cigar smokers to enjoy. Not only would these drinks not complement or cleanse the palate, they also are typically served at temperatures that would numb the palate. Below are some alternatives to highlight the cigar's flavor characteristics and nuances:

- Scotch
- Whiskey
- Bourbon
- Cognac
- Armagnac

- Aged rum
- Wine
- Port
- Craft beer

All of the drinks above will refresh the palate and are at their best at a temperature range of between 60 and 70 degrees, except for the beer. The 60- to 70-degree range allows the flavor molecules in the drinks to express their full potential. Any colder or warmer and you will not taste the full range of flavors they have to offer. Many craft beer gurus are going to challenge me on the temperature range for beer, but I'll remind them that our highlight of the evening is the cigar, not the beer. Beer is a little tricky, depending on the style: You may find that it is best served between 50 and 60 degrees with a cigar, but some heavy stouts do well at 60 to 70 degrees.

If you enjoy your beer on the cooler side and still want to enjoy your cigar, you can do the following: After taking a sip of cold beer, simply wait about 45 seconds to 1 minute for your mouth to come back to its normal temperature and salinity before continuing to smoke. You can also use this technique if you can't seem to break your habit of taking your scotch or whiskey on the rocks.

I have a friend who has a collection of the most exquisite, expensive, and rare scotches you could imagine. I would venture to say it is worth more than a new Lexus LS. In his bar, he also has whiskeys and bourbons for those he says can't appreciate a fine, well-aged, single malt scotch. He takes his high-quality scotch neat at room temperature in a $135.00 crystal snifter.

As much as I wanted to, I didn't dare challenge his way of taking his scotch, but one day the opportunity presented itself. We were enjoying an after-dinner cigar in his man cave and he asked me, "Why do you drink my good scotch in that weird glass and with a measured splash of cold water and chill it with those stainless steel ice cubes and check the temperature like a scientist?" I replied that I could prove to him that his treasured scotch and cigar would taste better if he took his scotch with a splash of water and at 64° in a flared rim wine glass, but he would have to take a blind taste test in order to prove my point. To my surprise, he said, "Sounds interesting—okay, prove it to me."

I prepared four scotches, two ounces each. The first one was in his crystal snifter, neat, at room temperature. The second was also prepared in his crystal snifter but with one teaspoon of cold water and chilled to 64° with stainless steel ice cubes. The third one was prepared with the scotch in a flared rim wine glass, neat, at room temperature. The fourth was prepared with the scotch in a flared rim wine glass along with one teaspoon of cold water and chilled to 64° degrees with stainless steel ice cubes.

I asked him to drink the first scotch and offer his impression, then do the same for the scotch in the second snifter. He responded, "The first scotch is good, but the second is better—what you poured in the second scotch, is it excellent?" I told him I'd let him know after he tasted all four scotches.

We moved on to the flared rim wine glass, neat, and finally to the fourth, also in the flared rim wine glass with added water and chilled. I asked his impression. "The third one is even better than the first one, and about the same as the second. The fourth scotch is amazing. Now tell me, what did you pour in those glasses?"

When I told him that I poured the same scotch in all four glasses, he looked at me in dismay and asked where he could buy a case of those weird wine glasses, fake ice cubes, and a thermometer.

Life: Complicated—Retro Hale: Not

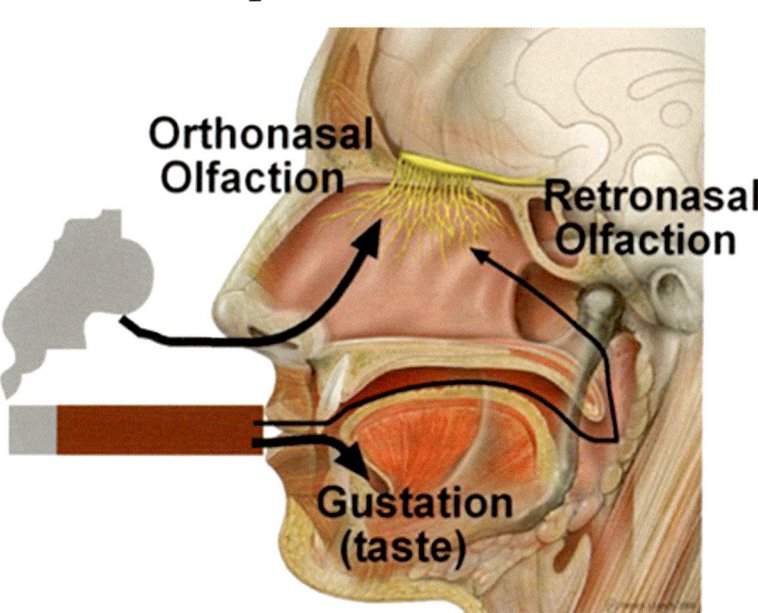

Every time we eat, we retro hale; otherwise we would taste only sweet, sour, salty, bitter, or savory, as the pinched-nose test in Chapter 3 proved. When we eat, we chew the food while we breathe in and out, which allows aroma molecules to travel up through our nasal cavity to the olfactory bulb. The aroma molecules bind or stick to the tiny hair-like receptors called cilia in the olfactory bulb, sending sensory signals to the brain to decode or match to a stored reference.

Now the taste options go from a mere five to hundreds. When we swallow, the soft palate blocks the food or liquid from going up through the nose, unless you cough or laugh, which will cause the food or liquid to travel up through the nose. I am sure this has happened to all of you at least once or twice in your lifetime. The opening and closing of the soft palate is a process that is beyond our control, unless you pinch your nose while you eat or drink.

If you can detect more than the five mouth tastes (sweet, sour, salty, bitter, and savory) while you eat, you have already mastered retro hale. Now all you have to do is apply this process to the way you smoke. Think of retro haling as learning to ride a bike, to water-ski or snow ski, or to parallel park. It's difficult until you know how. Then it becomes second nature.

Here are some suggestions to make retro haling your cigar second nature:

- Relax when you are smoking.
- Remember the 1 part per billion analogy.
- Each person's threshold may vary from a little to a lot—what matters is learning what your threshold is.
- Gently hold the cigar between your teeth and wrap your lips around the cigar. Take several short puffs while you gently inhale through your nose. Remove the cigar from your mouth, gently exhale the smoke from your mouth, and then inhale through your nose and exhale.
- Take two short puffs (one count each) and one longer puff (two counts) then exhale 1/3 of the smoke, then inhale through your nose and exhale another 1/3, then inhale through your nose and repeat this cycle one last time.
- Smoke as you normally do, but after you exhale all the smoke from your mouth, do a chewing motion with your mouth, while you breathe in and out through your nose.
- Smoke as you normally do, but after you exhale all the smoke from your mouth, inhale through your mouth and exhale through your nose.
- Smoke as you normally do, but while you are exhaling, tilt your head down then back up. This will push a very small amount of smoke up into your nasal cavity.

If you are experiencing a burning sensation in your nasal cavity, you are probably retro haling too much. The burning sensation is not a taste or a flavor note; it is a tactile sensation, like touching a hot burner, which is not desirable and not kind to the olfactory bulb in your nasal cavity.

Types of Blind Tasting

In a 2000 experiment, students from the oenology (the study of wine) program at the University of Bordeaux in France taste tested a white wine, a red wine, and a white wine that was dyed red so it looked like a red wine. The students' descriptions of the dyed white wine included many flavor descriptors usually used for red wine. Also, when they were told a wine was more expensive, even though it wasn't, the wine received better ratings.

If you want to avoid this bias trap of smoking the cigar band instead of the cigar, blind tasting will solve the problem. When you conduct a blind tasting, you can't smoke the cigar band or brand because it won't be wearing a cigar band—call it smoking a naked cigar, if you will.

An effective blind tasting—without seeing the cigar band or knowing what brand you are smoking—will challenge everything you thought you knew about cigars. Let's look at the three most common types of blind tastings.

Blind tasting is an outstanding way to develop and train your palate. It forces you to give the cigar all your attention and concentration. Also, you must focus deliberately on the different aspects of your sensory apparatus in order to decode the cigar's mystery and complexity. You have to rely on what you are actually sensing in the moment, rather than the preconceptions you have about a given cigar or cigar brand. With no prior knowledge of the cigar, you are forced to dig deeply, and in this process, you will have no choice other than to rely on your senses.

Although challenging and often humbling, you will find that blind tasting helps you understand how you personally identify individual taste characteristics of different tobaccos and their origins and style. When you are forced to rely solely on what you are sensing, you will learn to assess quality more accurately in terms of flavor profile, aroma, intensity, balance, and complexity. The goal is not to guess the tobacco origin or type or the cigar brand; instead, the purpose is to taste accurately and make an objective assessment of the cigar's style and quality. Given time, you will start to identify taste and flavor nuances of different tobaccos and may be able to identify their origin.

Due to the overwhelming quantities of high-quality cigars from Honduras, Nicaragua, Dominican Republic, and Cuba, it is not realistic to think that one can easily identify the origin or the brand. Many cigars are made with tobacco from the six major tobacco-growing regions and four minor regions. There are also a handful of what I will refer to as micro regions that creative blenders may explore from time to time, looking for flavor nuances that are new or different.

Major Regions:	Dominican Republic, Ecuador, Honduras, Mexico, Nicaragua, United States
Minor Regions:	Cameroon, Brazil, Indonesia, Peru
Micro Regions:	Columbia, Costa Rica, Florida, Panama, Pennsylvania

Blind tasting is a nurtured skill that requires patience and practice—it is not an innate ability. Through a well organized approach and mindful practice, you will find that your ability to taste will improve quickly. In a matter of months, not years, you may develop a palate that is the envy of a veteran smoker who puffs and puffs away with little thought as to a cigar's style.

It is imperative that you have a well organized approach that you use each time you conduct a blind tasting.

Cigar Style

- Simple: everyday cigar
- Puro: made with tobaccos from one country
- Exotic: a blend consisting of less common tobaccos, such as Amazon Basin, Costa Rica, Florida, Ometepe, Panama, Pennsylvania, Peru
- Classic: a complex flavor bomb that delivers opulent smoke that coats the palate with exotic flavors and has a finish that lingers on and on, leaving the smoker wanting for more

Keys Points for a Blind Tasting

Following are some suggestions that will make the process flow easily and effectively. Develop a systematic approach that feels right and works for you. Use the same approach for each blind tasting. Here is a suggested format:

- Be well organized and work in a systematic manner.
- Develop and use a descriptive and objective vocabulary.
- Find one or several cigar buddies who are also interested in further developing their palates and participating in a blind tasting.
- Decide on a tasting schedule: once a week, bimonthly, or monthly.

If you can't find a willing cigar buddy to join you, there are creative ways you can conduct a blind tasting on your own. Here are some suggestions:

What you will need:

- Have old cigar bands taken off of previously smoked cigars, preferable large ones: It is best not to remove the cigar band from an unsmoked cigar because you might tear the wrapper leaf.
- Have a glue stick and marker.
- Develop a random labeling system that will be difficult to remember: A through Z or 1 through 10 or combinations, such as A1-10 through H1-10. Don't always use same letter or number for a country or origin: Mix it up.
    - Here's an example for a Puro tasting: A1=Nicaragua, A3=Honduras, A2=Dominican.
    - Here's an example for a blend with a Habano Ecuador wrapper: B3=Nicaragua, B1=Honduras, B3=Dominican.
    - Here's an example for a blend with a Maduro wrapper: C5=Nicaragua, C4=Honduras, C6=Dominican

If you prepare the cigar a few days or a week before the blind tasting, you will probably forget your letter or number coding.

Blind tasting is based on tobacco theory. If you aren't familiar with the tobaccos, the growing regions, the blends, and the brands, your chances of being successful are zero. Knowing the classic tobacco-growing regions and the aroma, taste, and flavor characteristics of each tobacco is critical. Memorize the key characteristics of each tobacco and commit them to memory. In the beginning of the test, think in broad terms or categories and little by little narrow your focus to specific categories. Only then, make your final impressions.

Budgeting

Blind tasting is not easy on your wallet: It requires several cigars each session, so plan accordingly. If you have a limited budget, you might decide not to smoke two or three days before the blind tasting: Not only will this save you money for the cigars you are going to smoke during the blind tasting, but your palate will be fresh, more sensitive, and eager for palate stimulation.

Accurately describing a cigar's characteristics is one of the most important and rewarding skills for a cigar connoisseur to master. If you think you dislike full bodied, earthy Honduran cigars and know that you are smoking one, you will have already made certain decisions about the cigar. To be a good cigar taster requires concentration, knowledge, and, above all, awareness of your senses. When evaluating a cigar, personal opinion and enjoyment are not the focus. The purpose of evaluating a cigar is not only to enjoy it, but also to analyze the cigar and come to an understanding about its style and characteristics. It allows you to better identify and enjoy its qualities.

Tasting and the Environment

To evaluate a cigar, you must remain objective and analytical. Choose an environment that is free of distractions and competing aromas. If possible, taste in the same environment and at the same time of day. Before lunch or dinner is the optimal time, when your palate is fresh. Conducting a taste test in a crowded cigar lounge on Friday or Saturday night is not the ideal environment and will produce less than desired results. If you are going to conduct a blind tasting in a cigar lounge, schedule the tasting when the cigar lounge is quiet and free of secondhand smoke and noise distractions.

Ideal Environments to Conduct a Cigar Tasting

- Weather permitting, outside on your porch
- A cigar lounge at non-peak hours
- In your or your friends' man caves; in a garage if your man cave is still under construction and the temperature is in your comfort zone

Worst Environments to Conduct a Cigar Tasting

- On your hotel balcony facing the ocean
- On your porch with a stiff breeze or windy conditions
- In an environment you consider uncomfortably cold or hot
- A cigar lounge at peak hours
- At your favorite sports bar

- In a gentlemen's club
- Before or after Thanksgiving dinner or thirty minutes before Super Bowl kickoff

Blind tasting does not mean putting on a blindfold or closing your eyes when smoking; rather, it means that you do not know what you are smoking in advance.

However, the ultimate blind tasting would require you to wear a *blindfold*. This will eliminate all preconceived bias toward the cigar's wrapper type. In Chapter 2, we saw an example of how our sight can dramatically influence our perception. The only other bias that is left is the cigar size: how it feels in your hand and mouth.

Eliminating Bias

To eliminate a cigar's size bias, you can use the ProTip™, which I will discuss at the end of this section. With this device, I have demonstrated to many cigar smokers and connoisseurs that a small ring gauge cigar can have as much, or in some cases more, taste, aroma, intensity, balance, complexity, and finish as many larger ring gauge cigars. Also, small ring gauge cigars produce far less smoke and are easier to light, smoke, and control than larger ring gauge cigars.

When participating in a blind tasting, it is important to relax and remember that there are no right or wrong observations. No two humans are hardwired the same way; therefore, we smell and taste things differently based on our mental and physical health, our DNA, and our life experiences.

If you taste something different from another person, it doesn't mean you are wrong. Boldly share your impression, unless it is off-the-wall, like "blueberry pancakes" or "Red Bull." Always listen to others' comments—they may identify a taste note you didn't recognize or were unable to make an association with—but don't blindly agree.

> Fidel Castro's go-to cigar was a 38-ring gauge Lancero. For those of you who are not familiar with Fidel Castro, he owned an island called Cuba that is the birthplace of premium cigars. For over four decades, it is rumored that Castro smoked six to eight Lancero cigars a day. To eliminate concerns of someone putting poison in his Lancero cigars, his private stash of Lanceros were aged and stored under the bed of Liguito, the master blender who personally rolled all of Castro's cigars.
>
> Depending on the cigar size and shape, a cigar maker can make 100 to 150 cigars per day. Since Castro was smoking only six to eight cigars per day, what happened to the other 120 extra cigars? They were given to dignitaries to influence and win political favors. Even JFK was reportedly on the list—that is, until the Bay of Pigs fiasco.

Lead Tasting

This is the best type of tasting to start with. In lead tasting, you know something about the cigar's origin before you smoke it. For example, suppose that you want to become more familiar with the taste and flavor characteristic of Habano or Maduro wrappers. You will need to select cigars made with those wrappers from different regions or countries. For example, an Ecuadorian Habano versus a Nicaragua Habano, or a U.S. Broad Leaf versus a San Andres Maduro. Or you can conduct a lead tasting focusing on filler tobaccos grown in different regions such Corojo or Criollo grown in the Dominican Republic versus in Nicaragua or Honduras.

A tobacco seed variety—for example, Criollo 98—grown in the Dominican Republic versus in Nicaragua or Honduras will have different taste and aroma characteristics depending on which country and region in that country it was grown in. In many cases, the area will influence its flavor characteristics as much as or, in some cases more than, the seed variety. The reason some seed varieties are grown over others is due to both tradition or trial and error. Some seed varieties grow better in certain climates and soils and will express their full potential in those growing regions.

Another interesting setup for a Lead Tasting is to select cigars referred to as "Puro" (*pure* in English), which consists of all tobaccos from one country. You will need to purchase three Puros: one Dominican, one Nicaragua, and one Honduran. This will help you hone your taste to the unique flavor, taste, and aroma characteristics of tobaccos from the three major cigar producing countries.

You will find that true Puros are not as common as cigars that are made with Dominican, Nicaragua, or Honduras filler tobaccos with a wrapper or binder from another country such as Ecuadorian Habano/Sumatra, U.S. Conn., U.S. Broadleaf, or Mexican San Andres. These combinations are fine to use in a blind tasting, if it is noted in the score sheet. If you happen to get your hands on some Cuban cigars, you can add them to the mix for an interesting comparison.

If you don't finish all three or four cigars in the blind tasting, you can save the unfinished cigars to smoke the next day. In Florida, I have found that overnighting a cigar does best if the environment you leave them in has a humidity in the range of 55% to 75% and a temperature in the range of 60° to 85° degrees. I recommend that you do not put the cigars in a plastic bag, your humidor, or a cigar tube; instead, leave them in a clean ashtray, out of the direct sunlight, and away from an air conditioner vent if left indoors. A covered porch or garage will work in many cases. Also, I find it is best not to clip off the foot of the cigar behind the ash; instead, gently knock off the ash and place the cigar in the clean ash tray.

Vertical Tasting
- 2013 Vintage
- 2015 Vintage
- 2017 Vintage
- 2019 Vintage

Vertical Tasting is one of the most interesting types of blind tastings. You will need to select a cigar brand that you can secure multiple vintages of. The focus of this tasting is to see how the same cigars made from the same tobaccos and produced by the same manufacturer can vary from one vintage to another. This type of tasting can help you discern subtle differences that may occur from one crop to another as well as track the effects of aging.

You may notice differences that are the result of different growing conditions during each of the vintages. In warmer, drier vintages you might find a spike in the strength or intensity, whereas in vintages where the weather was cooler due to more rainfall, you might notice less strength but more delicate flavor nuances.

Vertical tastings are also an ideal way to see how a cigar ages. Take note as to how the cigars from older vintages differ from the cigars from younger vintages in terms of the following: aroma, strength, mouth taste, flavor, complexity, balance, and finish.

Horizontal Tasting

In this type of tasting, you will smoke several cigars from the same region made by different manufacturers. For instance, you can select cigars that were made in Nicaragua with Condega or Jalapa or Estelí tobaccos, by two or more manufacturers. In a horizontal tasting, you will learn to spot differences in how a cigar is blended and the effects of Terroir, which we will explore in the next section.

For blind tasting and smoking for enjoyment, it is important to have an unbiased and positive tasting mindset. Don't look for the taste characteristic you like in a cigar; rather, make note and enjoy what the cigar in your hand has to offer. Relish its attributes. Those who see their glass as always half empty will never enjoy their cigar nor their journey through life as much as those who always see their glass as half full.

- Jalapa
- Condega
- Estelí

Among Friends

From time to time, you may light up what seems like the best cigar you have had in a while, and you would like to share the taste sensations you are experiencing, but it is not a common practice to share a cigar with someone else—until now!

Let me introduce you to the ProTip™ kit. You can use these cigar-testing tips to take sample puffs of other smokers' cigars without the concern of passing germs through contact with another person's saliva.

The ProTip™

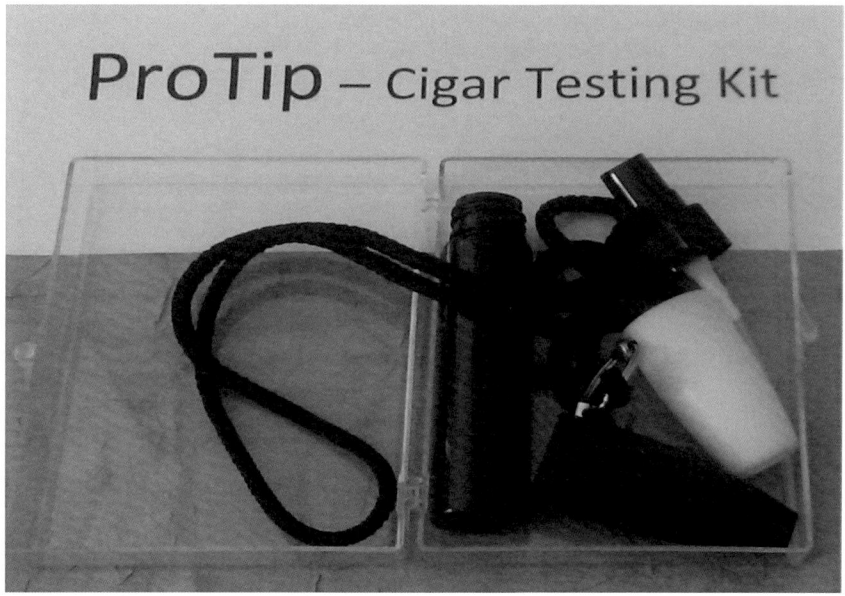

The ProTip™ is an excellent tool for all of the following:

- Getting an overall impression of a cigar's blend
- Determining if the blend is pairing well with the wrapper leaf
- Isolating the retro hale from the mouth taste influence
- Determining if it is a cigar you want to invest the time and money in

Advantages and Disadvantages of the ProTip™

The flavor profile of a cigar is the combination of the filler, binder, and wrapper leaf. When using the ProTip™, the smoker will bypass the influence the wrapper leaf has on mouth taste, which is an advantage in this situation but a disadvantage in the final stage of evaluating the overall cigar blend. A cigar blender can use the ProTip™ to isolate the filler and binder from the wrapper leaf to determine if the blend is what he is looking for, or if it's not pairing well with the current wrapper. He can save considerable time by pairing the blend with different wrappers to find a better combination instead of starting over. If used in this manner, the disadvantage becomes an advantage.

If you work in the cigar industry or in a cigar shop or lounge, you may find other uses for the ProTip™, such as when a cigar customer continuously complains about the blend or the draw not being right. An experienced salesman or shop owner can use the ProTip™ to quickly determine if the complainer is correct or just looking for another free cigar after he smoked two thirds of the cigar.

The ProTip™ is versatile, working with any cigar ring gauge from 38rg to 60rg. It will also work with most box-pressed cigars after the cigar head is moistened.

How a Cigar Size or Shape Affects Taste

We are all familiar with the admonition *Don't judge a book by its cover*. As mentioned above, many small ring gauge cigars can pack more flavor and intensity than large ring gauge cigars. Box-pressing a cigar can often intensify the blend, because the altered shape changes the dynamics in the way the filler leaves burn and how they stimulate the palate.

The other reason is that the filler to binder to wrapper ratio is changed. In order for a cigar wrapper not to crack or break when it is pressed, the cigar maker must "under bunch" (use fewer filler leaves) in the cigar bunch, or cigar core. Using fewer filler leaves allows the cigar to change from a cylindrical or round form to a flatten or box press form. This increases the wrapper to binder ratio, which influences the aroma, taste, and flavor of a cigar from a little to a lot.

If a cigar blender has created a cigar that has excellent flavor, but the balance or intensity isn't what he is looking for, he may decide to box-press the cigar without changing the blend. This may intensify its taste profile and improve the balance. On the other hand, if an excellent, round-format cigar is box-pressed, it may throw the cigar off balance. A master blender will make decisions based on experience, preferences, and trial and error.

A great way to experience differences stemming from a cigar's size is to purchase the same blend in several ring gauge sizes, as well as in a box-pressed format if available. Smoke one cigar size per day and record your impressions.

Most cigar smokers are true gentlemen or refined ladies. I've yet to see a fight break out in the cigar lounge, unlike other types of lounges, or, for that matter, sporting events, including little league baseball and soccer games. With that said, we come to a situation that occurred where a fight almost broke out in a cigar lounge, and, of all people, I was the main culprit.

This happened during the cigar boom. All forms of booms have an uncanny way of bringing out the worst in people. For those of you who were cigar smokers during the boom, you know it was an interesting time. Cigar shops and lounges were buzzing with excitement. Cigar smokers were jockeying to fill their humidors with their favorite cigars before they were sold out. After a long 12-hour day at the factory, I stopped off at a local shop to relax and smoke a cigar. I went into the humidor and selected a Lancero 7 x 38 ring gauge. As I was lighting up my cigar, someone in the lounge commented to his buddies that I was a cigar insider and made equipment that many of the major cigar factories used to make the cigars that they smoked. Then from across the room a cigar smoker, puffing away on a 60 ring gauge Maduro, commented, "Then why is he smoking a woman's cigar? Why doesn't he smoke a man's cigar [that is, one with a larger gauge]?"

Without thinking, I fired back, "I have no desire to put anything big in my mouth like some people." Before I realized what I had just said, he jumped up like a raging bull from the leather sofa and started coming towards me.

> Fortunately, I was rescued from my injudicious statement by some cigar comrades. The raging bull was ushered out of the lounge and not seen again for quite some time. Then one day, months later, someone sat next to me at the bar and asked me what Lancero cigar I recommended. I looked up and was startled to see the raging bull sitting next to me.
>
> I have to give the guy credit: He apologized for his naive remark months back and bought me a drink. I told him there are many excellent Lancero cigars, and this shop carried a handful, including Oliva, Casa Fernandez and Tatuaje Lanceros. I added that the cigar was on me. I was impressed: This guy had a very good palate. He was a highly intelligent man who had just started smoking and wanted to know everything about cigars—today.

After answering what seemed like an endless stream of questions, I said, "Look, let me put it this way: Variety is the spice of life." He smiled and said, "I'm glad my wife didn't hear you say that."

Terroir

Have you ever wondered how cigars, all made from aged tobacco leaves, can offer such a broad range of aromas, tastes, and flavors? There are many ways to think about terroir. The tobacco farmer or agronomist is an intricate part of the expression of terroir, because without his intervention, there is no expression of it. The quality of the tobaccos used to blend a cigar will affect our final sensorial experience when a cigar is smoked.

> Cigar makers (blenders) are unusual creatures, one part artist and one part mad scientist with the patience of the biblical figure Job. They wait months and sometimes even years to find out if their tobacco creations (blends) are bad, not so bad, just okay, so-so, good, very good, extraordinary.
>
> –Nick Cutro

Tobacco Plant Terroir

The French word *terroir* means soil. In relation to cigars, it has two very specific meanings. The first refers to the influence of the region: the soil and the climatic conditions in the specific region the tobacco is grown. The second refers to the quality of cigars produced from those tobaccos. Through robust agricultural practices, an agronomist can replicate soil conditions of regions that are known for high-quality tobaccos by amending the soil with nutrients. Even when these practices are followed, the tobaccos will still display unique qualities from the terroir in the region they are grown. In many cases, the terroir may have as much influence as the seed variety grown.

> Tobacco is the opiate of the masses:
> A cigar is the religion of the connoisseur.
>
> –Nick Cutro

What can't be replicated is seasonal rainfall and daytime high and nightly low temperatures. To experience evidence of terroir's influence, one has only to smoke a well blended Puro. Great terroir offers a diligent and insightful tobacco agronomist the opportunity to grow tobacco of exceptional quality, but then it is in the hands of the cigar blender with an exceptional palate to bring out the hidden secrets that lie dormant within the terroir.

In the last several decades, new terroirs have captured the attention of the cigar world and have been developed, most notably for use in the production of the following tobaccos.

- San Andreas from Mexico for wrapper and binder
- Habano and Sumatra from Ecuador for wrapper and binder
- Arapiraca, Mata Fina, Amazon Basin from Brazil for wrapper, binder, and filler
- Filler from Peru
- Jalapa, Condega and Estelí, Nicaragua for wrapper, binder, and filler
- Ometepe, Nicaragua for filler

Tobacco Agronomist

All of these tobaccos offer exceptional and unique aroma and taste characteristics.

The blender can purchase from an array of distinct tobaccos to work with, but the agronomist has a different set of elements that he must know and understand to grow healthy, robust, and aromatic tobacco plants. If the terroir has too much or too little of any of the elements listed below, the tobacco plant will produce inferior tobacco. An experienced agronomist not only tests the soil at different intervals, but uses his keen eye to study the tobacco plant as it is growing in the fields, looking for visual clues that will alert him to potential deficiencies in the soil. As you read the list below, I am sure you will have an even greater appreciation for tobacco agronomists and farmers next time you light up a cigar.

Macronutrients (Derived from Air and Water

- Carbon
- Hydrogen
- Oxygen
- Macronutrients (Primary)
- Nitrogen
- Phosphorus
- Potassium

Macronutrients (Secondary)

- Sulfur
- Calcium
- Magnesium

Micronutrients

- Iron
- Molybdenum
- Boron
- Copper
- Manganese
- Sodium
- Zinc
- Nickel
- Chlorine
- Cobalt
- Aluminum
- Silicon
- Vanadium
- Selenium

Excerpt from an Interview with John Oliva, Jr.

President, Oliva Tobacco Company

TAMPA, FLORIDA, SEPTEMBER 2020

Nick: Your father and grandfather are legendary tobacco growers and processors and your grandfather Angel Oliva, Sr., is an inductee in the class of 1997 *Cigar Aficionado* Hall of Fame. What were the most important lessons they taught you about growing and fermenting tobacco that would produce extraordinary aroma and taste?

Johnny: One main emphasis that was always stressed to me was the soil. The soil is what gives the tobacco its unique characteristics. Tobaccos from Ecuador will taste different from tobaccos from Dominican, Nicaragua, or Honduras. He also insisted that we took care of the tobacco leaf in the fields and in the processing facilities. For example: During fermentation everything was always done gently. You wanted to let it go through the fermentation process slowly, and that's what brings out the unique flavors. The only time you want to stress the tobacco is at certain times during the growing stage, but never during the fermentation stage.

Nick: At what point do you know you have an extraordinary tobacco crop—when it's in the field or when it's in the processing facility?

Johnny: If you have a beautiful crop in the field, you can get some ideas about its quality, but to me, the most important thing is how the tobacco comes out of the barn (processing facility). I've seen beautiful tobacco in the field and I've seen it completely destroyed in the processing barn. When you know you have a good or extraordinary crop is when you see the tobacco after it goes through fermentation.

JOSE MENDEZ
QUALITY TOBACCOS SINCE 1972

Excerpt from an Interview with Fito Maruschke Mendez

ALMACEN DE TABACO JOSE MENDEZ & COMPANY,
S.R.L., MOCA, DOMINICAN REPUBLIC, FEBRUARY 2020

Nick: Fito, what are the most important lessons that your father and grandfather taught you about growing and processing tobacco leaf that will offer unique aromas and taste characteristics?

Fito: The first lesson they taught me is to never take nature for granted—every crop you grow is different. What worked out for you on the last crop may not necessarily work out on the next one. Secondly, you have to be always on the lookout, because things can go from very good to very bad in a matter of days or even hours.

Nick: So it's a never ending task. Right now we're sitting in the midst of a sea of tobaccos. What distinguishes one tobacco bale of tobacco from another?

Fito: A lot has to do with your knowledge and the connection you have with tobacco plants and the tobacco fields. What you do to the tobacco here in the processing facility and in the fermentation and selection processes are all important, but a big part is played by Mother Nature. Mother Nature is what can give you a favorable wind to reach the ultimate goal, which is to achieve an excellent crop.

Nick: At what point do you realize you have an exceptional tobacco—in the growing stage, in the fermenting stage, or both?

Fito: That is an interesting question. You can have an excellent crop when tobacco is more or less developed in the fields. But when the tobacco is in the curing barns and you are seeing the tobacco leaves and open the leaf, you more or less have the idea or perception that the crop is going to be a good group or an excellent one. You have some idea. But like everything in life, that is just phase one of the story. It's like a book, and that is the first part of the story.

The second part starts when you are fermenting the tobacco. It is then, when you open up the first fermentation bulk and smell the tobacco and look at the tissue of the tobacco and see its properties. It is in this second stage that you will know if you are going to have an excellent crop.

Nick: This morning I conducted a workshop with the ProPalate® Training System with your tobacco team consisting of agronomists, fermentation specialists, and supervisors. What would you like to share with our readers regarding your experience with this training system?

Fito: I have to congratulate you. Not only is it fun to realize things you have been doing without a real systematic or objective approach, this system can open you up to experience all the different sensations and give you the tools to work with.

Nick: What are your thoughts regarding using DNA testing to determine your mouth taste sensitivity to better understand your taste preferences?

Fito: DNA testing, along with other things, can help you reposition yourself to better understand your preferences. It's a very interesting method, and I feel it can be very useful for anyone interested in developing their palate: people who work in the cigar industry and also for the general cigar consumers.

Tobacco: Understanding the Raw Material

Tobacco Wrappers 101

Here are the three main categories for classifying wrappers:

Shade Grown: This is typically the mildest of the three wrapper types. As the name suggests, it is grown under a shade cloth. It is primarily known for light, aromatic, and roasted taste notes. Below are taste notes to look for. If you don't find all of the taste notes listed in one cigar, you are on the right track, because every cigar won't have every taste note listed below; it may have only a few depending on the quality and the region it was grown.

- Light: floral, fresh hay, herbaceous, citrus
- Aromatic: cedar, cinnamon
- Roasted: roasted nuts (cashews, hazelnut and almonds)
- Complex: caramel, vanilla, graham cracker

The initial mouth taste may seem a little sour or acidic to some smokers, but this acidity typically fades way after a few minutes into the cigar and may be replaced with a creamy, honey-like mouth taste.

Natural Shade Grown: This is a subcategory of wrapper leaf that is primarily grown in Ecuador in mountainous regions that offer an abundance of cloud cover that acts similarly to the shade screen used to grow U.S. Conn. shape wrappers. These wrappers offer the similar taste notes as shade grown, but with a little deeper flavor and intensity and with less mouth taste acidity.

- Light: floral, fresh hay, herbaceous, citrus
- Aromatic: cedar, cinnamon
- Roasted: roasted nuts (cashews, hazelnut and almonds)
- Complex: caramel, vanilla, graham cracker

Natural: These are tobaccos that are grown without shade covering from shade cloth or cloud cover, so the color range can go from a little darker than natural shade grown to a medium brown. Below are taste notes to look for:

- Light: floral, fresh hay, citrus
- Aromatic: black pepper, cedar, cinnamon, nutmeg
- Roasted: roasted nuts, wood smoked
- Earthy: Barnyard, woody, leather
- Complex: chocolate, coffee, caramel, graham cracker

Maduro: This translates in English to "ripe" or "mature" and is a term used to describe a fermentation process the wrapper leaf undergoes to achieve a dark brown to a charcoal black to a radiant dark mahogany. There are three primary methods used to turn thick tobaccos leaves into a Maduro wrapper.

The first is referred to as "natural Maduro." Thick wrapper leaves are selected for this process and are aged in pilons, or piles of leaves stacked one on top of the other. The thicker wrapper leaves can handle higher (hotter) fermentation temperatures resulting in a sweet and flavorful wrapper.

The second process is referred to as "sweating." In this process the tobacco leaves are processed with steam. The final process is referred to as "cooking." In this process, the tobacco leaves are soaked in hot water, hence the name "cooked."

The sweating and cooking processes produce the darkest leaves, referred to as Oscuro. In these processes, many of the oils in the tobacco leaf are extracted resulting in a dull, but very dark and even charcoal-colored leaf, which has less flavor and taste than wrappers that are naturally fermented.

Maduro wrappers offer a sweet taste with complex aroma. Below are some taste notes to look for:

- Dried fruit: fig, plum, raisin, dark sweet cherry
- Aromatic: paprika, cedar, nutmeg
- Earthy: barnyard, leather, dried shitake mushroom, smoked wood
- Complex: chocolate, coffee, caramel

Don't let the color of Maduro wrappers fool you. In many cases, they may not be as strong as shade or natural wrappers due to the way they are processed, which extracts more nicotine through longer and hotter fermentation or by steaming or cooking them. The reason many Maduro cigars are considered medium-plus to full bodied is due to the types of the filler leaves used in the blend. Richer, heavier filler leaves are often used by blenders so a rich flavorful Maduro wrapper doesn't overpower the cigar's overall taste profile, but there are many well blended Maduro cigars that are medium bodied.

Tobacco Plant Field

Hybrid Versus GMO

For thousands of years, humans have used traditional modification methods such as selective breeding and crossbreeding to develop plants and animals with more desirable traits. Hybrid tobaccos are created by geneticists and agronomists working with Mother Nature. If a given tobacco is a hybrid, it doesn't mean that it is better than non-hybridized tobaccos or vice versa. Hybrid tobaccos are created for various reasons:

- To create a tobacco plant that is more resistant to funguses or insects
- To create a tobacco plant that is more robust in a given growing region
- To create a tobacco plant that offers unique taste characteristics and flavor

Several hybrid tobaccos were developed to resist diseases such as black shank (a root fungus) and blue mold (a wind-blown spore). Below are the most commonly used hybrids:

- Criollo 98 and 99
- Corojo 99
- Habanos 2000

Because our palate is directly linked to our general health and well-being, I feel compelled to share with you what I know about foods made with GMO, or genetically modified organisms, also referred to as bioengineered. Hybridization should not be confused with GMOs, which were first used in food crops in 1994 to increase crop yields and were touted as the magic bullet that would end world hunger. Unfortunately, the promise of GMOs has not panned out. World hunger has increased significantly, while the profits of the companies that make and sell GMO products has skyrocketed.

The good news is that tobacco hybrids were created by introducing different genetic material via cross-pollination into the host plant. If Mother Nature feels it's a good match, she will allow it to hybridize, creating a new variation of a tobacco plant. In GMOs, the geneticist directly alters an organism's DNA, most of the time counter to Mother Nature's wisdom. The best example is GMO corn that is resistant to herbicides, which allows the farmer to spray glyphosate, commonly known as Roundup, on the target plant without killing the target. In order to do this, the geneticist must alter the plant's DNA code and insert the glyphosate gene, producing a plant with a poison DNA gene.

While geneticists were altering the corn's DNA, they also inserted a pesticide gene known as Bacillus Thuringiensis, or Bt, to the same corn seed so the farmer no longer has to spray a pesticide that kills worms on the crop—it, too, is now part of the corn's DNA. Bt is a soil bacterium that destroys the worm's digestive system: One bite of the host plant and the worm dies. I hate to think of what it can do the human digestive system.

Monsanto pioneered this process by covering up or challenging all the scientific data that showed the dangers of long-term consumption of foods made from plants grown with GMO seeds. To date, there are 17 foods commonly sold in the supermarket that are produced from plants grown with what many opposing advocates call Frankenstein seeds.

Most European countries prohibit farmers from using GMO seeds in agricultural practices for growing foods for human consumption. India was one country that bought the GMO dream and is suffering greatly due to the negative side effects associated with GMO crops: They are currently trying to pass a bill to ban GMO seeds sold and used in their country. The company Monsanto was purchased by Bayer AG in 2018. Shortly after the acquisition, Bayer was faced with an avalanche of lawsuits. In June of 2020 Bayer agreed to pay $10.9 billion to settle 95,000 of the 125,000 US lawsuits claiming the widely used weed killer Roundup caused cancer and cancer related deaths.

Many of the cigar connoisseurs I talk with are also "foodies" and prefer to eat the best quality natural foods available. For those of you who are not foodies yet, but are interested in learning more regarding what is in the foods you consume, allow me to give you some useful tips so you can make an informed decision regarding the foods you and your family consume.

Many of the available genetically modified plant varieties are considered commodity crops. These crops are grown and harvested for processing into a wide range of frequently used ingredients. Below are two lists. The first list consists of genetically modified crops currently approved for growing and selling in the United States. The second is a list of the GMO fruits and vegetables that are currently sold in the US.

Commodity Crops

- alfalfa canola oil
- cotton (cottonseed oil)
- corn oil
- soybean oil
- sugar beets

All of the oils listed above, as well as fructose sugar, corn syrup, and beet sugar, are made using plants grown with GMO seeds. It should be noted that currently corn and beets sold in the produce sections at grocery stores are not grown with GMO seeds.

After harvesting, these GMO crops are manufactured into many of the common ingredients found in today's packaged foods, such as amino acid(s), alcohol, aspartame, ascorbic acid, sodium ascorbate, citric acid, sodium citrate, ethanol, flavorings, high fructose corn syrup, hydrolyzed vegetable protein, lactic acid, maltodextrin, molasses, monosodium glutamate (MSG), sucrose, textured vegetable protein, xanthan gum, vitamins, vinegar, yeast products, and others.

Almost all processed foods use plants that were grown using GMO crops unless they are labeled organic. The next time you pick up a bottle of salad dressing, a box of cereal, chips, or dip, take a look at the labeling. Chances are that you'll see several of the ingredients listed above.

Fresh Fruits and Vegetables Grown with GMO Seeds

- Arctic apple
- Innate potato
- Zucchini
- Yellow squash
- Rainbow papaya from Hawaii

Because the number of GMOs available for commercial use increases every year, we as consumers need to be vigilant if we wish to avoid buying and consuming these products, which are now known for placing humans and the environment at risk.

Organic: Your Best Bet to Avoid GMOs in Food

The organic label is a federal standard for how food is produced, and it requires a product to contain no GMO ingredients. This includes not only organic crops but beef, pork, chicken, and turkey: Animals must eat only organically grown feed for their meat to be labeled organic. Organic foods come with other benefits, too. For instance, they can't be grown with toxic pesticides or synthetic fertilizers or treated with chemicals or irradiated.

Cigar Aging

Most cigars with few exceptions are designed to be enjoyed once they leave the manufacturer's facility. A respectable cigar brand owner will not put his name on a cigar that is not ready to smoke. Cigars that leave his factory have gone through rigorous taste samplings, and only then does the brand owner give the okay to put on the cigar band, pack them in a box, and make them available to the consumer.

Every cigar blend is a reflection of the cigar brand and the blender's passion for his creation. A cigar blender is like a boxer who has to step into the center ring wearing only boxer shorts, with nothing to hide behind, putting himself on the line with each new release. So be gentle and considerate with your comments if you smoke a cigar that doesn't taste the way you like a cigar to taste. You can simply say, "It's a well made cigar and draws well but it's too intense or too earthy for my liking" or "It's has a beautiful tasty wrapper, but doesn't have enough strength for me" or "It's has a lot of flavor, but it's too spicy for my palate."

On rare occasions, a few cigar blends may undergo a magical transformation and develop unique flavor characteristics that challenge and excite our palate. These rare experiences will turn a cigar smoker into a connoisseur looking forward to their next cigar rapture.

Cigars that need aging may taste young with an abundance of vigor, and their flavor nuances may seem particularly pronounced: too intense or edgy. During additional aging, the harsh edges may smooth out, producing a smoother texture and an overall more harmonious cigar, just as when people age, their vigor may be less obvious and replaced with subtleness and the desire for a more harmonious life experience.

> The *best environment* to overnight a cigar is around 70% relative humidity, plus or minus 5% in either direction. In Florida and most southern states, during certain times of the year a cigar can overnight in the ashtray and still be smokable and enjoyable the next day. Low humidity under 60% or very high humidity 80+% will have a negative impact on a cigar.

If you have a box or several boxes of cigars in your humidor, here are some suggestions to help you decide which cigars to age and which ones to enjoy now.

- The cigar is extremely intense and sometimes over the top, but it offers complex aromas and tastes nuances that you find intriguing.
- The cigar seems to taste better after you let it go out and rest and then continue to smoke, later that day or night.
- You leave the unfinished cigar in the *right environment*, finishing it the next day. Its intensity continues to subside and the harsh edges soften while it still excites your palate.
- You cut off both ends of the cello to allow the cigar to breathe.

Keep Notes

- When aging cigars, it is imperative that you keep good records.
- A small to medium size note pad is convenient and easy to use and store. You can also use a 5" x 7" note card or your smart phone or tablet.

Always begin each entry with the date; then add your comments. Take your note pad with you to your smoking area so you can write down your observations as you experience them.

The safest way to age a cigar is to cut the foot and head off the cello as mentioned above. This will allow it to still off gas, while protecting it from picking up other or undesirable aromas that may be in the humidor.

The most important thing to remember is that, without some type of record, your chance of reproducing a positive result is slim to none. Set up a schedule and follow it so you can see if your observations were correct. If you put away a box of cigars and later find them with no reference, smoke one or two and make the decision: to age, to smoke, or to give away.

Once you decide which cigars to rest, experiment: Smoke one bimonthly or monthly until you notice an improvement or lack thereof. Follow your instincts. When there is a noticeable improvement, continue to age them. When there is no noticeable improvement, it's time to put them in your rotation or share them with your cigar buddies. As with people, wine, and whiskey, some cigars age gracefully, but they all have a life expectancy, and after their prime, they don't get any better. If aged too long, they will start to lose their intensity and flavor. If that happens, share them with cigar comrades who enjoy light bodied cigars. As the old adage goes, one man's trash is another man's treasure.

Cigar Ambassador

Damion was a dear friend who was the living embodiment of a cigar ambassador. We were neighbors, but for several years we rarely spoke, other than the passing, "Hello, how are you?" To most people, we would have appeared to be complete opposites. He was a tall, robust man, highly educated with a PhD in literature and was a past president and vice president of respected universities. I am an average size man, self-educated with no degree or titles to my name other than an occasional "Mr." One warm summer evening when I was sitting outside smoking, I was surprised when Damion walked up to my back porch and told me that the aroma of the cigar I was smoking was intoxicating. At first, I thought he was going to ask me to be a good neighbor and stop smoking on my back porch, but instead he told me that he was fresh out of cigars, desperately needed a good cigar to smoke, and wanted to buy one from me. I told him that I did not sell cigars but would be happy to share one with him.

I led him into my house and invited him to select a few cigars from my upright humidor. He looked at me and said, "Wow, which ones are your favorites?" I told him they were all my favorites, so grab a few and let's go light them up. We sat on the porch and smoked several cigars and sipped Scotch until the wee hours of the night. From that night until his untimely death, he would walk over after dinner and we would smoke and have a drink.

One evening, after we got to know each other better, I mentioned that it seemed strange that he used a taxi to get around when we lived in the suburbs. Why didn't he just buy a car and drive? He asked me to pour another round and he would explain.

After taking a sniff and sip of a vintage scotch, he told me his story. He explained that he was in a special program that didn't allow him to drive. As I probed further, he told me his license had been taken away after his third DUI. I asked him if that special program was called AA, and he asked me if I had ever attended an AA meeting. I told him no, I didn't have a drinking problem—why would I want to go to an AA class? He replied that if I attended a class, it would be an eye-opening experience for me. So the next night I drove him to class and sat in on my first AA meeting. It really was an eye-opening experience: The attendees ranged from those suffering in the midst of economic, emotional, and physical misery to those who, from the outside would appear to be extremely successful men and women.

I became Damion's good friend and designated driver. For me, it was like attending a university on wheels. He was brilliant: the author of several academic books; an art collector; a classical music, opera, and ballet buff; a cigar, wine, and scotch connoisseur; and a foodie. Not only was he super-intelligent, he was one of the kindest human beings I have ever had the pleasure of knowing. He loved to share his knowledge and his treasure with everyone around him.

To set the record straight, Damion and I were not partners or a couple; we are both 100% heterosexual alpha males. One of the main differences between us was that Damian was a metrosexual. For those of you not familiar with this term, it refers to a refined man who is fastidious about his appearance, who uses hand and face lotions and goes to a salon once or twice a month to have his hair washed, styled and blow-dried followed by a manicure and pedicure.

One night, like many, he drank too much and handed me the bill and his credit card and asked me how much the damage was. I told him $200.00 for the food and $400.00 for the wine and scotches. I asked him how much he would like to leave for the tip. He caught me off guard by asking how much I recommended. I responded that 20% is $120.00. He criticized me for using a percentage and asked me what the experience we had that evening was worth. I was perplexed by his question and said the first thing that came to my mind: "Priceless." He said, "Now you are learning—put down $300.00 for the tip. I should have just followed his instructions, but I carelessly responded, "But, Damion, that is 50% of the bill." He fired back, "When was the last time you dined out and the chef came to your table to ask you what you would like him to prepare for your meal—off the menu?" I responded, "Never."

He said, "If you want to have an extraordinary dining experience, you have to be extravagant."

One evening we dined in a swanky restaurant that had indoor and outdoor seating; we sat in the outdoor smoking section. Because of the orientation of the outside deck, the breeze coming off the water usually blew the smoke away from the nonsmoking seating area. This night, however, the breeze was not cooperating and was blowing our cigar smoke in the direction of the nonsmoking area. Since we had already finished our dinner and were enjoying an after-dinner cigar, our waitress politely asked if we would mind changing our seats because our smoke was interfering with the other guests who were still eating.

Before I could dig my heels in and remind the waitress that we were sitting in the smoking section, Damion beat me to the punch and told her we would be happy to move. I didn't want to challenge Damion in front of others, and we were ushered to another table. I asked Damion why he was willing to give up our table in the smoking area. He explained that he, too, did not appreciate smelling other people's secondhand smoke when he was dining. I had to agree.

Later that evening a woman walked up to us and thanked us for being understanding and considerate gentlemen. Then she surprised us both and asked if she could buy one of our cigars for her husband. Damion told her that we did not sell cigars, but before he could finish his sentence, she added, "I'll happily give you $100 for a cigar. As I reached in my shirt pocket to make a quick hundred bucks, Damion told her that he would be happy to share one of his extra cigars with her husband.

Damion asked if her husband had a clipper and lights, and she told him no. Damion said not to worry and proceeded to clip and light the cigar for her husband. As Damion was preparing the cigar, she opened up and told us the reason for her strange request. Her husband had recently been diagnosed with pancreatic cancer.

Damion handed the woman the lit cigar and told her that she and her husband were welcome to join us. To my surprise, the couple joined us, and we smoked and drank the night away, sharing cigar stories.

I will call the lady Samantha and her husband Bill. I don't think Bill had smoked a cigar in a long time. He burned through a Quesada Special Edition R Series Churchill in less than twenty minutes. Damion always had two cigar carrying cases, just in case—no pun intended. Before Bill burned his mustache, Damion offered him another cigar, this time a Partagas Spanish Rosado.

Bill seemed to be having the time of his life, especially in light of a recent cancer diagnosis. We learned that the previous week his doctor told him that he had twelve weeks to live with the aggressive type of cancer he had unless he started treatment immediately. The doctor had explained to Bill that he would need to match the cancer with aggressive treatment. The doctor recommended that Bill walk down the hall and schedule an appointment to have a feeding tube inserted in his stomach within the next couple of days and prepare for surgery.

Bill told the doctor that the treatment sounded a little extreme. The doctor asked Bill whether or not he wanted to live. Bill asked the doctor about his chances of survival, and the doctor told him survival rate was 15%, but only if he started treatment immediately.

Bill was an accountant, so he knew those odds were dismal and was well aware of the side effects of radiation and chemotherapy. He asked the doctor about the quality of life he could expect after the surgery and treatment regime he was recommending. The doctor told him that he might lose his taste and have to keep the feeding tube in his stomach for a year and have to use a wheelchair to get around.

Bill smiled at Damion and me. "I looked the doc in the eye and told him I'd rather go out with my boots on." Then he turned to Samantha and asked her to tell the rest of the story. She shared with us that the doctor told Bill not to be selfish and only think about himself—instead, he should think about his wife and kids. Bill told the doctor that is exactly who he was thinking about: "I don't want to be a burden to them."

At the end of the night, we exchanged business cards, and over the next three years we shared many dinners followed by our favorite cigars. One night towards the end of his journey, Bill shared with us that the last three years had been the most memorable and enjoyable of his life. He told Damion, "You have been an inspiration to me. You showed me by example, not to feel sorry for myself and to be grateful for all the good things I've had and still have."

Bill said that he had lived more in the last 3 years than the previous 60 years. He added, "I learned to live in the moment, because you helped me realize that is the only thing you can be sure of."

The moral of the story is this: A true cigar ambassador is a gentleman, treating others the way he would like to be treated and is considerate of others who don't smoke or want to smell someone else's cigar smoke. And he always takes responsibility for the direction his cigar smoke travels.

Excerpt from an Interview with Klaas Kelner

Grand Ambassador, Davidoff of Geneva

USA CORPORATE HEADQUARTERS, PINELLAS PARK, FLORIDA, USA, DECEMBER 2019

Nick: After reviewing the ProPalate® System and calibrating your palate using this method, what would you like to share with our viewers about your experience with the ProPalate® Kit?

Klaas: You have designed a very standardized process of defining and resetting your palate so you can be able to identify different aromas. Whether you use the ProPalate® Kit or some other kind of training, it is definitely something that can help somebody identify or memorize certain types of aromas. Then when they are enjoying a cigar, they're going to better understand the complexities that are inside premium cigars. So, I would definitely suggest for cigar smokers to test their palate and train their nose to these certain types of aromas.

The nice thing about the ProPalate® is that you're able to try 25 different aromas that you can become familiar with and start memorizing, so you can start picking them up in cigars.

So, it's definitely a good exercise and can be very helpful for consumers. Also, what I like about this kit is that if you follow Davidoff's theory, a good cigar has to has to be balanced. When you blend a cigar that has each one of these pillars or columns on your calibration board, it is a good way of saying yes, I have a cigar that is complex and not one dimensional. Ultimately, a good blender will try to make a blend that is complex, and is balanced.

Nick, thank you for bringing the kit. It's fun. It's a good exercise.

Nick: I'm glad you enjoyed working with the kit and I appreciate you having me here today and taking the time to analyze the kit and offer of your comments.

Klaas: It was my pleasure. Thank you, Nick.

Excerpt from an Interview with John Oliva, Jr.

President, Oliva Tobacco Company

TAMPA, FLORIDA, SEPTEMBER 2020

Nick: Earlier I demonstrated how the ProPalate® Training System works. What would you like to share with our readers regarding your experience going through the system?

Johnny: First, one of the most important things was the diversity of aroma references you have in the kit. It gives you a benchmark to associate with the aromas and flavors you are trying to find in a cigar that you are smoking.

And second, to actually be able to smell exact references first and then attempt to find those aromas in a cigar was an eye-opening experience for me. It takes all the guesswork out of conducting a cigar tasting, and it limits personal bias. For instance, I don't have a lot of exposure to nutmeg, so actually smelling it in the spice jar, like you explained to me, will take me back to a stored reference, which in my case was eggnog, which I drink every year on Christmas Eve; it's my favorite drink to have on that occasion. If I don't have a nutmeg reference to go back to, then I am creating one now, by smelling it your kit and knowing what I'm smelling—this is amazing.

Nick: Do you have any closing thoughts you would like to share will our readers?

Johnny: This system is going to help everyone in the cigar industry, from the tobacco growers, to the cigar manufacturer, and most importantly to the consumer. It is amazing how you broke all this down into a training system that everyone can use to develop their cigar palate. Every industry has their mad scientist and now the cigar industry has theirs. Thank you, Nick, for reaching out to me and inviting me to participate in this interesting project that you have developed.

Chapter 6:

The Ultimate Experience: CIGAR BLISS

"Tobacco is a plant that converts thoughts into dreams."
—Victor Hugo

Of all things, *time* is the most precious—once lost, it can never be regained. Let's make sure we spend our time wisely, whether developing our palate or savoring our favorite cigars with comrades or in solitude in search of our cigar bliss.

In Chapter 3 we discussed the many reasons we smoke, which all come down to one word: enjoyment. Also we compared watching sports and listening to music to smoking cigars and showed that the more you know about a subject, the more you will enjoy it.

So now I'm going to throw you a curve ball about fully enjoying your cigar smoking experience. You need to know when to forget everything you've learned about cigars so you can reach the ultimate experience: Cigar Bliss.

Let's use sports and music to demonstrate my point. A professional baseball batter has swung his bat a thousand times over, but he still continues to go in the batting cage and hit ball after ball. There are times when he can hit any pitch thrown at him and other times he can't seem to get even a piece of the ball.

At practice a coach instructs the pitcher to throw inside and outside curve balls, knuckle balls, fast balls, right down the middle, low fast balls, and high outside fast balls—you get the point. When Babe Ruth stepped into the batter's box on game day, was he thinking of what the coach drilled into his head (step into a breaking curve, step away from an inside slider, step straight into a fast ball)? When a baseball is coming towards a batter at 100+ miles per hour, the batter has only a fraction of a second to react: His only chance of hitting the ball is to rely on his instinct.

> Smoking cigars is like falling in love. First, you are attracted by its shape, you stay for its flavor, and you must always remember never, never to let the flame go out.
>
> —Winston Churchill

The same holds true for a cigar smoker. After developing your palate through conscious effort, you will reach a point where smoking becomes second nature, allowing you to sense different aromas, tastes, and flavors from a rainbow of options. But like the batter who had to first make a concerted effort to be in charge of his bat, you will have to do the same to be charge of your palate.

Let's get out of our right brain for a moment and turn again to our left brain to gain some more knowledge and information that will help guide us to our Cigar Bliss.

CIGAR BLISS!
How to Create Those Memorable Smoking Experiences Over and Over Again

As mentioned in Chapter 2, we live in a world of amplified distractions, a punishing drumbeat of constant input broadcast through our cellphones, tablets, iPads, TV news channels, and radios. This cacophony follows us like a shadow: to and from work, into our homes, and into our bedrooms, seeping into our minds, bodies, and souls. We need to be conscious of how these distractions potentially influence our state of mind and smoking experience.

For a true cigar connoisseur, there is but one poultice for his raw nerve endings: a great cigar that delivers a memorable smoking experience.

> A burning cigar is a Memoir documenting its journey from seed to smoke. It pays tribute to the hands that caressed its leaves, a hundred times over, before it found its way into your hand, was set on fire, and went up in smoke.
>
> —Nick Cutro

Many of us have read or watched interviews where cigar smokers share their most memorable smoking experiences. These cigar connoisseurs typically recall one event above all others that left a lasting impression that was branded in their brains, not their forearm, chests or backside. Wouldn't it be nice if there were a formula to recreate those memorable smoking experiences over and over again?

There just might be. Let's examine other life events that run parallel with many of those memorable experiences.

- Being on vacation with the worries of the world left behind
- Enjoying perfect weather: sweater temperature, low humidity, and a faint breeze
- Spending time in the company of true friends or loving cigar-friendly family members
- Being excited about a forthcoming trip to a Big Smoke or a trip to the DR, Nicaragua, or Honduras
- Getting in a great workout at the gym or on the racquetball court, or almost shooting par if it wasn't for the nine waterhole shots
- Being unable to smoke for a few days or, worse, a week or two; then lighting up

- Receiving the gift of a vintage Cuban Puro from a dear cigar buddy
- Enjoying a great meal, skipping dessert, and walking away from the table before you overindulged
- Coming off some type of victory, whether a round of golf when you were making shots that Tiger Wood would envy or closing a business deal that you were convinced would never close
- Enjoying a few drinks instead of a few too many

Now let's look at a few things that probably didn't occur before that memorable moment.

- Getting home from work late, grabbing a go-to cigar, and smoking while you did some yard work
- After a grueling day at the office or in the field, rushing to your favorite cigar lounge and drinking a pint of ice-cold craft beer or throwing back five shots of whiskey while finishing of a Churchill in less than ten minutes
- Using a two-for-one dinner coupon, including appetizers and desserts, while dining alone
- Just getting laid off from a career job
- Being overexcited about your youngest kid finally getting a real job and moving out of the house
- Having a blowout argument with a close friend or family member
- Waking up at the crack of dawn on Sunday morning, lighting up your first cigar at 8:00 am, and starting work on your "honey do" list so the "missus" would allow you to host a Cigar and Super Bowl Party that afternoon
- Finishing off a meal that included your entrée, two baskets of extra rolls, two desserts, and your spouse's half-eaten baked potato while she was in the restroom
- Smoking a Gordo (60rg gauge) outside in dead winter with a wind chill factor of 10°
- Smoking a Double Corona in Florida while playing golf in 90° heat and 80% humidity
- Indulging in your third or fourth cigar of the day

I would venture to say we all agree that the second list of scenarios didn't produce one of those memorable smoking experiences. If you want to recreate a memorable smoking experience, identify as many of the things that you did or didn't do when you had such an experience and attempt to replicate as many as possible.

Closing Thoughts

It has been a pleasure writing this book and sharing what I have to offer, but my greatest joy would be to know that I was able to show you a few things that will enhance your next smoking experience and every one thereafter. If you feel inclined to share a story or make a comment, you can visit me at ProPalate.net.

I'll leave you with four thoughts to contemplate while enjoying your next cigar.

A First Thought

There are five things in life money can't buy:

- Health
- Love
- Happiness
- Class
- A sophisticated palate

...And one thing that money can buy:

- A memorable cigar

A Second Thought

In your less productive moments, light up one of your favorite cigars and find solace in your solitude while contemplating this: *How can I become a more fully realized human being and assist those around me in doing the same?*

A Third Thought

The quality of your life will be determined by the quality of the questions you ask yourself and others—and the quality of the cigars you smoke!

And Finally

- Bliss is a state of pure joy and harmony: In a Blissful state, one wants for nothing more or nothing less.
- Bliss often comes at unexpected times; and is never achieved through effort.
- In the state of Bliss, time is irrelevant. Hours can pass in what seem like minutes or mere seconds.
- Bliss is a state of being Lost in the Moment.

So, light up one of your favorite cigars and enjoy your journey, finding your *Cigar Bliss!*

My Story: Why I Wrote This Book

One day after a grueling day of dealing with life's improbabilities, I lit up one of my favorite cigars and reflected on my heritage and career in the cigar industry, and the inspiration was born.

My paternal great grandparents, like many Italians who were raised in Tampa, Florida, in the early 1900s, came from a small village on the Island of Sicily, via Ellis Island, to roll cigars in historic Ybor City. Their daughter, my grandmother, married a cigar factory laborer who died before I was born. *Grandma* became a master cigar maker at the Regensburg Cigar factory, which is now owned and operated by the legendary J.C. Newman family. Her talents extended far beyond crafting handmade cigars.

Never has there lived a better Italian cook than this cigar-rolling grandma. To this day, I have yet to eat a gourmet meal that equals her creations. Her kitchen looked like a food lab. At any given time, you could spot fresh produce, strings of garlic bulbs, and hot red peppers hanging from the window frame. Better yet was the delicious aroma of various meats marinating and herbed veggies leaping in and out of pots simmering on a gas stove. This woman didn't just bake a classic eggplant parmigiana. She painstakingly subjected lovely purple-rimmed slices of eggplant to a salt leaching process to remove inherent bitterness. Her process took 10 to 12 hours, which meant she started prepping the eggplant at 5:30 am. What patience she had for the end result! Whether making dinner or dessert, she got it right every time. You could compare her to Maria, the cook in the award-winning movie *Like Water for Chocolate*. (It is a must-see for any "foodie" who enjoys a non-violent, action-free, but entertaining and inspirational movie.)

On my mother's side, my grandmother and grandfather emigrated from Cuba prior to the embargo. Cuba is considered the *birthplace* of pedigreed cigars although most experts agree the epicenter of quality has migrated to the Dominican Republic, Nicaragua, and Honduras. My grandpa avoided working in the Tampa cigar business, choosing instead self-employment, driving a soda-pop truck. Even though Grandpa didn't earn a living from cigars, except from some extra money he made selling them on his soda truck route, he indulged on a regular basis and took pride in being a connoisseur.

He was Cubano, after all! He introduced me to my first premium cigar at the age of 15. When he caught me smoking a Swisher Sweet, he took me into the back room and scolded me: "If you don't want me to tell your father, you have to promise to never smoke one of those things again." From that day on, he would allow me to puff from his cigars when no one was looking. He also encouraged me to smell the smoke wafting from the end of his cigar. He would often say, "A fine cigar is a treat for everyone close enough to *smell the aroma*."

I must add that his mother, my great-grandmother, affectionately called "Bonita," which means "Little Cutie," smoked cigars. She lived with my grandparents. This 4' 11" Cubana smoked one Churchill cigar every day. You can imagine what my American adolescent friends thought when they saw this 80+-year-old cigar smoking grandma with a Churchill hanging out of her mouth. Most would never step foot in her house, thinking she might be some kind of witch.

I consider myself fortunate to have grown up in a diverse family with old-world values. My father was an extremely wise man—wise, in that he had an innate sense about things. Like most kids, I rarely listened to my parents because I lived with them and knew their faults. As I got older, my father got smarter. No, he didn't take night classes; as I got older and matured, I came to realize the importance of the things he was trying to teach me. My father had tremendous insight. His lessons were grounded in art, science, and the laws of nature, in spite of the fact that he had dropped out of school at 16 to travel as a saxophone player with a big band. The war had just ended, dancing was a favorite pastime, and the music of the day was swing and jazz. In those days kids often quit school so they could earn money to help support the family. Today, parents juggle two jobs so they can pay for their kids' smart phones, tablets, video games, and designer labels. Enough said on that.

My father was a student of life—always curious as to how things worked and why. Although he had no formal education, he proved to be a gifted teacher. My friends, the neighborhood kids, and I learned more about life from him than from all our schoolteachers combined. For example, he could take the worst baseball team in the neighborhood league and in 8 weeks turn it into a contender for the playoffs.

Dad owned and operated a small music store in downtown Tampa for 43 years. He encouraged me to learn music by studying world-class musicians via record albums. He also trained himself to be a master woodwind technician. As a teenager, I remember sitting in his office when recording artists called from New York and played their instruments over the speakerphone. My father could diagnose pesky technical problems by just listening to the unique quality of sound. Witnessing his skill firsthand heightened my capacity to detect subtle musical nuances. My senses were coming alive: hearing and touch through my dad, taste and smell through my grandparents.

Job offers poured in from major instrument manufacturers, including Yamaha, an up-and-coming company located in Japan in the 60s. Now Yamaha is the largest music company in the world. Although my dad turned down those offers, he served as a consultant, traveling to Japan to teach his method of setting up woodwind instruments. Yet money didn't motivate him. You couldn't buy him, no matter the price. He lived his life as he desired—remaining self-employed.

Once I got out on my own, I realized that most folks didn't understand how common household items worked, nor did they try to learn. They couldn't begin to fix appliances, radios, TVs, air-conditioning window units, nada. On the other hand, they mastered the simple art of collecting a paycheck, buying the latest TV, or watching sports. I began to realize that the knowledge my father imparted to me was not the norm. Like him, I enjoy sharing whatever I have acquired that might be of value to others. Hence, another reason for this book.

Most things of substance are comprised of parts, so I must mention the other half of the equation—my mom. His opposite! That's what made them a great team. She was always happy and fun to be around, ever willing to receive visits from friends and family. Mom was gifted with an eye for fashion and design. To this day, at 85 years young, she still looks better than most women her junior. She is not easy to keep up with, whether twirling on the dance floor, hiking at high altitudes in Peru, or trekking the trails of the Great Wall of China.

Back to how I joined the cigar industry. In the early 90s, I wholesaled cigars made in the Dominican Republic. Unbeknownst to me, a cigar boom was smoldering and would soon explode. *Cigar Aficionado* magazine, the first of its kind, played a key role in the growth. I am sure most of you are aware of the magazine and many are regular readers. If not, you owe it to yourself to pick up a copy. Another key factor credited for the explosive growth in the cigar industry was a book titled *The Ultimate Cigar*. Although outdated, this book can serve as a starting point for the growth that occurred during the cigar boom.

Cigar Aficionado offered a taste rating section where they described the taste of cigars using taste notes. As I read those descriptions, I wondered, "Why was I born with such a pathetic palate?" I had smoked cigars for some 20-odd years and all I could taste were tobacco and smoke. Forget flavor subtleties such as aged or fresh leather, smoked oak or hickory, hints of baker's spice, the bright, lively sweet top note of black pepper, or the pungent earthy note of white pepper. *Cigar Aficionado*'s rating scale ranged from 1 to 100. *I* used a much simpler 3-part system: bad cigar, good cigar, and great cigar. A paradigm shift loomed, and I didn't even know what the word meant.

As the old adage goes, "Timing is everything." During booms in any industry, when demand/buyers outnumber supply/sellers, manufacturers don't need good sales reps. Factories could not make cigars fast enough. What factories needed was more efficient tools; that's where I saw opportunity and stepped in. Since "necessity is the mother of invention," I decided to manufacture cigar equipment, starting with the ProPress™ cigar mold. This plastic mold helped pioneer the replacement of wood molds. Today, probably 90% of all premium cigar bunches are pressed in plastic molds. My ProSeries™ consists of several other products—ProBox Press™, ProEnd Cut™, ProGlue™, ProGauge™, ProStand™, ProTip™, ProKey™ and ProRuler™.

I've been very fortunate over the last 25 years to supply almost all major and midsize cigar factories with equipment that I replicated, redesigned, or designed. Because I was an equipment manufacturer and not a cigar maker or cigar salesman, I was never treated as an advisory spy or potential competitor. Today I walk freely through most factories, gleaning every bit of knowledge I can from legends in the business. When I ask sincere questions, master cigar blenders respond in like manner. They can't wait to share their love of the leaf with those who relish their creations.

I must share three stories with you. The first two marked turning points in my career, and the third sealed my fate in the cigar industry. The first two stories took place in the mid-90s as I dabbled in making cigar equipment.

First Turning Point

I lived and worked in Tampa, Florida, once known as the cigar capital of the world. In the 1920s, 500,000 million handmade cigars were produced in 126 cigar factories in West Tampa and Ybor City. Many cigar icons trace their roots back to Tampa: Frank Llaneza, John Oliva, J.C. Newman, Arturo Fuentes, and Armando Garcia.

One day I received a phone call from a man I did not know who would soon introduce me to another giant in the cigar industry. Armando Garcia, one of the legendary machinists in the machine-made cigar business, called and asked if he could pay me a visit. Armando had retired from Hava-Tampa cigars, a well known brand that sold worldwide for decades. He still did consulting work into his late seventies. From the moment he arrived, I knew I was in the presence of a master of his trade and a true gentleman.

Armando seemed pressed for time and, after shaking my hand, started drilling me with technical questions. As I answered them, he took notes on a small pad he'd pulled from his shirt pocket. He wanted to know the type of material I was using, the size tolerances I could hold, and the type of cutters I was using—carbon or tool steel. Then he asked to see one of my cigar molds.

After he studied it and took countless measurements, he put the mold down and told me he wanted to introduce me to Frank Llaneza, the owner of Villazon Cigar Company located on Armenia Avenue in Tampa. General Cigar purchased the building several years later during the cigar boom. Today it is owned by the Oliva Tobacco Company.

Armando made me aware that I was to meet a giant in the cigar world, and he gave me specific instructions: Show up early, dress nice, tuck your shirt in, wear a belt, don't talk too much, just answer Mr. Llaneza's questions honestly, and bring two samples of your product. Our meeting was set for 9:00 am, and I showed up at 8:30 am, finding Armando in the parking lot waiting for me. I was definitely nervous.

As we walked towards the massive 4-story half-a-block-long cigar factory, Armando reminded me again not to talk too much and to answer Sr. Llaneza's questions honestly. After Armando introduced me to Sr. Llaneza, he left, and there I was, all by myself in front of a cigar icon. Within the first two minutes I was completely relaxed, feeling like I was instead in front of a loving grandfather. But I remembered Armond's advice, "Don't talk too much and be honest."

Our 30-minute meeting lasted over three hours, followed by lunch. When I told Sr. Lleneza my favorite cigar was the Excalibur, he lit up and asked me if I would like to smoke one with him. I hesitated at first, because Armando told me not to smoke during our meeting, so I asked Sr. Llaneza if it would be okay if I showed him my cigar mold samples first, then enjoyed the Excalibur. His response was, "Armando trained you well."

After I showed him my cigar molds, he asked my production capability, and I could hear Armando's advice, "Be honest." So I told him the truth. "Right now we are maxed out; for new orders, the delivery time is 16 weeks, *but* we are running only two shifts, and I can run a third shift and start on your order immediately if necessary." He asked why I didn't buy more machines. I told him that my father had taught me that in the business cycle there are always highs and lows and a good businessman doesn't overextend himself so that he can ride out the low cycles. What I didn't tell Sr. Llaneza was that I still had a safety deposit box full of silver and gold coins that I should have sold in the late 70s during the precious metal boom, but in that case, of course, I had ignored my father's advice. Anyway, he told me that my father had taught me well and that he would test my molds in the factory. If they performed well, he would start placing orders.

Then we lit up two Excaliburs, and for the rest of the morning he patiently demystified the art of growing great tobaccos and blending world-class cigars; *at least in my mind*. Toward the end of our meeting I remember asking Sr. Llaneza, what tobaccos he used to create the Excalibur blend. He hesitated, then responded with a serious look on his face. "The blend is top secret and kept under lock and key." That silenced me—did I cross the line and insult him with such a bold inquiry? I hesitated in responding to his remark, afraid I might make matters even worse. You could hear a pin drop in the room and then he broke the silence. "I'll tell you my secret, but only if you promise to never tell anyone." I assured him his secret was safe with me. Since that meeting took place well over 20 years ago and the statute of limitations for secrets is 20 years, I'll go ahead and reveal it now, so you aren't tempted to start skipping pages to find the secret. If anyone ever accuses me of giving away or selling trade secrets, I'll deny it:

To succeed in the cigar industry, it takes a do or die mindset, foresight, insight, and oversight; passion, purpose, and courage to "bet the farm on the next crop." Perhaps most important, you need to respect Mother Nature and work with whatever she gives.

So now that you know Sr. Llaneza's secret, is anyone interested in starting a cigar factory? Not so fast. Before you decide, let me share a popular insider's joke that goes something like this: "What does it take to have a million-dollar stake in the cigar business? Start with two million; it won't take long before you go through your first million and your stake will be worth one million."

Second Turning Point

The second pivotal moment in my cigar career centers on my second major customer. In the mid-90s I was flying back and forth to the Dominican Republic so often that I didn't know if I was coming or going. When you wake up in a strange bed and it takes you a few seconds to realize where you are or, worse, what country you are in, it is a sign that something has to change. So I moved to the Dominican Republic and lived in a single room condo that I had bought back in the mid-80s when I was playing in a band on Norwegian Caribbean Cruise Line. We used to dock in Puerto Plata every Sunday after being at sea for two days. We all had cabin fever, so I'd walk around the city with my band mates and try to stay out of trouble.

While I was living in the Dominican, I tried to visit every cigar factory twice a week. I was having a problem getting past the security guards at some of the factory front gates, so I hired Yovani, a local who knew *the lay of the land and the way of the land*. Every time we showed up at a factory's front gate, he would talk to the security guard and offer him a cigar. If he didn't smoke cigars, he would offer him a pack of cigarettes—back then a pack of ten cigarettes cost about RD$0.50, the equivalent of US$0.16.

Eventually we would get past the front gate and I would have an opportunity to show the production manager or factory owner my equipment. A few months, a box of cigars, and a few cartons of cigarettes later, we made it past most of the factory front gates and into the galleria—the large room where cigars are hand crafted; but there were still a few that we were having difficulty with.

We were told by several managers and owners that there was an important and large factory in Villas Gonzalez, a little out of the way, but worth a shot. After 16 tries to get past the guardhouse, I was ready to throw in the towel and give up. I told Yovani this was the last time we were going to call on this company. As we drove north of the cigar zone in Santiago to Villas Gonzalez, I remembered one of a few things I did learn in school. It was a phrase one of my wise schoolteachers used to say: "A sure sign of insanity is doing the same thing over and over, and expecting different results," a line he had borrowed from Einstein.

I told Yovani to take everything out of the giveaway box, which was where we kept cigars that production managers or factory owners were gracious enough to give us to smoke, and then we would re-gift them to front gate guards. I put one of my cigar molds in the empty box and told the guard I had a very important package from the United States for their engineer, Manuel Batista, and that I was told to put in *his hands only*. To my surprise, that got us escorted to the front door of the office. Now all I had to do was convince the office manager to let us into the waiting room.

It was around 2:00 in the afternoon, and the heat was brutal. We had been driving around Santiago visiting factories in a small pickup truck with no air conditioning since 7:00 am. As luck would have it, the office manager, too, bought my story and invited us in, offering bottled water and stale cookies. I hadn't eaten since 6:00 am and had smoked at least 4 cigars on an empty stomach, so stale cookies were better than nothing. The office manager asked me if I would like to come back tomorrow, because Sr. Batista was in a meeting with Sr. Kelner and the meeting was probably going to last a long time. I told her that I'd already visited all my clients and would gladly wait as long as it took.

Minutes turned into hours, and at 5:00 the office manager locked up and didn't ask again if I wanted to come back tomorrow. She knew by this time that I had dug my heels in and was going to see Sr. Batista, come hell or high water. So there I was, locked in the office at the Davidoff Factory, hearing bits and pieces of Sr. Batista and Sr. Kelner's conversation regarding which new blends to put into production.

Around 5:30 Sr. Batista walked into the office to get something and was surprised to see us still waiting. He said that he thought we'd left and were coming back tomorrow. I told him that I was flying back to the States tomorrow and wanted to give him a sample cigar mold to test. Luckily he asked to see the mold, then he told me to follow him back to the office where he was working with Sr. Kelner. The large desk in Sr. Kelner's office was covered with cigars in small bundles with paper bands holding them in place, each with different codes identifying distinctive blends. Sr. Batista moved a few cigar bundles off the desk so Sr. Kelner could inspect the cigar mold. After quick inspection, he asked if I would leave it with him so he could test it tomorrow. Sr. Batista took my pager number and told me to expect a message in the next day or two.

The next day Sr. Batista's secretary paged and asked me to call the office. When I called, she asked when I would be back in DR. I told her I had had to reschedule my flight, so I could tie up some lose ends. She asked me to hold the line, and when she came back, she asked when I could stop by the factory to meet with Sr. Batista. I told her I was at the restaurant across the street from the front gate, and she laughed. I was telling the truth—we were on our way back to Puerto Plata and Villas Gonzales was just off the main highway, so we parked ourselves there—just in case we got the call.

When we drove up to the guardhouse, the gate opened and we went to the office, this time unescorted. Sr. Batista got right to the point: How many molds did I have in inventory? I showed him the list of well over one thousand molds, and he wanted them all. In addition, he wanted me to make many more molds with different sizes and different shapes, or Figurados, as they are referred to in the industry, such as Perfecto, Torpedo, Belicoso, and Salamon. I am proud to say that over the last two and a half decades all of the Davidoff and Avo cigars have been made using cigar molds that my company has proudly manufactured.

Final Turning Point
This final story sealed my fate in the cigar industry. After the cigar boom went bust in the late 90s, no one was ordering cigar molds and, to make matters worse, all the companies that went bust were unloading their cigar making equipment for pennies on the dollar.

One afternoon I received a call from a man who had a very strong Spanish accent. He introduced himself as Lazaro Lopez from Oliva Tobacco. He asked if I would like to make cigar molds for them and I told him, "It depends."

"Depends on what?"

"Depends on how many you need."

"*Muchísimos.*"

That got my attention, so I asked if we could meet and discuss the order in person. Then the conversation went south literally when he told me that first I needed to visit the factory in Nicaragua.

"*Nica-what?*"

"Ni/ca/rra/gua," he enunciated slowly.

The first thing that came to my mind was the Sandinista revolution that took place in the '80s. I told Sr. Lopez that I had no desire to go to a communist country. He fired back, "Nicaragua isn't a communist country. It's was a quasi-socialist dictatorship."

That was bad enough for me. "No thanks," I told him. Fortunately for me, he wasn't taking no for an answer and convinced me to at least consider it. I told him to give me a few days to think about it and I would get back to him.

I called my sister, who is a travel consultant, and asked if it was safe to travel to Nicaragua. She said that Nicaragua was definitely not a vacation destination, but it was not on the list of "Do not travel" countries for US citizens. So, I thought, what the hell, I need a vacation and maybe I could sell a few of the large inventory of molds I still had left over from the cigar boom. The next week I was on a plane to *Nica-what*.

The flight from Miami to Nicaragua was rough. There were summer storms brewing in the Gulf of Mexico causing a lot of turbulence. As the passengers started to prepare for landing, I looked out of the window and, based on what I saw, I thought we were making an emergency landing on a military base. There was just a single runway, and it was short to boot. There was no terminal to off-load passengers. As we walked across the airfield towards a small building, we were met by two men wearing dark sunglasses who looked like Nicaragua's version of secret service agents. One of them took our passports, which concerned me, but Sr. Lopez seemed okay with it, so I figured it was part of the routine. We were escorted to a small VIP lounge in a hangar-type building where we had a few drinks and a cigar while trying to relax after the rough flight. As we were unwinding, Sr. Lopez gave me great news, I would be staying in a house owned by Sr. Llaneza and Sr. Oliva, so I started to feel much better about this trip.

The drive from the airport to our destination was about 1½ hours. As we drove through lush green mountainous terrain to a small village called Estelí, it was hard to imagine how a country so beautiful and rich in resources could be so poor. The landscape in Nicaragua is a sight to behold, both majestic and humbling. If you catch the winter blues and can't seem to shake them off or if you are just feeling sorry for yourself because you can't have everything you want in life, buy a plane ticket and hotel accommodations in Nicaragua for under a $1,000 dollar: You will get an attitude adjustment that could last you a lifetime—while smoking some world-class cigars.

When we arrived at the guesthouse, I met Gustavo "Gus" Cura, a tobacco rep and now operations manager for NACSA (Nicaraguan American Cigars SA). We were practically neighbors back in Tampa. He owned the "Golden Ring" Cuban sandwich shop around the block from an Art Center for under privileged kids that I built and ran. This trip was starting to feel surreal. My friendship with Gus had grown over years, and I affectionately called him "The Ambassador." There isn't a nicer, more generous, more knowledgeable tobacco man that I know.

The next morning Gus's driver dropped me off at the factory where I was to spend the next couple of days. After meeting the office personnel and having a shot of espresso, I was taken to the "Galeria." I had visited large factories during the cigar boom, but this factory was enormous. The sound of 1,000 cigar makers all working at a feverish pace with the clacking sound of their chavetas cutting and slicing the tobacco leaves, was deafening; and the tobacco aroma was intoxicating.

As I settled in, I started to analyze the cigar molds they were using, and tried to figure out why their molds were not giving the cigar bunches the correct press, I was asked what type of cigar I would like to smoke—suave (light), mediano (medium), o forte (strong)? I had already learned my lesson during the cigar boom not to smoke while I was working, so I asked the production manager if I could have one of each size to smoke later that evening. He obliged and brought me 3 Lancers, 3 Coronas, 3 Robustos, 3 Toros, 3 Churchills and 3 double Coronas—what a gentleman.

I measured and remeasured mold after mold for 2 days and could not find a common pattern; the sizes were all over the map. On the third day, I asked the production manager in broken Spanish, if he had any molds that were giving him the press he needed. He smiled and handed me a mold that had 3 pieces of aluminum air-conditioning tape in the bottom of the mold slot. Placed one on top of another, they measured 0.0750, or $1/128^{th}$, of an inch, which is one half of a cigar ring gauge or the thickness of 3 sheets of common copy paper. With that information everything started to make sense.

Nicaragua's climatic conditions and rich volcanic soil produced tobacco plants with robust and luscious foliage. The binder and wrapper leaves they were using were thicker than the tobaccos that were used to make cigars in the Dominican. So, when I returned to the States, I made sample molds using a new formula. These molds passed inspection. We were off to the races.

On my second to last day, Gus told me that he wanted to introduce me to some folks who are making some excellent cigars. I'll never forget walking into their factory late one very hot afternoon. The factory had a low ceiling, which was common for most buildings at that time. Lighting was dim due to weak power supplied by the municipality. The air was still and stale. As we were walking to the back of the factory, three men approached us. They gave Gus a firm handshake followed by a bear hug. Then Gus introduced me to Gilberto Oliva, Sr., Gilberto Oliva, Jr., and Carlos Oliva.

They, too, were having trouble getting the right press with their cigar molds. As they drilled me with questions, I started to feel nauseous from the heat, secondhand cigar smoke, and my empty stomach. Gilberto, Jr., must have noticed I was looking a little ghostly and offered me a soda and some crackers from a box he had on his desk—probably kept there for moments like the one I was experiencing. I must confess that, when I walked into their factory, I was less than impressed. I actually felt sorry for them—how naïve of me. Little did I know that they were in the mist of building a state-of-the-art factory across the street. They told me that they would need "lots and lots of cigar molds" in the near future. And so they did.

A few years later I developed relationships with other cigar manufacturers and sold them molds: Joya de Nicaragua, Padron, Drew Estates, Rocky Patel, Casa Fernandez (Aganorsa), A. J. Fernandez, PENSA, and Plasencia, which has factories in both Nicargua and Honduras. I also ventured into Danlí, Honduras, which is a couple of hours north of Estelí. Crossing the border at "Frontera Los Manos" is always an adventure as it can take from an hour to a half a day to pass through immigration. If you are the impatient type and get frustrated easily, I highly recommend you think twice before attempting this border crossing. If you think that boasting to an underpaid overworked fully armed Honduran immigration officer "I'm an American" will make a difference, think again. You may wish you never uttered those words when wake up lying on the pavement face down wondering what just happened.

In Honduras I met Julio, Christen, and Justo Eiroa with the Eiroa Tobacco family, Conrado Plasencia, Rick Rodriguez and Agustin Garcia, Jorge Maradiaga with STG and the Davidoff Honduran team.

I feel fortunate to have had the opportunities to work with all of the people I've mentioned in this book—and too many more to name. Over the years I have enjoyed friendships with many industry icons. They will always be a part of my Cigar Bliss.

Understanding Humidity & How it Effects Your Cigars

There are two types of humidity: Relative and Absolute. In order to maintain your cigars' optimum quality, it is important to understand the difference. Relative humidity is cited in weather forecasts as it relates to the temperature and affects how we feel. Your cigar will fare much better if you monitor this type of humidity. Let's discuss both types so you can understand this phenomenon and know how to keep your cigars in the optimum humidity.

Absolute humidity is the measurement of water vapor (moisture) in the air, regardless of temperature.

Relative humidity also measures water vapor but *relative* to the *temperature* of the air. It is expressed as the amount of water vapor in the air as a percentage of the total amount or water vapor that *could* be held at its current temperature. Warm air can hold far more moisture than cold air; meaning that the relative humidity of cold air would have to be far higher than warm air, if their absolute humidity levels were equal.

For storing cigars you want to monitor the relative humidity. If not, you may have some unintended surprises; such as, an infestation of tobacco weevil and over humidified cigars that will be difficult to keep lit. Also, these cigars may taste bitter, lacking the flavors they are capable of offering. To use the chart below, match the temperature with the RH; this will give you the same humidity ratio as the 70°/70%.

Relative Humidity Chart

Temperature (°F)	RH(%)
75	59
74	61
73	63
72	65
71	68
70	70
69	72
68	75
67	78
66	80
65	83
64	86
63	89
62	92
61	96
60	No RH Level

Two Ways to Describe a Cigar
Subjective and Objective

Subjective/Indirect/Poetic Description (Example)

"This is a smooth, straight forward cigar with a very attractive wrapper. It offers a melody of appealing aromas, with ample amounts of smoke, punctuated by delicate flavors. It will pair well with a double expresso with or without sugar or a Frappuccino. It has a nice, delicious finish that offers many interesting aroma notes and nuances. A very approachable cigar that is easy to enjoy after lunch or dinner. Highly recommended for both the novice and the connoisseur."

Objective/Direct/Factual Description (Example)

"This is medium plus strength cigar. The 1st third offers strong notes of aged leather and cedar with hints of citrus and cinnamon. As you smoke into the 2nd and final 3rd of the cigar, the citrus and cedar notes are replaced with black pepper, licorice, dark chocolate and a hint of roasted hazel nuts. The cigar has a long finish that is creamy, with notes of fresh hay, caramel, and vanilla."